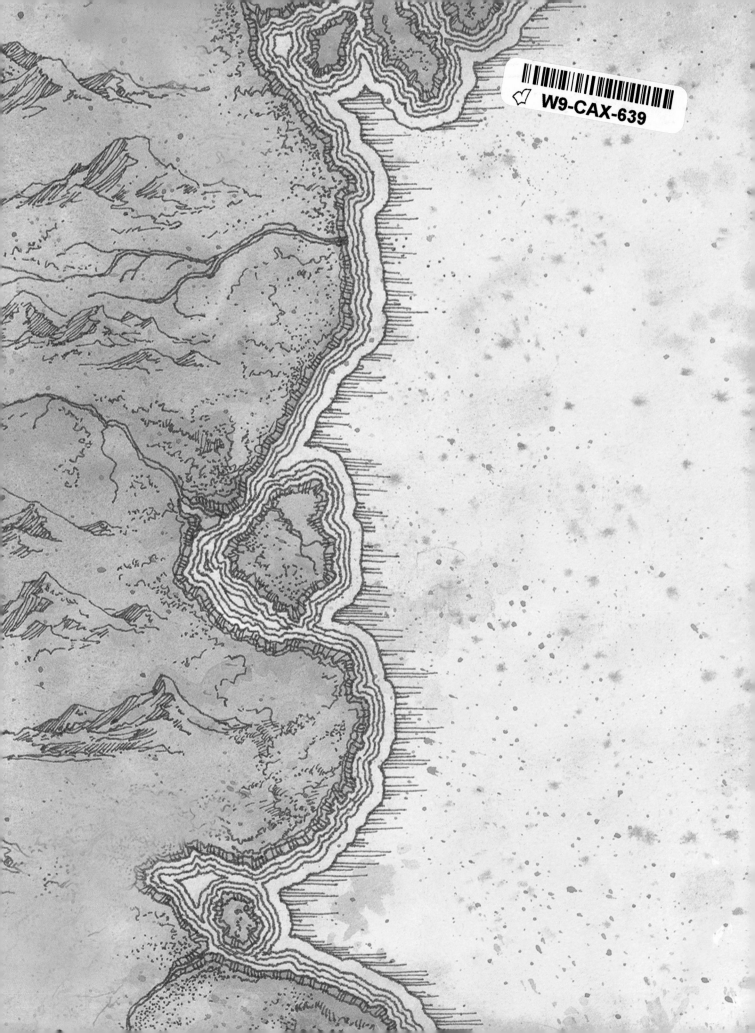
W9-CAX-639

LIVING IN OUR

WORLD

Series Authors

Dr. Richard G. Boehm

Claudia Hoone

Dr. Thomas M. McGowan

Dr. Mabel C. McKinney-Browning

Dr. Ofelia B. Miramontes

Series Consultants

Dr. Alma Flor Ada

Dr. Phillip Bacon

Dr. W. Dorsey Hammond

Dr. Asa Grant Hilliard, III

HARCOURT BRACE & COMPANY

Orlando Atlanta Austin Boston San Francisco Chicago Dallas

New York Toronto London

SERIES AUTHORS

Dr. Richard G. Boehm
Professor
Department of Geography and Planning
Southwest Texas State University
San Marcos, Texas

Claudia Hoone
Teacher
Ralph Waldo Emerson School #58
Indianapolis, Indiana

Dr. Thomas M. McGowan
Associate Professor
Division of Curriculum and Instruction
Arizona State University
Tempe, Arizona

Dr. Mabel C. McKinney-Browning
Director
Division for Public Education
American Bar Association
Chicago, Illinois

Dr. Ofelia B. Miramontes
Associate Professor
School of Education
University of Colorado
Boulder, Colorado

SERIES CONSULTANTS

Dr. Alma Flor Ada
Professor
School of Education
University of San Francisco
San Francisco, California

Dr. Phillip Bacon
Professor Emeritus of Geography and
   Anthropology
University of Houston
Houston, Texas

Dr. W. Dorsey Hammond
Professor of Education
Oakland University
Rochester, Michigan

Dr. Asa Grant Hilliard, III
Fuller E. Callaway Professor of Urban
   Education
Georgia State University
Atlanta, Georgia

MEDIA AND LITERATURE SPECIALISTS

Dr. Joseph A. Braun, Jr.
Professor of Elementary Social Studies
Department of Curriculum and Instruction
Illinois State University
Normal, Illinois

Meredith McGowan
Youth Librarian
Tempe Public Library
Tempe, Arizona

GRADE-LEVEL CONSULTANTS AND REVIEWERS

Diana Birdsong
Assistant Principal
Edward Titche Elementary School
Dallas, Texas

Carol Brooks
Curator
Arizona Historical Society
Yuma, Arizona

Mary Carl
Teacher
Culver Elementary School
Evansville, Indiana

Tonda M. Edmunds
Teacher
Greenwood Elementary School
Florence, South Carolina

Julie H. Honeycutt
Teacher
Little Creek School
Norfolk, Virginia

Diane Hoyt-Goldsmith
Children's Author
Square Moon Productions
Orinda, California

Dr. Barbara Talbert Jackson
Executive Director
Grants Administration (Retired)
District of Columbia Public Schools
Washington, D.C.

Darlena Ohlensehlen
Teacher
Horizon Elementary School
Jerome, Idaho

Sandra Wren
Teacher
Pope Elementary School
Arlington, Texas

Copyright © 1997 by Harcourt Brace & Company

All rights reserved. No part of this publication may be reproduced or transmitted in any form or by any means, electronic or mechanical, including photocopy, recording, or any information storage and retrieval system, without permission in writing from the publisher.

Requests for permission to make copies of any part of the work should be mailed to: Permissions Department, Harcourt Brace & Company, 6277 Sea Harbor Drive, Orlando, Florida 32887-6777.

HARCOURT BRACE and Quill Design is a registered trademark of Harcourt Brace & Company.

Acknowledgments and other credits appear in the back of this book.

Printed in the United States of America

ISBN 0-15-302039-3

5 6 7 8 9 10   032   99   98   97

CONTENTS

UNIT 1

UNIT 2

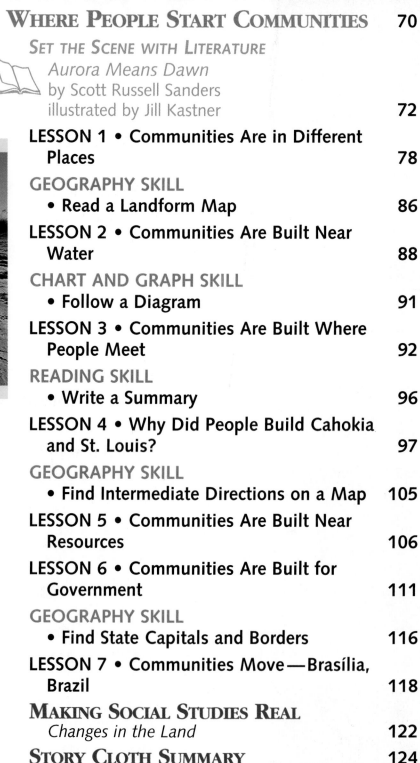

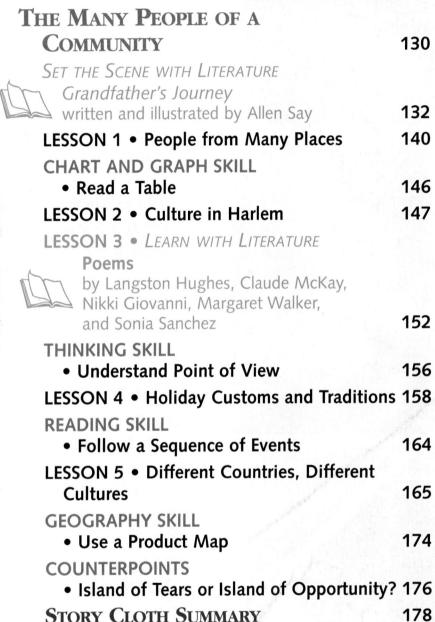

UNIT 3

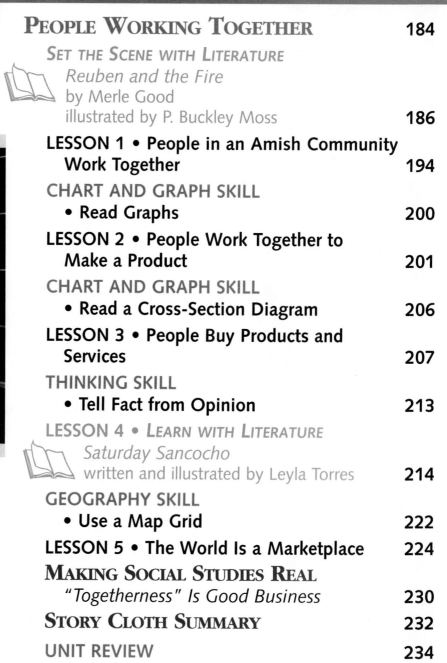

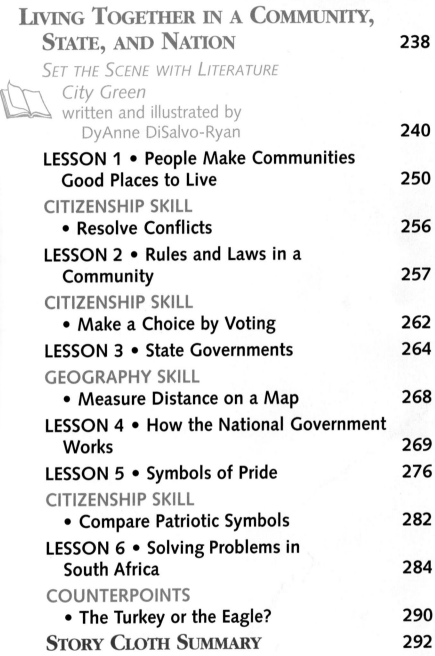

UNIT 6

F.Y.I.

MAPS

CHARTS, GRAPHS, DIAGRAMS, TABLES, AND TIME LINES

ATLAS

CONTENTS

THE WORLD: POLITICAL

180° 160° W 140° W 120° W 100° W 80° W 60° W

ARCTIC OCEAN

80° N

Greenland
(DENMARK)

ALASKA
(U.S.)

60° N

CANADA

NORTH AMERICA

40° N

UNITED STATES

Azores
(PORTUGAL)

Bermuda
(U.K.)

ATLANTIC OCEAN

Area of inset

MEXICO

Tropic of Cancer

20° N

Midway Islands
(U.S.)

CAPE VERDE

HAWAII
(U.S.)

PACIFIC OCEAN

VENEZUELA   **GUYANA**
                 SURINAME

COLOMBIA   FRENCH GUIANA
                 (FRANCE)

Equator

Galápagos Islands
(ECUADOR)

ECUADOR

BRAZIL

Tokelau
(N.Z.)   **KIRIBATI**

PERU

SOUTH AMERICA

WESTERN SAMOA   *American Samoa*
                      (U.S.)   *Cook Islands*
                                     (N.Z.)   *French Polynesia*
                                                    (FRANCE)

BOLIVIA

20° S

TONGA

PARAGUAY

Niue
(N.Z.)

Pitcairn
(U.K.)

Tropic of Capricorn

Easter Island
(CHILE)

CHILE

URUGUAY

40° S

PACIFIC OCEAN

ARGENTINA

Falkland Islands
(U.K.)

South Georgia
(U.K.)

60° S

Antarctic Circle

80° S

180° 160° W 140° W 120° W 100° W 80° W 60° W

UNITED STATES

30° N

Gulf of Mexico

100° W

BAHAMAS

ATLANTIC OCEAN

Tropic of Cancer

Turks and Caicos **(U.K.)**

20° N

MEXICO

CUBA

20° N

Puerto Rico
(U.S.)   Anguilla **(U.K.)**

DOMINICAN REPUBLIC   St. Martin **(FRANCE AND NETH.)**
HAITI   **ANTIGUA AND BARBUDA**
                           Montserrat **(U.K.)**

Cayman Islands
(U.K.)   **JAMAICA**

Virgin Islands
(U.S. AND U.K.)   Guadeloupe **(FRANCE)**

ST. KITTS AND NEVIS   **DOMINICA**
                            Martinique **(FRANCE)**

Caribbean Sea   **ST. LUCIA**
                    BARBADOS

BELIZE

Aruba
(NETH.)   *Netherlands Antilles*
                (NETH.)   **ST. VINCENT AND THE GRENADINES**

GUATEMALA   **HONDURAS**

EL SALVADOR   **NICARAGUA**   **GRENADA**

TRINIDAD AND TOBAGO

PACIFIC OCEAN

10° N

Panama Canal

10° N

A2

| 0 | 200 | 400 Miles |
| 0 | 200 | 400 Kilometers |

Azimuthal Equal-Area Projection

COSTA RICA

PANAMA

VENEZUELA   **GUYANA**

COLOMBIA

90° W   80° W   70° W   60° W

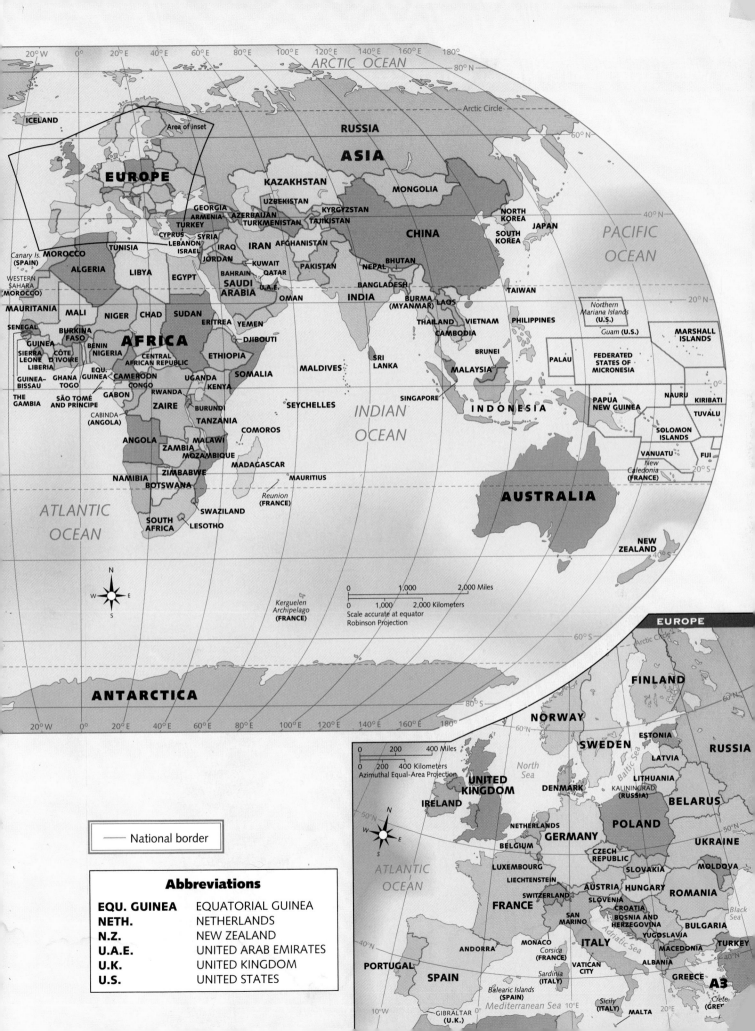

ARCTIC OCEAN

80°N

Arctic Circle

60°N

ICELAND

EUROPE

Area of inset

RUSSIA

ASIA

40°N

KAZAKHSTAN

MONGOLIA

GEORGIA
ARMENIA
TURKEY
AZERBAIJAN
TURKMENISTAN
UZBEKISTAN
KYRGYZSTAN
TAJIKISTAN

NORTH
KOREA

JAPAN

SOUTH
KOREA

PACIFIC
OCEAN

CYPRUS
LEBANON
ISRAEL
SYRIA
IRAQ
IRAN
AFGHANISTAN
CHINA

Canary Is.
(SPAIN)
MOROCCO
TUNISIA
JORDAN
KUWAIT
PAKISTAN
NEPAL
BHUTAN

WESTERN
SAHARA
(MOROCCO)
ALGERIA
LIBYA
EGYPT
BAHRAIN
QATAR
SAUDI
ARABIA
U.A.E.
BANGLADESH
TAIWAN

20°N

MAURITANIA
MALI
NIGER
CHAD
SUDAN
OMAN
INDIA
BURMA
(MYANMAR)
LAOS

Northern
Mariana Islands
(U.S.)

SENEGAL
ERITREA
YEMEN
THAILAND
VIETNAM
PHILIPPINES
Guam (U.S.)
MARSHALL
ISLANDS

GUINEA
BURKINA
FASO
AFRICA
CENTRAL
AFRICAN REPUBLIC
ETHIOPIA
DJIBOUTI
CAMBODIA

SIERRA
LEONE
LIBERIA
BENIN
NIGERIA
CÔTE
D'IVOIRE
EQU.
GUINEA
CAMEROON
UGANDA
SOMALIA
MALDIVES
SRI
LANKA
BRUNEI
PALAU
FEDERATED
STATES OF
MICRONESIA

0°

GUINEA–
BISSAU
GHANA
TOGO
CONGO
RWANDA
KENYA

THE
GAMBIA
SÃO TOMÉ
AND PRÍNCIPE
GABON
ZAIRE
BURUNDI
SEYCHELLES
SINGAPORE
INDONESIA
PAPUA
NEW GUINEA
NAURU
KIRIBATI

CABINDA
(ANGOLA)
TANZANIA
INDIAN
OCEAN
TUVALU

COMOROS
SOLOMON
ISLANDS

ANGOLA
MALAWI
ZAMBIA
MOZAMBIQUE
MADAGASCAR
VANUATU
New
Caledonia
(FRANCE)
FIJI

20°S

NAMIBIA
ZIMBABWE
BOTSWANA
MAURITIUS
Reunion
(FRANCE)
AUSTRALIA

ATLANTIC
OCEAN

SOUTH
AFRICA
SWAZILAND
LESOTHO

NEW
ZEALAND

40°S

N
W E
S

Kerguelen
Archipelago
(FRANCE)

0   1,000   2,000 Miles

0   1,000   2,000 Kilometers

Scale accurate at equator
Robinson Projection

60°S

EUROPE

Arctic Circle

80°S

60°N

ANTARCTICA

FINLAND

NORWAY

SWEDEN

ESTONIA

20°W 0° 20°E 40°E 60°E 80°E 100°E 120°E 140°E 160°E 180°

60°N

LATVIA

North
Sea

LITHUANIA

KALININGRAD
(RUSSIA)

RUSSIA

BELARUS

0   200   400 Miles

0   200   400 Kilometers
Azimuthal Equal-Area Projection

UNITED
KINGDOM

DENMARK

50°N

IRELAND

NETHERLANDS

GERMANY

POLAND

50°N

BELGIUM

CZECH
REPUBLIC

UKRAINE

N
W E
S

LUXEMBOURG

SLOVAKIA

MOLDOVA

LIECHTENSTEIN

AUSTRIA
HUNGARY

ROMANIA

ATLANTIC
OCEAN

SWITZERLAND

SLOVENIA
CROATIA

FRANCE

BOSNIA AND
HERZEGOVINA

YUGOSLAVIA

BULGARIA

Black
Sea

SAN
MARINO

40°N

ANDORRA

MONACO
Corsica
(FRANCE)

ITALY

VATICAN
CITY

MACEDONIA

ALBANIA

TURKEY

A3

PORTUGAL

SPAIN

Sardinia
(ITALY)

GREECE

10°W

Balearic Islands
(SPAIN)

Sicily
(ITALY)

MALTA

Crete
(GRE

GIBRALTAR
(U.K.)

Mediterranean Sea 10°E

20°E

─── National border

Abbreviations

EQU. GUINEA	EQUATORIAL GUINEA
NETH.	NETHERLANDS
N.Z.	NEW ZEALAND
U.A.E.	UNITED ARAB EMIRATES
U.K.	UNITED KINGDOM
U.S.	UNITED STATES

ARCTIC OCEAN

Beaufort Sea

Baffin Bay

Greenland (DENMARK)

Bering Strait

Viscount Melville Sound

Davis Strait

Arctic Circle

ALASKA (U.S.)

Fairbanks

Anchorage

Whitehorse

Juneau

Gulf of Alaska

Bering Sea

Yukon River

Mackenzie River

Liard River

Great Bear Lake

Great Slave Lake

Yellowknife

Foxe Basin

Hudson Strait

Labrador Sea

60° N

CANADA

Peace River

Athabasca R.

Lake Athabasca

Saskatchewan R.

Hudson Bay

James Bay

Edmonton

Calgary

Saskatoon

Regina

Winnipeg

Lake Winnipeg

Thunder Bay

St. John's

Vancouver

Seattle

Portland

Puget Sound

Columbia R.

Snake R.

Boise

UNITED STATES

Salt Lake City

Great Salt Lake

Missouri R.

Great Lakes

St. Lawrence River

Ottawa

Quebec

Montreal

St. John

Gulf of St. Lawrence

Halifax

Detroit

Toronto

Albany

Boston

Chicago

Cleveland

New York City

Reno

Denver

St. Louis

Indianapolis

Philadelphia

Washington, D.C.

San Francisco

Las Vegas

Colorado R.

Memphis

Richmond

Norfolk

Los Angeles

San Diego

Phoenix

El Paso

Dallas

Atlanta

Raleigh

Charleston

Tucson

Rio Grande

Houston

New Orleans

Savannah

Jacksonville

30° N

Hermosillo

San Antonio

Tampa

Miami

BAHAMAS

Nassau

ATLANTIC OCEAN

Honolulu

HAWAII (U.S.)

Tropic of Cancer

Chihuahua

MEXICO

Monterrey

Gulf of Mexico

Havana

CUBA

HAITI

Port-au-Prince

Durango

León

Tampico

PUERTO RICO (U.S.)

PACIFIC OCEAN

Guadalajara

Mexico City

JAMAICA

Santo Domingo

DOMINICAN REPUBLIC

Puebla

Veracruz

BELIZE

Kingston

Acapulco

GUATEMALA

Belmopan

Guatemala

HONDURAS

Caribbean Sea

San Salvador

Tegucigalpa

EL SALVADOR

Managua

Maracaibo

NICARAGUA

San José

Caracas

GUYANA

SURINAME

COSTA RICA

PANAMA

Panama City

VENEZUELA

Paramaribo

Cayenne

Medellín

Georgetown

FRENCH GUIANA (FRANCE)

Cali

Bogotá

0° Equator

Quito

COLOMBIA

Rio Negro

Amazon R.

Belém

Galápagos Islands (ECUADOR)

Guayaquil

ECUADOR

Iquitos

Manaus

Tapajós River

Fortaleza

Trujillo

PERU

Xingu R.

Recife

Lima

BRAZIL

Tocantins R.

São Francisco R.

FRENCH POLYNESIA (FRANCE)

Papeete

Cuzco

Brasília

Salvador

Lake Titicaca

La Paz

Belo Horizonte

Arequipa

BOLIVIA

Goiânia

Sucre

Campo Grande

Rio de Janeiro

Tropic of Capricorn

Antofagasta

PARAGUAY

São Paulo

Salta

Asunción

Curitiba

San Miguel de Tucumán

Paraná R.

30° S

CHILE

Córdoba

Pôrto Alegre

Valparaíso

Rosario

URUGUAY

Santiago

Buenos Aires

Montevideo

La Plata

Río de la Plata

Concepción

Mar del Plata

Valdivia

Bahía Blanca

0   1,000   2,000 Miles

0   1,000   2,000 Kilometers

Miller Cylindrical Projection

ARGENTINA

National border

⊛ National capital

• City

N
W   E
S

A4

Punta Arenas

Falkland Islands (U.K.)

South Georgia (U.K.)

150° W   120° W   90° W   60° W   30° W

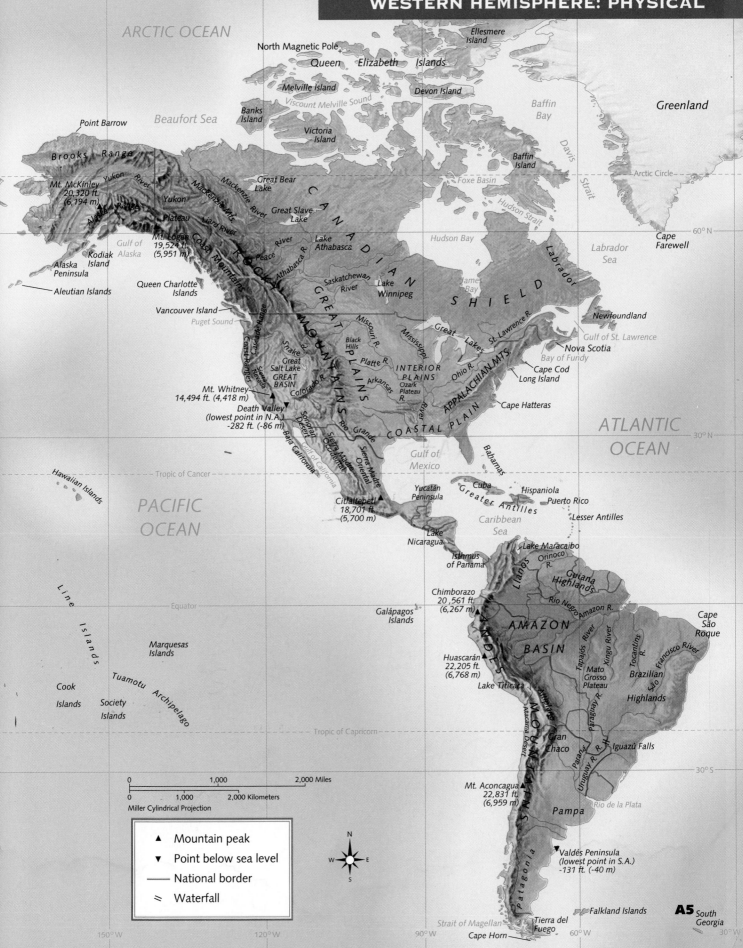

ARCTIC OCEAN

North Magnetic Pole

Queen Elizabeth Islands

Ellesmere Island

Melville Island

Devon Island

Baffin Bay

Greenland

Banks Island

Viscount Melville Sound

Beaufort Sea

Victoria Island

Point Barrow

Brooks Range

Yukon River

Great Bear Lake

CANADIAN

Baffin Island

Foxe Basin

Davis Strait

Arctic Circle

Mt. McKinley 20,320 ft. (6,194 m)

Yukon

Plateau

Mackenzie Mts.

Mackenzie River

Great Slave Lake

Hudson Strait

60° N

Alaska Range

Liard River

Peace River

Hudson Bay

James Bay

SHIELD

Labrador

Cape Farewell

Mt. Logan 19,524 ft. (5,951 m)

Coast Mountains

ROCKY

Athabasca R.

Lake Athabasca

Labrador Sea

Gulf of Alaska

Kodiak Island

Alaska Peninsula

Aleutian Islands

Queen Charlotte Islands

Vancouver Island

Puget Sound

Cascade Range

Coast Ranges

Columbia R.

Snake R.

Great Salt Lake

GREAT BASIN

Sierra Nevada

Mt. Whitney 14,494 ft. (4,418 m)

Death Valley (lowest point in N.A.) -282 ft. (-86 m)

MOUNTAINS

GREAT PLAINS

Missouri R.

Black Hills

Platte R.

Arkansas R.

Colorado R.

Saskatchewan River

Lake Winnipeg

Great Lakes

Mississippi R.

INTERIOR PLAINS

Ozark Plateau

Ohio R.

St. Lawrence R.

Newfoundland

Gulf of St. Lawrence

Nova Scotia

Bay of Fundy

Cape Cod

Long Island

APPALACHIAN MTS.

Cape Hatteras

ATLANTIC OCEAN

30° N

Colorado R.

Rio Grande

Sierra Madre Occidental

Sierra Madre Oriental

Sonoran Desert

Baja California

Gulf of California

COASTAL PLAIN

Gulf of Mexico

Bahamas

Greater Antilles

Cuba

Hispaniola

Puerto Rico

Lesser Antilles

Tropic of Cancer

Hawaiian Islands

PACIFIC OCEAN

Citlaltépetl 18,701 ft. (5,700 m)

Yucatán Peninsula

Lake Nicaragua

Isthmus of Panama

Caribbean Sea

Lake Maracaibo

Orinoco R.

Llanos

Guiana Highlands

Rio Negro

Amazon R.

Line Islands

Equator

Marquesas Islands

Galápagos Islands

Chimborazo 20,561 ft (6,267 m)

AMAZON BASIN

Tapajós River

Xingu River

Tocantins R.

São Francisco River

Cape São Roque

Cook Islands

Society Islands

Tuamotu Archipelago

Huascarán 22,205 ft. (6,768 m)

Lake Titicaca

ANDES

Mato Grosso Plateau

Paraguay R.

Brazilian Highlands

Tropic of Capricorn

Atacama Desert

Gran Chaco

Paraná R.

Uruguay R.

Iguazú Falls

30° S

Mt. Aconcagua 22,831 ft. (6,959 m)

Pampa

MOUNTAINS

Rio de la Plata

Valdés Peninsula (lowest point in S.A.) -131 ft. (-40 m)

Patagonia

Falkland Islands

South Georgia

Strait of Magellan

Tierra del Fuego

Cape Horn

1,000   2,000 Miles

0   1,000   2,000 Kilometers

Miller Cylindrical Projection

▲ Mountain peak

▼ Point below sea level

— National border

≈ Waterfall

N W E S

150° W   120° W   90° W   60° W   30° W

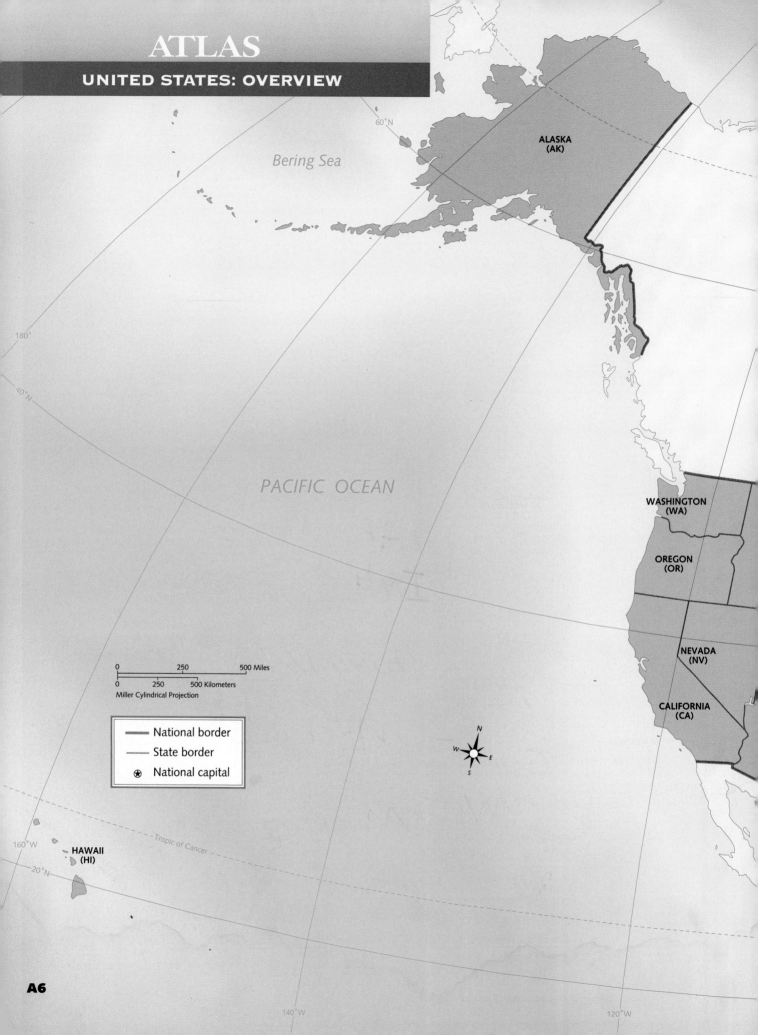

Bering Sea

60°N

ALASKA
(AK)

180°

40°N

PACIFIC OCEAN

WASHINGTON
(WA)

OREGON
(OR)

NEVADA
(NV)

CALIFORNIA
(CA)

| 0 | 250 | 500 Miles |
| 0 | 250 | 500 Kilometers |

Miller Cylindrical Projection

National border
State border
National capital

N
W   E
S

160°W

Tropic of Cancer

HAWAII
(HI)

20°N

140°W

120°W

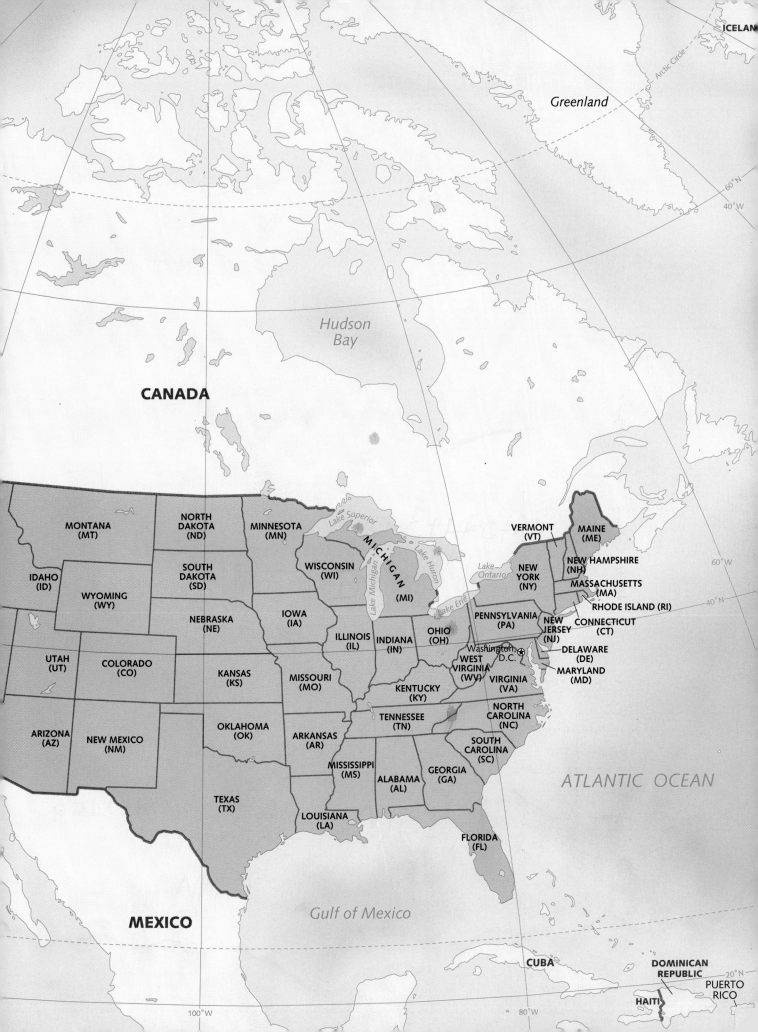

CANADA

RUSSIA

ARCTIC OCEAN

Alaska
(AK)

CANADA

Bering
Sea

Juneau

PACIFIC OCEAN

Washington
(WA)
Olympia

Montana
(MT)
Helena

Salem

Oregon
(OR)

Boise

Idaho
(ID)

Wyoming
(WY)

Cheyenne

Great
Salt
Lake

Salt Lake City

Sacramento

Carson City

Nevada
(NV)

Utah
(UT)

Denver

Colorado
(CO)

PACIFIC
OCEAN

California
(CA)

Santa Fe

Arizona
(AZ)
Phoenix

New
Mexico
(NM)

Honolulu

Hawaii
(HI)

PACIFIC
OCEAN

MEXICO

N
W E
S

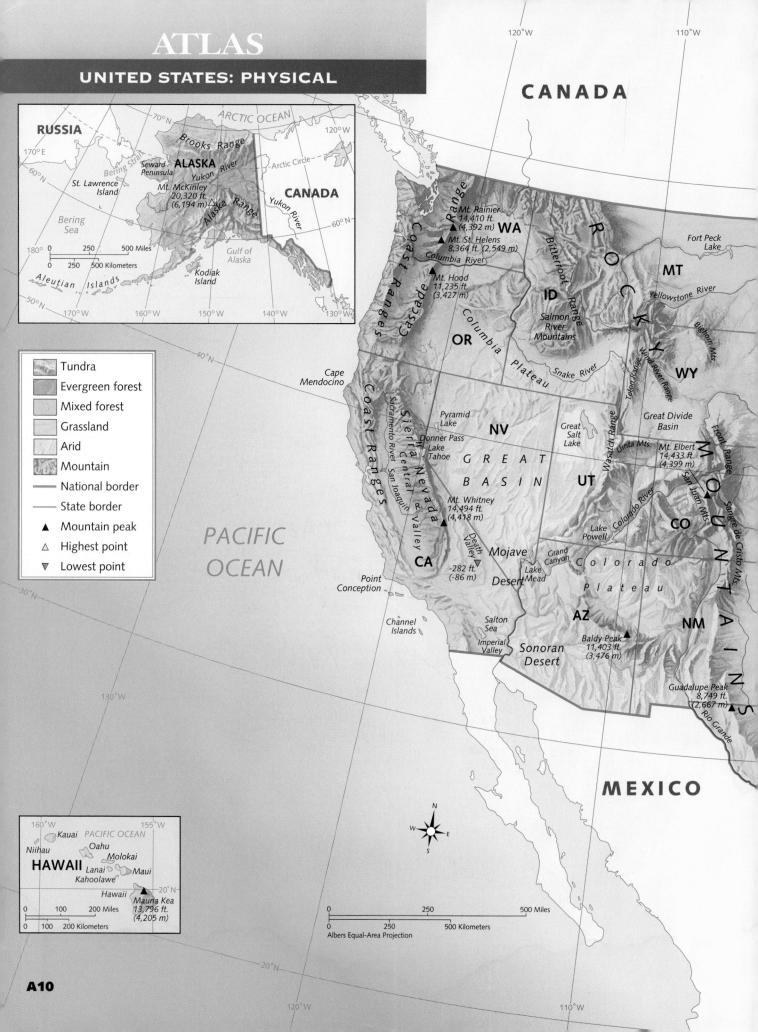

RUSSIA

ARCTIC OCEAN

Brooks Range

170° E

70° N

Seward Peninsula

ALASKA

Yukon River

Arctic Circle

60° N

St. Lawrence Island

Mt. McKinley 20,320 ft. (6,194 m)

Alaska Range

CANADA

Yukon River

60° N

Bering Strait

Bering Sea

Gulf of Alaska

250

500 Miles

180°

250

500 Kilometers

0

Kodiak Island

Aleutian Islands

50° N

170° W

160° W

150° W

140° W

130° W

CANADA

120° W

110° W

Fort Peck Lake

Mt. Rainier 14,410 ft. (4,392 m)

WA

R O C K Y

Bitterroot Range

MT

Mt. St. Helens 8,364 ft. (2,549 m)

Columbia River

ID

Salmon River Mountains

Yellowstone River

Bighorn Mts.

40° N

Mt. Hood 11,235 ft. (3,427 m)

OR

Columbia Plateau

Snake River

Teton Range

Wind River Range

WY

Cape Mendocino

Pyramid Lake

NV

Great Salt Lake

Wasatch Range

Great Divide Basin

Front Range

Uinta Mts.

Mt. Elbert 14,433 ft. (4,399 m)

M
O
U
N
T
A
I
N
S

Donner Pass

Lake Tahoe

G R E A T

B A S I N

UT

Colorado River

San Juan Mts.

Sangre de Cristo Mts.

CO

Sacramento River

Sierra Nevada

San Joaquin Valley

Central Valley

Mt. Whitney 14,494 ft. (4,418 m)

Lake Powell

Colorado

Plateau

Coast Ranges

CA

Death Valley -282 ft. (-86 m)

Mojave Desert

Grand Canyon

Lake Mead

PACIFIC

Point Conception

Channel Islands

Salton Sea

AZ

Baldy Peak 11,403 ft. (3,476 m)

NM

OCEAN

30° N

Imperial Valley

Sonoran Desert

Guadalupe Peak 8,749 ft. (2,667 m)

Rio Grande

Legend

	Tundra
	Evergreen forest
	Mixed forest
	Grassland
	Arid
	Mountain
——	National border
——	State border
▲	Mountain peak
△	Highest point
▽	Lowest point

MEXICO

N

W E

S

160° W

155° W

Kauai

PACIFIC OCEAN

Niihau

Oahu

Molokai

HAWAII

Lanai

Maui

Kahoolawe

Hawaii

20° N

Mauna Kea 13,796 ft. (4,205 m)

0   100   200 Miles

0   100   200 Kilometers

0   250   500 Miles

0   250   500 Kilometers

Albers Equal-Area Projection

20° N

130° W

120° W

110° W

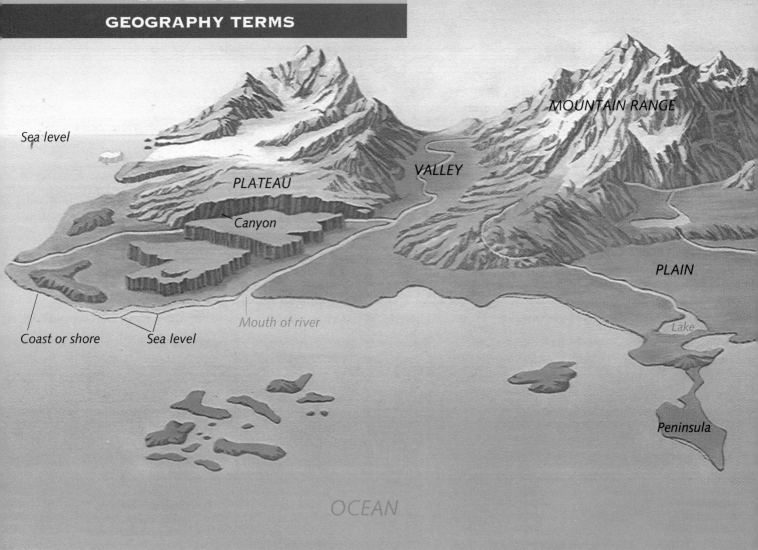

Sea level

MOUNTAIN RANGE

VALLEY

PLATEAU

Canyon

PLAIN

Coast or shore   Sea level

Mouth of river

Lake

Peninsula

OCEAN

bay part of a lake, sea, or ocean with land around some of it

bluff high, steep face of rock or earth

canyon deep, narrow valley with steep sides

cliff high, steep face of rock or earth

coast land along a sea or ocean

delta triangle-shaped area of land at the mouth of a river

desert dry land with few plants

foothills hilly area at the base of a mountain range

gulf body of water with land around some of it, but larger than a bay

harbor area of water where ships can dock safely near land

hill rolling land that rises above the land around it

island land that has water on all sides

lake body of water with land on all sides

mountain highest kind of land

mountain range row of mountains

mouth of river place where a river empties into another body of water

oasis area of water and fertile land with desert on all sides

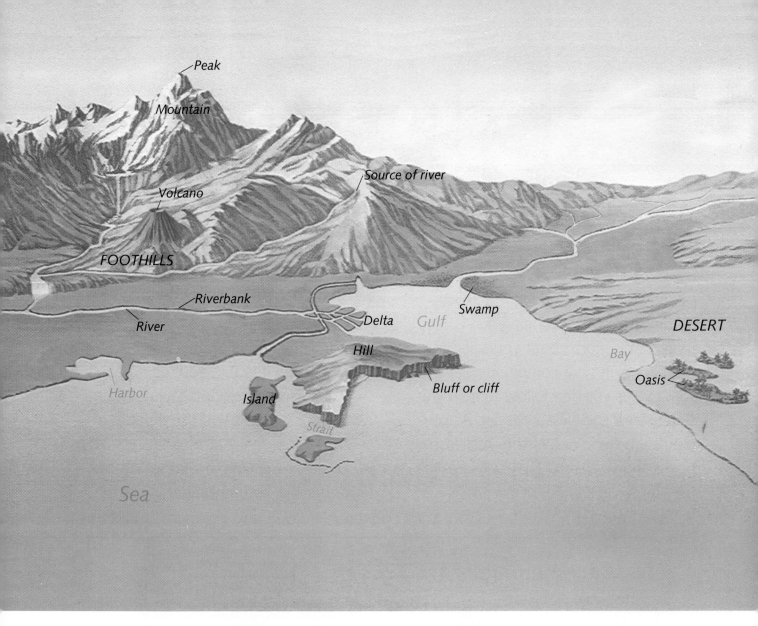

Peak

Mountain

Source of river

Volcano

FOOTHILLS

Riverbank

River

Delta

Gulf

Swamp

DESERT

Hill

Bay

Harbor

Island

Bluff or cliff

Oasis

Strait

Sea

ocean body of salt water larger than a sea

peak top of a mountain

peninsula land that has water around most of it

plain flat land

plateau large area of high, flat land with steep sides

river large stream of water that flows across the land

riverbank land along a river

sea body of salt water smaller than an ocean

sea level level that is even with the surface of an ocean or sea

shore land along the edge of a lake, sea, or ocean

source of river place where a river or stream begins

strait narrow body of water that joins two larger bodies of water

swamp area of low, wet land with trees

valley low land between hills or mountains

volcano mountain that has poured out hot rock

Read Your Social Studies Book

Why Is This Skill Important?

The stories you read in this Social Studies textbook will help you understand more about yourself and the people in your community. Here are some steps you can follow to help you understand each lesson better. As you read each step, look at the small lesson pages shown below. They will explain the steps you should follow.

Understand the Process
Before You Read the Lesson

A. Find the title of the lesson. The title is in large letters at the top of the page. The title tells you what you will be reading about. The number in the circle tells you the number of the lesson.

B. Look for the Link to Our World box under the lesson number. Read the

---

A

LESSON 6

Communities Are Built for Government

Link to Our World

Why would location be an important reason for building a city or town?

Focus on the Main Idea
Read to find out why location was important in building Washington, D.C., and other places of government.

Preview Vocabulary
capital city
capitol
state capital
county
county seat

B

The early leaders of the United States decided it was time to build a new city where the country's laws would be made. The people of Virginia and Maryland gave the country some land along the Potomac River on which to build the new city.

The Story of Washington, D.C. **C**

George Washington rode out on his horse to look at the land along the Potomac River. The new nation was going to build a **capital city** where the leaders of the country could meet and work. President Washington wanted to find a good place to build this city. **D**

Each day from the middle of October until the end of October in 1791 he rode along the riverbank. It was hard to choose just the right place to build the nation's capital. George Washington talked with Thomas Jefferson about the problem. He talked with other leaders, too. At last a good place was chosen. Washington, D.C., was soon to be built.

E A painting of George Washington, the first President of the United States

From this drawing by Pierre L'Enfant, the city of Washington, D.C., began to take shape.

Who?

Benjamin Banneker 1731–1806

This picture of Benjamin Banneker was drawn when he was a young man. Thomas Jefferson knew that Banneker had many skills. So Jefferson told George Washington that Banneker would be a good person to help lay out the streets of Washington, D.C.

F

Two former clock makers, Andrew Ellicott and Benjamin Banneker, measured the land. An engineer, Pierre L'Enfant (pee•AIR lahn•FAHN), used their measurements to plan the city's streets and buildings. The first thing built was the **capitol**, the building where lawmakers meet. Where you find a capitol building, you will find a capital city.

C ✔ Why was the capital city located in the middle of the nation?

question in the top of the box. Think about what this question means to you. Then read the sentence under Focus on the Main Idea. The question and the sentence will help you understand why the lesson is important.

Read the words under Preview Vocabulary. These are important words for understanding the lesson. You will find these words highlighted, or colored, in yellow. The meaning of each word will be given right after it is highlighted.

C. Quickly look through the lesson and read the headings that are printed in red. Also read the questions that have a large check mark beside them. Doing this will help you find out what the lesson is about. You can also look at the pictures, maps, and charts. Ask yourself these questions.

- What do I already know about this subject?
- What will I learn about this subject?

While You Read the Lesson

D. Read part of the lesson before you study the pictures that go with it. Start at a heading that is printed in red, and read until you come to a question with a check mark. As you

read, stop and look up words you do not know. Take your time, and reread any paragraphs you do not understand.

E. When you have finished reading, study the pictures and maps that go with this part of the lesson. Then read the captions, or words, that explain each picture or map. Pictures and their captions tell you more about a subject or help explain what you read in the lesson.

F. Read the sections titled Who?, What?, When?, or Where? These sections add interesting facts to what you have read.

After You Read the Lesson

Ask yourself these questions.

- What new things did I learn about this subject?
- Is there something more I want to know?

Think and Apply

Use the steps listed above as you read the first lesson. Then read them again before you begin other lessons. You may wish to use them as you read lessons in the rest of the book. How can steps like these help you read other textbooks or magazines and newspapers?

What Is a Community?

A community is a place. ➡

People in a community work together to solve problems. ➡

A community is a group of people who live and work together in the same place. People all over the world live and work in all kinds of communities. Some of those communities look much like yours. Others look very different. No matter where they are or how they look, communities are alike in many ways. In this unit you will read about the things that are the same in all communities. You will also learn what makes each community different.

← **Children in a park in Orlando, Florida**

Communities are made up of different groups of people. →

⬆ **Communities change over time.**

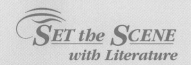
ROXABOXEN

by Alice McLerran   illustrated by Barbara Cooney

**In this story some children build an imaginary
community on a hillside in their neighborhood. Using
old boxes and desert stones, they build a place where
wonderful things can happen.**

Marian called it Roxaboxen.
(She always knew the name of everything.)
There across the road, it looked like any rocky hill—
nothing but sand and rocks, some old wooden boxes,
cactus and greasewood and thorny ocotillo—
but it was a special place.

The street between Roxaboxen and the houses curved like a river,
so Marian named it the River Rhode.
After that you had to ford a river to reach Roxaboxen.

Of course all of Marian's sisters came:
Anna May and Frances and little Jean.
Charles from next door, even though he was twelve.
Oh, and Eleanor, naturally,
and Jamie with his brother Paul.
Later on there were others, but these were the first.

Well, not really the first.
Roxaboxen had always been there
and must have belonged to others, long before.

When Marian dug up a tin box filled with round black pebbles
everyone knew what it was:
it was buried treasure.
Those pebbles were the money of Roxaboxen.
You could still find others like them if you looked hard enough.
So some days became treasure-hunting days, with everybody trying to
    find that special kind.
And then on other days you might just find one without even looking.

A town of Roxaboxen began to grow, traced in lines of stone:
Main Street first, edged with the whitest ones,
and then the houses.
Charles made his of the biggest stones.
After all, he was the oldest.
At first the houses were very plain, but soon they all began to
    add more rooms.
The old wooden boxes could be shelves or tables or anything you wanted.
You could find pieces of pottery for dishes.
Round pieces were best.

Later on there was a town hall.
Marian was mayor, of course;
that was just the way she was.
Nobody minded.

After a while they added other streets.
Frances moved to one of them and built herself a new house outlined
    in desert glass,
bits of amber, amethyst, and sea-green:
a house of jewels.

And because everybody had plenty of money,
there were plenty of shops.
Jean helped Anna May in the bakery—
pies and cakes and bread baked warm in the sun.
There were two ice cream parlors.
Was Paul's ice cream the best, or Eleanor's?
Everybody kept trying them both.
(In Roxaboxen you can eat all the ice cream you want.)

Everybody had a car.
All you needed was something round for a
    steering wheel.
Of course, if you broke the speed limit you had to go to jail.
The jail had cactus on the floor to make it uncomfortable,
and Jamie was the policeman.
Anna May, quiet little Anna May, was always speeding—
you'd think she liked to go to jail.

But ah, if you had a horse, you could go as fast as the wind.
There were no speed limits for horses,
and you didn't have to stay on the roads.
All you needed for a horse was a stick and some kind of bridle,
and you could gallop anywhere.

Sometimes there were wars.
Once there was a great war, boys against girls.
Charles and Marian were the generals.
The girls had Fort Irene, and they were all girl scouts.
The boys made a fort at the other end of Roxaboxen, and they were
    all bandits.

Oh, the raids were fierce, loud with whooping and the stamping
    of horses!
The whirling swords of ocotillo had sharp thorns—
but when you reached your fort you were safe.

Roxaboxen had a cemetery, in case anyone died,
but the only grave in it was for a dead lizard.
Each year when the cactus bloomed, they decorated the grave
    with flowers.

Sometimes in the winter, when everybody was at school and the
    weather was bad,
no one went to Roxaboxen at all, not for weeks and weeks.
But it didn't matter;
Roxaboxen was always waiting.
Roxaboxen was always there.
And spring came, and the ocotillo blossomed,
and everybody sucked the honey from its flowers,
and everybody built new rooms, and everybody decided to have
    jeweled windows.
That summer there were three new houses on the east slope
and two new shops on Main Street.

And so it went.
The seasons changed, and the years went by.
Roxaboxen was always there.

The years went by, and the seasons changed,
until at last the friends had all grown tall,
and one by one, they moved away
to other houses, to other towns.
So you might think that was the end of Roxaboxen—
but oh, no.

Because none of them ever forgot Roxaboxen.
Not one of them ever forgot.
Years later, Marian's children listened to stories of that place
and fell asleep dreaming dreams of Roxaboxen.
Gray-haired Charles picked up a black pebble on the beach
   and stood holding it,
remembering Roxaboxen.

More than fifty years later, Frances went back
and Roxaboxen was still there.
She could see the white stones bordering Main Street,
and there where she had built her house
the desert glass still glowed—
amethyst, amber, and sea-green.

Where on Earth Is Roxaboxen?

Why might you need to find out where places are?

Focus on the Main Idea
Learn the ways to describe where a community is found.

Preview Vocabulary
location
map
continent
globe
hemisphere
equator

You have just read a story about a place called Roxaboxen. Marian and her friends started Roxaboxen. Working together, they built streets, homes, stores, and other buildings. Then they pretended to live and work in the community they built. If someone asked you how to find Roxaboxen, what could you say?

Where on a Map?

The children built Roxaboxen on a hill in their neighborhood. The hill was at the corner of 2nd Avenue and 8th Street. This corner was Roxaboxen's location. A **location** is where something is found.

To show someone where to find Roxaboxen, you might draw a map. A **map** is a picture that shows the location of something. A map can show the whole Earth or just a small part of it, such as a neighborhood. This map shows where Roxaboxen was located.

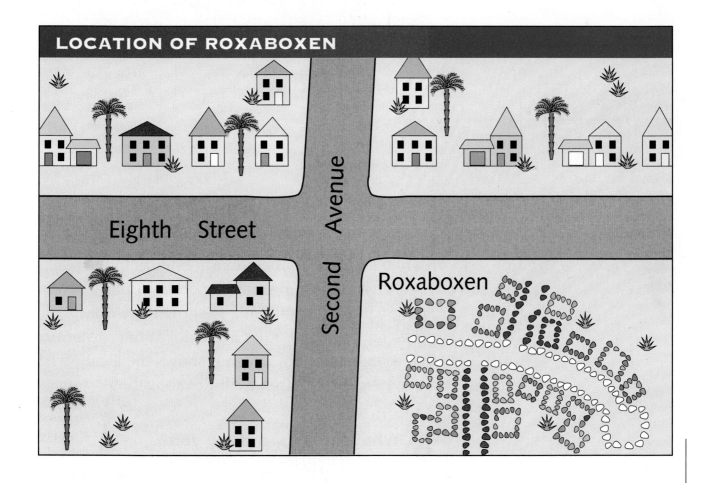

LOCATION OF ROXABOXEN

Eighth Street

Second Avenue

Roxaboxen

A NEIGHBORHOOD IN YUMA, ARIZONA

Map Key
- Location of Roxaboxen
- Railroad

Marian's imaginary neighborhood was in the real city of Yuma. The map shows a part of Yuma. There are too many streets in Yuma to show the whole city on a small map. Look for the dot at the corner of 2nd Avenue and 8th Street. It shows the location in Yuma where the children built Roxaboxen.

 **What can a map show you?**

Where Is Yuma?

The city of Yuma is located in Arizona. Arizona is one of the 50 states that make up our country. Our country is the United States of America. Most people call it the United States for short.

The map shows all 50 states in the United States. It shows you the location of Arizona in the United States. The dot tells you the location of Yuma in the state of Arizona.

How many states make up the United States of America?

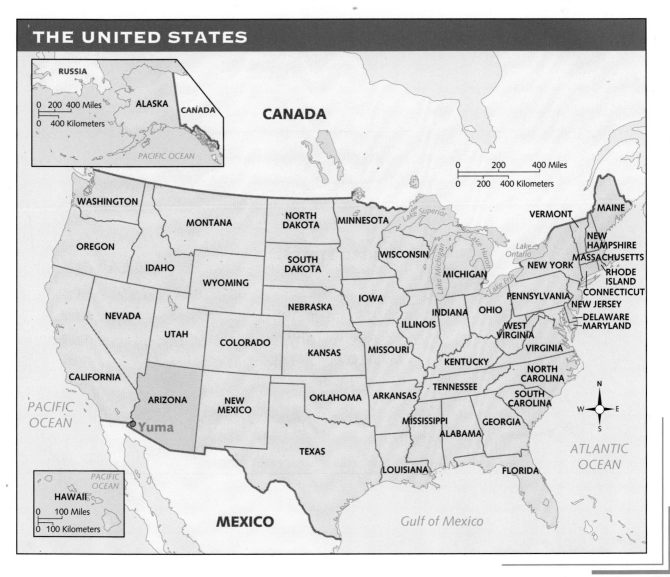

THE UNITED STATES

Countries and Continents

The United States is one of the countries on the continent of North America. A **continent** is one of the seven main land areas on the Earth. The United States, Canada, and Mexico are the countries that make up the biggest part of North America. This map shows where Yuma, Arizona, is located in North America.

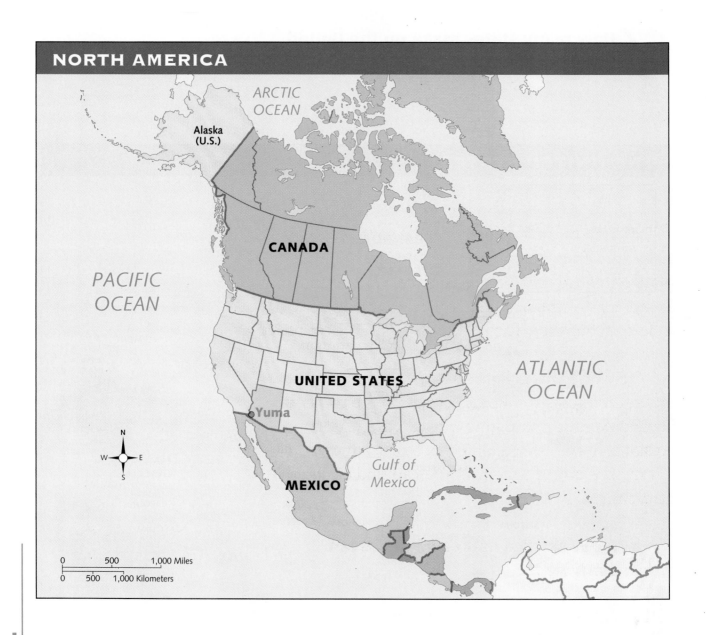

NORTH AMERICA

ARCTIC OCEAN

Alaska (U.S.)

CANADA

PACIFIC OCEAN

UNITED STATES

ATLANTIC OCEAN

Yuma

MEXICO

Gulf of Mexico

N
W   E
S

0   500   1,000 Miles
0   500   1,000 Kilometers

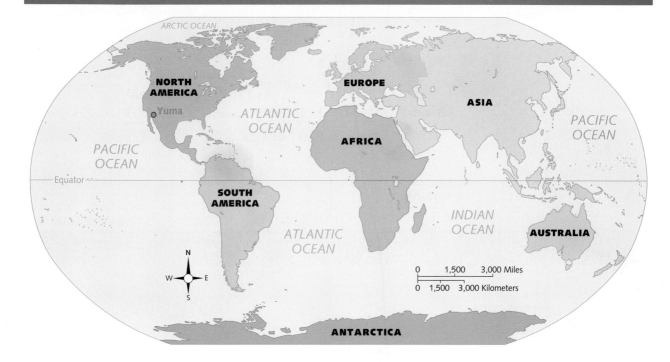

This map of the world shows the seven continents. They are Africa, Antarctica, Asia, Australia, Europe, North America, and South America. Each continent, except for Australia and Antarctica, is made up of different countries. There are more than 190 countries in the world today.

Where on Earth is Roxaboxen? You can now answer the question. Roxaboxen is on the corner of Second Avenue and Eighth Street. It is in Yuma, Arizona, in the United States, in North America.

Where is North America? You can find out on the next page.

 What are the names of the seven continents?

Hemispheres

Maps of the whole Earth do not always show the true shape of the planet or the true sizes of all the continents. That is because maps are flat, and the Earth is round. A **globe** is a better model of the Earth because it is round, too. However, a map is easier to carry with you.

Each of the pictures above shows half the Earth. Another way of saying "half the Earth" is to use the word **hemisphere** (HEH•muh•sfir). *Hemi* means "half." *Sphere* means "ball" or "globe."

If you cut a globe in half from the North Pole to the South Pole, you get two hemispheres. One half would be the Western Hemisphere. The other half would be the Eastern Hemisphere.

Another way to divide the Earth is along the equator. The **equator** is an imaginary line that is halfway between the North Pole and the South Pole. If you cut a globe in half at the equator, you still get two hemispheres—the Northern Hemisphere and the Southern Hemisphere.

You can see that North America, including Yuma, Arizona, is north of the equator. It is in the Northern Hemisphere. It is also in the Western Hemisphere. Every place on the Earth is in two hemispheres at the same time.

 In which two hemispheres is Roxaboxen?

LESSON 1 REVIEW

Check Understanding

1. **Recall the Facts**   What line divides the Northern from the Southern Hemisphere?

2. **Focus on the Main Idea**   How would you tell someone where to find Roxaboxen?

Think Critically

3. **Link to You**   What words would you use to tell someone your location on the Earth? Which of the words you used were vocabulary words?

Show What You Know

 **Map Activity**   Use the map on page 33 to draw the shape of your state. Show where your community is located. Then explain your map to a family member.

How To

Read a Map

Why Is This Skill Important?

Maps can help you find a location. They can also tell you a lot about a place. They show places to visit, such as parks, museums, and shopping malls. They show which way you must go to get to a place. They also show how far away something is. Suppose you are visiting the city of Yuma for the first time. You can use a map to help you get where you need to go.

Understand the Process

Most maps have the same parts. If you know what each part does, you can read a map more easily.

- **Title**—The title tells you what a map is about. The title is often at the top or bottom of a map. What is the title of the map shown on page 39?
- **Map Key**—Most maps use **symbols** to stand for something that is real on the Earth. Some symbols do not look exactly like what they stand for. Look at the box that is at the bottom of the map. This is called the map key. A **map key** tells what the symbols on the map stand for. What symbol stands for the sheriff's office? What symbol stands for a park?
- **Scale**—The map of Yuma has a **distance scale**. You can use it to measure the distance, or how far it is, between two places on the map. To do this, you need a sheet of paper. Place the paper on the map, just below Carver Park and City Hall. Make one mark on the paper right where Carver Park is. Make another mark where City Hall is. Then line up the first mark with the zero on the distance scale at the top of the map. Check to see where the second mark lines up. The marks you made on the paper should line up with the marks for one mile on the distance scale. It is one mile from Carver Park to City Hall. Now, use the distance scale to find out how far it is from the library to the Arts Center Museum.

- **Directions**—Find the drawing that shows the letters **N**, **S**, **E**, and **W**. This drawing is called a compass rose. A **compass rose** tells you directions, or which way to go. **N** means north, **S** means south, **E** means east, and **W** means west. These four directions are called **cardinal directions**. Suppose you are at City Hall. In which direction would you go to get to Fort Yuma?

Think and Apply

Write five questions about finding location and distance. Then ask a classmate to use this map to answer your questions. Now try your hand at answering his or her questions!

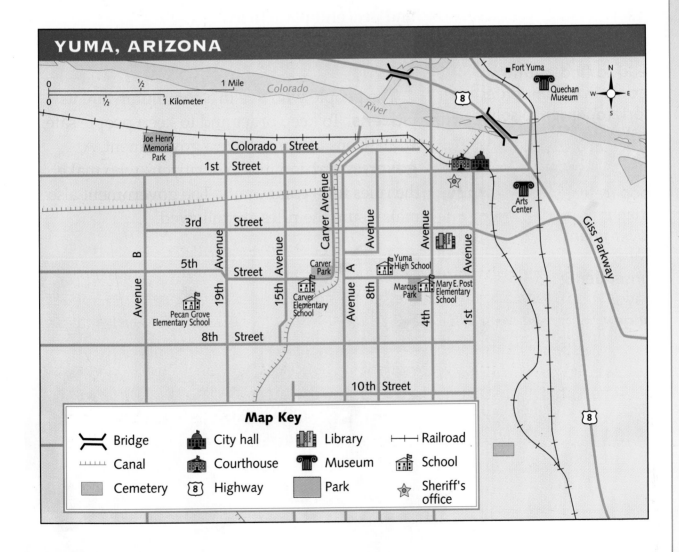

YUMA, ARIZONA

Map Key

Bridge	City hall	Library	Railroad
Canal	Courthouse	Museum	School
Cemetery	Highway	Park	Sheriff's office

Getting Along in a Community

Link to Our World

Why do people in your community need to work together?

Focus on the Main Idea
Read to find out how people in communities work together to solve problems.

Preview Vocabulary
cooperate
citizen
government
law
consequence
mayor
judge

Like the children in Roxaboxen, people in real communities such as Yuma, Arizona, do things together. Sometimes they get along. Sometimes they do not. People must learn to **cooperate**, or work together, to keep their community a safe and peaceful place to live.

Governing a Community

The people who live in a community are its **citizens**. To keep order and to keep people safe, the citizens of Yuma have a government. A **government** is a group of citizens who make the rules for a community. The government also makes sure the rules are followed.

Citizens working together

A community government makes rules called laws. **Laws** are written to make the community a safe place to live. Traffic laws are rules that tell citizens how to travel safely through the community's streets. Without traffic laws, many people might be hurt in accidents. They might ride their bikes without stopping at stop signs and be hit by cars.

If people break laws, they may face the consequences of their actions. A **consequence** is something that happens as a result of an action. Being hurt in an accident is one type of consequence. Paying a fine, or money, is another type of consequence. If a very important law has been broken, a person may have to go to jail. In Roxaboxen the children went to jail if they drove too fast.

Jamie was the police officer in Roxaboxen. Police officers in Yuma and other communities work to keep people safe and to see that all citizens follow the laws.

Police officer in Roxaboxen

Police officer in Yuma

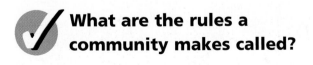
What are the rules a community makes called?

The mayor of Roxaboxen

How Laws Are Made

Each community has a way to make laws and to see that they are followed. In Roxaboxen, Marian was the mayor. A **mayor** is the leader of a city or town government. The mayor's job is to see that things get done that will make the community a good place to live.

In Yuma, groups of citizens are chosen to make laws for all the people in the community. They meet with the mayor to talk about problems in the community. Then they decide how to solve them.

City of YUMA, Arizona

MARILYN R. YOUNG
MAYOR

The mayor of Yuma

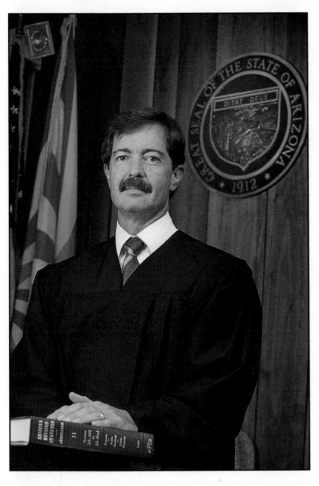

A judge in Yuma

Courts make up another part of the government in Yuma and in most other communities. **Judges** are citizens who are chosen to work as leaders in the courts. Judges decide if a person has broken the law. They also decide the consequences for people who break the law. Judges work in the courts to make certain that citizens are treated fairly.

 What is the leader of the city government called?

LESSON 2 REVIEW

Check Understanding

1. **Recall the Facts** What is a government?
2. **Focus on the Main Idea** How do people in real communities work together to solve problems?

Think Critically

3. **Personally Speaking** Think about some rules your school has. What are some consequences you might face if you do not follow the rules?

Show What You Know

 **Poster Activity** Think about how laws can keep you safe in your community. Choose one law, and make a poster that shows why people should follow it. At the bottom of your poster, write a sentence that tells what could happen if the law is not followed. Hang up your poster in the classroom, and discuss it with classmates.

How To

Act as a Responsible Citizen

Why Is This Skill Important?

Each citizen in a community has responsibilities. **Responsibilities** are duties citizens have. One of these responsibilities is to understand and obey the law. When citizens obey the law, they help keep their community safe and peaceful.

Remember What You Have Read

Many community laws are like the traffic laws you read about in Lesson 2. They are made for a reason. Laws help people in a community live together safely and peacefully. If someone does not obey the law, he or she may face consequences. Responsible citizens know that laws are important, so they obey them.

Understand the Process

As you have just read, it is the responsibility of all citizens to obey laws. Here are some ways you can be a responsible citizen.

- **At Home**—Pick up after yourself. Put away your books and games so someone does not trip over them.

- **At the Park**—Put your trash in a trash can. Play sports only in places where signs say you can play safely.
- **At School**—Follow the directions of the crossing guard. Look both ways before crossing.

What other ways can you show that you are a responsible citizen?

Think and Apply

Some laws are made to keep people safe. Is there a law in your community that people must wear seat belts when riding in a car? Should laws like this be followed? Explain your answer.

BUILDING CITIZENSHIP

How We Get What We Need

Link to Our World

What kinds of things do you need to live?

Focus on the Main Idea
Read to find out how people in communities meet their needs.

Preview Vocabulary
resource
volunteer

In order to live, people need food, clothing, and shelter. People in real communities can help one another meet these needs. They can work together like Marian, Charles, and others did in Roxaboxen.

Meeting Needs with Resources

Some of the needs people have can be met with resources. A **resource** is something that people use to make what they need. The children in Roxaboxen used big white stones to mark their streets. They used old wooden boxes to make shelves and tables. The stones and boxes were resources the children used to meet their needs. People in Yuma use many resources, too. Soil, water, and plants are important resources.

A worker in Yuma uses many resources to build a house.

The children used resources to build Roxaboxen.

45

A community has another important resource—its people. People are a source of work and skills in a community.

The children of Roxaboxen used their skills in many ways. Jamie was the police officer. Marian was the mayor. Jean and Anna May worked in the bakery. In Yuma some people cook meals and some sell clothing. Others build roads, while still others paint buildings and keep them clean.

In any community there are many jobs that need to be done. People depend on one another in many ways.

 What are some important resources in a community?

Workers at a bakery in Roxaboxen

Workers at a bakery in Yuma

People Make a Difference

Some people work in a community without being paid. These people are **volunteers**. Many volunteers spend their free time doing things to make their community a good place to live.

Volunteers help solve problems in the community. For example, community food banks collect food given by people. Then volunteers take it to places where people who have no food can get a meal free.

Volunteers help people when there has been an earthquake or a flood. They collect food, clothing, blankets, and medicine for people who need them.

In some cities in Arizona, volunteers give their free time to help with a project called "Habitat for Humanity." A habitat is a place to live. On weekends these volunteers work together to help people who are not able to build or fix up their own homes.

Volunteers at a food bank

 How do volunteers help make their communities good places to live?

Volunteers in Yuma help with a community project.

LESSON 3 REVIEW

Check Understanding
1. **Recall the Facts** Why are people important resources?
2. **Focus on the Main Idea** What kinds of resources help people in communities meet their needs?

Think Critically
3. **Link to You** What are some ways you can help in your community as a volunteer?

Show What You Know

Collage Activity
Look through magazines for pictures of resources. Make a collage to show resources you and your family have used in the last week. Along with your classmates, put your collage in a binder that everyone can look through.

A Community Has a History

Link to Our World

Why is learning about the past important?

Focus on the Main Idea
Read to find out how Yuma has changed over the years.

Preview Vocabulary
history
ancestor
missionary

Every community has a history. **History** is the story of what has happened in a place. The story begins when people begin to live and work there. Roxaboxen's history started when Marian set up its first streets and buildings and gave the place its name. Many real communities have a long history. For example, Yuma's history started hundreds of years ago.

Long, Long Ago

The first people to live in the place that is now called Yuma were the Quechan (KET•chan) Indians. They farmed land along the Colorado River. The Quechan were part of a larger group of Indians known as the Yuma. Many people who live near Yuma today have ancestors who were Yuma Indians. An **ancestor** is someone in a person's family who lived a long time ago, such as a great-great-grandparent.

This photograph of Quechan Indians was taken in 1882.

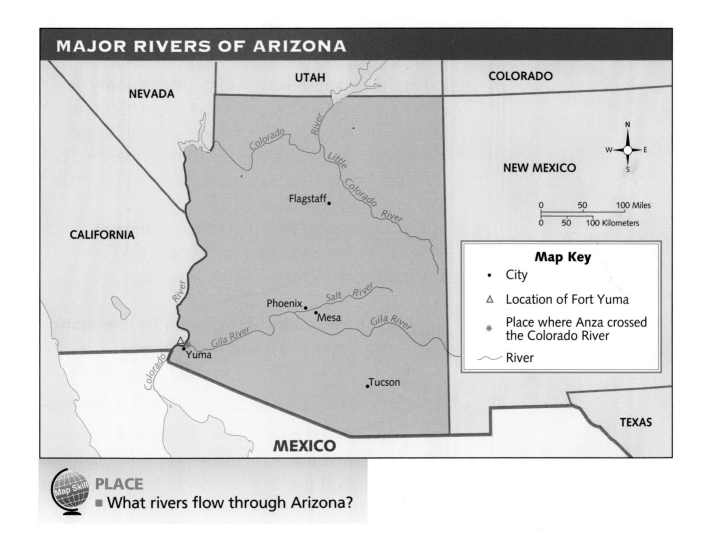

MAJOR RIVERS OF ARIZONA

NEVADA

UTAH

COLORADO

Colorado River

Little Colorado River

Flagstaff.

CALIFORNIA

NEW MEXICO

River

Phoenix.

Salt River

Mesa

Gila River

Gila River

Yuma

0   50   100 Miles

0   50   100 Kilometers

Map Key

• City

△ Location of Fort Yuma

✳ Place where Anza crossed the Colorado River

~ River

.Tucson

TEXAS

Colorado River

MEXICO

PLACE
- What rivers flow through Arizona?

Beginning in the 1500s explorers from the country of Spain explored the land along the Colorado River. One of those explorers was Juan Bautista de Anza (HWAN bow•TEES•tah day AHN•sah). In 1774 he looked for a way to cross the Colorado River. The river was wide and rough. It was hard to cross from one side to the other. Anza learned that the best place to cross the river was near where Yuma is now.

Anza knew that he would need the help of the Quechan Indians to cross the river. He gave gifts of clothing to the Quechan leader. In return the Quechans helped Anza cross the river. Then they made a large meal for everyone. The Quechans served watermelons that had been buried in the sand to keep them cool.

More Spanish people came to the Yuma area in 1780. A group of missionaries came to teach the Indians the Spanish way of life. A **missionary** is a person who is sent to tell others about his or her beliefs. The Spanish missionaries built a mission, or church, and tried to change the Indians' beliefs. The Quechan Indians turned against the missionaries in 1781 and made them leave.

In 1821 Yuma became part of the country of Mexico. The ancestors of many people who live in Yuma today were Spanish or Mexican.

 Who were the first people to live along the Colorado River near Yuma?

Anglos and Chinese Move to Yuma

In 1850, United States soldiers built a fort across the river from Yuma. Soon many people began to travel through Yuma on their way to look for gold in California. In 1854 an agreement with Mexico made Yuma a part of the United States. Then many people gave up looking for gold. They stopped in Yuma and stayed. The Spanish people of Yuma called these new citizens Anglos. Anglos are persons whose ancestors came from Europe and were not Spanish.

This painting shows how Fort Yuma looked in 1850.

Another group of people who moved to Yuma were the Chinese. In 1877 thousands of Chinese workers came to help build the railroads. Chinese families still live in Yuma.

 Why did Anglos move to Yuma?

Changes over Time

Over the years there have been many changes in Yuma. The name of the town has changed three times. First, it was Colorado City. Then, it was Arizona City. Finally, the town was called Yuma. That was the name of the large group of Indians the Quechan Indians belonged to.

Yuma grew from just a few small buildings into the large, modern city it is today. The pictures on these pages show some of the ways Yuma has changed in over 100 years.

The photograph on the left shows how Main Street in Yuma looked during a parade in 1909. The photograph above shows how it looks today.

Many changes have taken place, but much has stayed the same. The weather in Yuma is still sunny and warm. People still live and work in this town next to the Colorado River. They raise their families and enjoy the location and weather.

Knowing a community's history can help you better understand the people who live in the community today. Many groups have made Yuma their home—Yuma Indians and Spanish, Mexican, Chinese, and Anglo people. They all have interesting stories to tell about how they came to live in Yuma.

 What has stayed the same in Yuma over the years?

The Sunshine Capital

Yuma is known for its sunny weather. There are more sunny days each year in Yuma than in any other city in the United States.

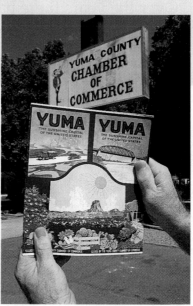

 These children are enjoying the Pig River Festival in Yuma.

LESSON 4 REVIEW

Check Understanding

1. **Recall the Facts**   What groups of people have lived in Yuma over the years?

2. **Focus on the Main Idea**   How has Yuma changed over time?

Think Critically

3. **Think More About It**   Why do you think the Indians made the Spanish missionaries leave?

Show What You Know

Interview Activity
Find a person who has lived in your community for a long time. Make a list of the questions you would like answered. Then interview the person to find out what changes he or she has seen. Share what you learn with your classmates.

How To

Read a Time Line

Why Is This Skill Important?

When you study Social Studies, you sometimes need to keep track of when events happened. To help you keep these dates in order, you can use a time line. A **time line** shows when important events took place.

Understand the Process

You read most time lines from left to right, just like a sentence. The things on the left happened first. The things on the right happened later. Look at the time line shown here. The first thing it shows is that the Yuma Indians helped the Spanish explorer Anza cross the Colorado River in 1774. The last thing the time line shows is when Chinese workers started to build the railroads. In what year did that happen?

Think and Apply

Use the time line to help you answer these questions.

1. Which was built first, Fort Yuma or the Spanish mission?

2. Did Yuma become part of the United States before or after the building of Fort Yuma?

3. In what year did Anza cross the Colorado River?

4. In what order did the Spanish, the Chinese, and the Anglos arrive in Yuma?

5. When did Yuma become part of the United States?

TIME LINE OF YUMA'S HISTORY

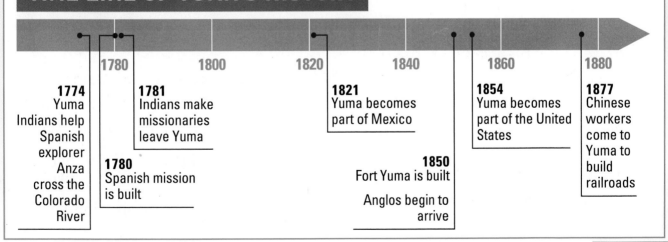

1774 Yuma Indians help Spanish explorer Anza cross the Colorado River

1780 Spanish mission is built

1781 Indians make missionaries leave Yuma

1821 Yuma becomes part of Mexico

1850 Fort Yuma is built

Anglos begin to arrive

1854 Yuma becomes part of the United States

1877 Chinese workers come to Yuma to build railroads

1780 1800 1820 1840 1860 1880

Many People, Many Ways of Life

LESSON 5

Link to Our World

Why do you think most communities are made up of different groups of people?

Focus on the Main Idea
Read to find out how groups of people come to live together in some communities.

Preview Vocabulary
custom
culture
founders

In most communities people with the same interests or background form groups. In Roxaboxen, the girls formed one group and the boys formed another. Today the city of Yuma, like most other large communities, has many groups of people. Native Americans and people whose ancestors came from Asia, Mexico, Europe, Africa, and other places all live there.

Many different people live in Yuma.

What Makes Groups of People Special?

In any community the people in a group often share the same customs. A **custom** is a way of doing something. In the United States, one custom is for people to greet each other by shaking hands.

In the United States, it is a custom for people to shake hands when they meet.

In Saudi Arabia one custom is for women and girls to cover all parts of their bodies when they go out in public. They even cover the lower part of their face with a cloth called a veil.

The customs that people have are part of their culture. The **culture** of a group is the people's way of life. The people of a culture usually speak the same language and often have the same beliefs. They may enjoy the same art, music, dance, and literature.

 What makes up the culture of a group of people?

Women in Saudi Arabia wear veils.

Captain George Vancouver pointing to the land that would later become the city of Vancouver

How Do Groups of People Start Communities?

A community begins when a group of people first live together. The people who start the community are called its **founders**. Marian and the other children who started Roxaboxen were its founders.

Some communities are made up of just one group of people who share the same culture. Other communities are made up of many groups with different cultures, all living and working together.

Vancouver is a city in Canada, the country to the north of the United States. Like Yuma, Vancouver is a community made up of many groups of people from different parts of the world. The Musqueam (MUS•kwe•um) Indians were the first people to live on the land where the city was built. Some people who live in Vancouver today have Musqueam ancestors.

Vancouver is named for British sea captain George Vancouver, who explored the area in 1792. He said that the land and the water would become part of his country, Great Britain. However, George Vancouver was not the founder of the city. The founders of Vancouver were the people who built a lumber mill there in 1865. The area around the lumber mill later became the city of Vancouver.

 Who are the founders of a community?

The founders of Vancouver

VANCOUVER, BRITISH COLUMBIA

CANADA

BRITISH COLUMBIA

PACIFIC OCEAN

150   300 Miles
150   300 Kilometers

•Vancouver

UNITED STATES

Map Key
🌲 Forest

ARCTIC OCEAN

BRITISH COLUMBIA   CANADA
•Vancouver

PACIFIC OCEAN

UNITED STATES
•Yuma

MEXICO   Gulf of Mexico

ATLANTIC OCEAN

700 Miles
700 Kilometers

HUMAN-ENVIRONMENT INTERACTIONS
The founders of Vancouver built a lumber mill.
■ What resource was there for them to use?

Different People Make Up a Community

The groups of people who make up a community often have different customs and cultures. However, they can still get along with one another.

People from many parts of the world have made Vancouver their home. Many who live there today have Native American ancestors. The children and grandchildren of people who came from Russia, England, Scotland, and Ireland live in Vancouver, too. People also came to Vancouver from other countries in Europe, such as Germany and Italy. In the 1850s miners came from the United States and Australia to search for gold. In the 1880s thousands of Chinese workers came to help build the railroads. Then, in 1904, a large group of Sikhs (SEEKS) moved to Vancouver from India to cut timber in Canada's forests.

A Vancouver street in 1902

Sikh timber cutters

This classroom in Vancouver is filled with children of many different cultures. It is an interesting place to learn.

Today four out of every ten students in Vancouver speak English at school and another language at home. Having different languages can make it hard for people to talk with one another. Different customs can make it hard for people to understand one another. But the differences between people make Vancouver an interesting place to live and work.

 What were three main reasons people moved to Vancouver from other countries?

Chinese people in Vancouver celebrate the Lunar New Year.

Communities Celebrate

The people of the different groups in a community like to celebrate their own holidays. In Vancouver the Chinese people celebrate the Lunar New Year. They hold a parade and set off fireworks. This day most often comes in February.

At other times all the people of a community celebrate a holiday together. On July 1 everyone in Vancouver celebrates Canada Day, their nation's birthday. This holiday is like the Fourth of July in the United States. Canadians gather to watch parades and fireworks. They listen to speeches and sing their national anthem.

Fireworks in the night sky over Vancouver

Each group that lives in Vancouver has its own customs and culture. But all the people are Canadian citizens. They are proud of their flag and their country.

 How do citizens of Vancouver celebrate Canada Day?

When?

July 1, 1867

Before 1867 Great Britain ruled Canada. However, on July 1, 1867, an important event took place. A new law was passed that gave Canadians the right to form their own central government. This important day became Canada Day, a holiday celebrated by all Canadian citizens every July 1.

This photograph shows the Canadian leaders working together in 1867.

LESSON 5 REVIEW

Check Understanding

1. **Recall the Facts** What kinds of things do people of the same culture share?
2. **Focus on the Main Idea** How do different groups of people come to live together in a community?

Think Critically

3. **Explore Viewpoints** Why might people with the same interests or backgrounds want to form groups?

Show What You Know

 **Bulletin Board Activity** Collect pictures showing customs from around the world. Cut out pictures from old magazines, or draw pictures to show what you have seen yourself or read about in books. Write a paragraph that explains each custom. Give your paragraph a title. Then add your pictures to a class bulletin board.

MAKING SOCIAL STUDIES REAL

A Community GUIDANCE CARD

The tiny community of Kotzebue (KAHT•suh•byoo) had a problem. Over the years some people had lost their feeling of responsibility to the community. There were problems with fighting and crime. Members of the community wanted to do something to help bring the community back together. So they created a community guidance card.

On the card is a list of ideas about the community that are important to the people of Kotzebue. "They give us all a sense of belonging, a sense of peace," says Rachel Craig, a community leader. Some of these ideas are

- Cooperation

- Family roles

- Hard work

- Humor

- Love for children

- Respect for nature

- Respect for others

- Responsibility to community

- Sharing

Many community members, young and old, carry these cards with them wherever they go. The cards help remind the people of the ideas that are most important to them. Today there are fewer problems in Kotzebue. A small card has made a big difference in this community.

With guidance and support from Elders, we must teach our children Inupiaq values.

knowledge of language
sharing
respect for others
cooperation
respect for elders
love for children
hard work
knowledge of family tree
avoidance of conflict
respect for nature
spirituality

OUR UNDERSTANDING OF OUR UNIVERSE AND OUR BELIEF IN

Iñupiat Iḷitqusiat

EVERY IÑUPIAQ IS RESPONSIBLE TO ALL OTHER INUPIAT FOR THE SURVIVAL OF OUR CULTURAL SPIRIT, AND THE VALUES AND TRADITIONS THROUGH WHICH IT SURVIVES. THROUGH OUR EXTENDED FAMILY, WE RETAIN, TEACH, AND LIVE OUR IÑUPIAQ WAY.

KOTZEBUE, ALASKA

ARCTIC OCEAN

RUSSIA

Kotzebue

Arctic Circle

Nome

Fairbanks

CANADA

A L A S K A

Anchorage

Bering Sea

Gulf of Alaska

Juneau

N
W · E
S

0   200   400 Miles
0   200   400 Kilometers

PACIFIC OCEAN

THINK AND APPLY

BUILDING CITIZENSHIP

Now it is your turn to make a guidance card. First, brainstorm a list of ideas that are important to you and your classmates. Then, pick five of the most important ideas. Next, cut out a blank card from cardboard or construction paper. Last, write the ideas on the card. Carry your card with you, and show it to a family member. Explain why the ideas on it are important to you and your classmates.

STORY CLOTH

Follow the pictures shown in this story cloth to help you review the things you read about in Unit 1.

Summarize the Main Ideas

1. A community has a location on Earth.

2. Citizens in a community form governments and work together to solve problems.

3. People in a community use resources to meet their needs.

4. A community changes over time.

5. A community is made of different groups of people that live and work together.

Make a Puzzle Picture Compare the community you live in to the pictures that are shown here. Then tell about your community by making a puzzle picture. Draw the outlines of puzzle pieces on a sheet of heavy paper. Now write a sentence and draw a picture on each puzzle piece. The sentence should describe and the picture should show something interesting about your community. Cut out the puzzle pieces. Ask a classmate to put them back together again.

COOPERATIVE LEARNING WORKSHOP

Remember

- Share your ideas.
- Cooperate with others to plan your work.
- Take responsibility for your work.
- Show your group's work to the class.
- Discuss what you learned by working together.

Activity 1
Demonstration

Role-play customs that citizens in your community follow. For example, a member of your group might show how his or her family celebrates a birthday. Talk about how customs in your community are alike and how they are different.

Activity 2
Write a History

As a group, write a history of your community. List ways you can find information. One way might be to ask a librarian for help. You might also talk to people who have lived in your community for a long time. Make a booklet that tells what your group has learned.

Activity 3
Make a Model

Roxaboxen was a community made by a group of children. They built Roxaboxen with old boxes and stones. Work with a group of classmates to make a model of your own imaginary community. Plan where you will have your community, and then build it. You can use empty boxes and rinsed milk cartons for buildings. You can cut paper to make roads and sidewalks. Work together to make your model community a safe and peaceful place to live.

CONNECT MAIN IDEAS

Use this graphic organizer to show how the unit's main ideas are connected. First, copy the organizer onto a separate sheet of paper. Then, write one detail about each community that will support each main idea.

Lesson 1
A community has a location on Earth.
Roxaboxen _____
Yuma _____

Lesson 2
Citizens in a community form governments and work together to solve problems.
Roxaboxen _____
Yuma _____

What Is a Community?

Lesson 5
A community is made up of different groups of people who live and work together.
Roxaboxen _____
Yuma _____

Lesson 3
People in a community use resources to meet their needs.
Roxaboxen _____
Yuma _____

Lesson 4
A community changes over time.
Roxaboxen _____
Yuma _____

USE VOCABULARY

Roxaboxen was an imaginary community. Think of your own imaginary community, and write sentences about it. Use each word below in your sentences.

citizen   custom   founder   law   location

WRITE MORE ABOUT IT

Write a Postcard Imagine that you are visiting the community of Vancouver. Make a postcard that shows the city. Then fill out the postcard telling a friend about the people you have met.

CHECK UNDERSTANDING

1. How can you find your community on a map?

2. Why can people be thought of as a resource?

3. Why is Vancouver made up of different groups of people?

THINK CRITICALLY

1. **Link to You** What is one law in your community that is important to you and your family? Tell why it is important.

2. **Personally Speaking** How can people from different cultures make your life more interesting?

3. **Cause and Effect** What might happen if people stopped volunteering to help others?

APPLY SKILLS

How to Read a Map Use the map to answer the following questions.

1. What symbol stands for an airport?

2. Suppose you were at the zoo. In which direction would you travel to reach the hospital?

3. How far is it from the school to city hall?

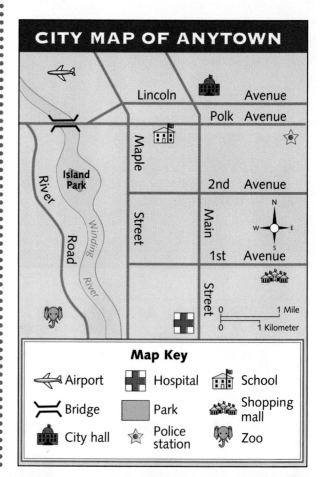

CITY MAP OF ANYTOWN

Lincoln Avenue
Polk Avenue
Maple
Island Park
River
Winding River
Road
Street
2nd Avenue
Main
1st Avenue
Street
0 1 Mile
0 1 Kilometer

Map Key

Airport   Hospital   School

Bridge   Park   Shopping mall

City hall   Police station   Zoo

How to Be a Responsible Citizen

Think about the rules you must obey at school. List three of those rules, and explain why each is important. Then explain what the consequences are for not obeying these rules.

How to Read a Time Line

The time line below shows when things happened in an imaginary community named Happytown. Use the time line to help you answer these questions.

1. Which was built first, the city park or the new movie theater?

2. When did Tina Smith become mayor?

3. When did citizens from Sadville move to Happytown?

4. For how many years was the town without a movie theater?

READ MORE ABOUT IT

The Big Orange Splot by Daniel Manus Pinkwater. Hasting House. One day Mr. Plumbean decides to paint his house every color of the rainbow. His neighbors are unhappy about this. Read to find out if Mr. Plumbean and his neighbors work out their problems.

The House I Live In by Isadore Seltzer. Simon & Schuster. What kinds of homes do people live in? In this book you will discover some of the places people live, such as houseboats, old farmhouses, and trailer homes.

How My Family Lives in America by Susan Kuklin. Bradbury. The stories in this book tell how people of different cultures share their customs, songs, games, and languages with others.

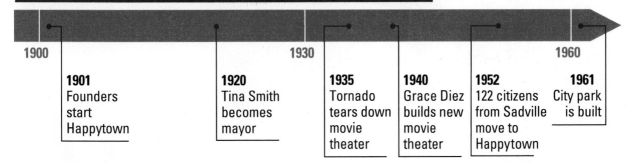

TIME LINE OF HAPPYTOWN'S HISTORY

1900

1901
Founders start Happytown

1920
Tina Smith becomes mayor

1930

1935
Tornado tears down movie theater

1940
Grace Diez builds new movie theater

1952
122 citizens from Sadville move to Happytown

1960

1961
City park is built

UNIT 2
Where People Start Communities

Some communities are built near water. →

Some communities are built where roads meet. →

People do not choose just any place to start a community. They have reasons for their choices. In this unit you will read about where people have built cities and towns and why they have built them there.

← **The Last Dollar Ranch near Telluride, Colorado**

← **Some communities are built near resources.**

Location is important to places of government. →

71

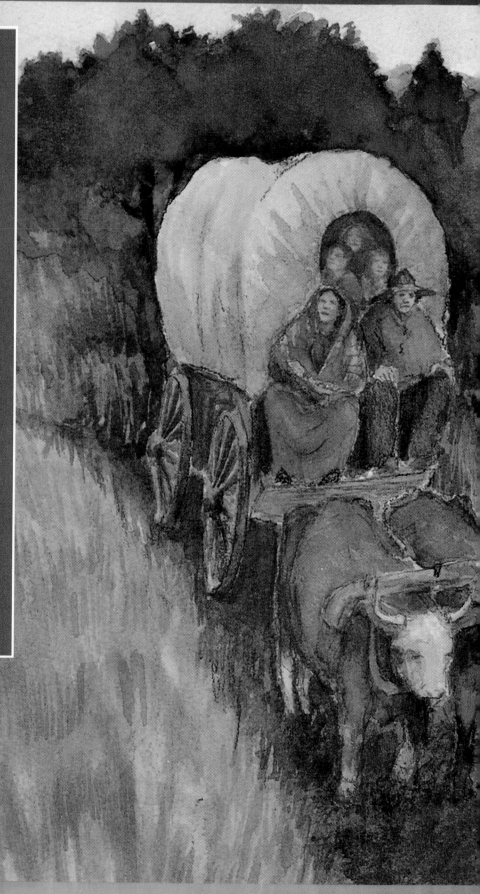

Read this story about the first family to live in the town of Aurora, Ohio. The family arrived in the year 1800, when Aurora had a name but no people.

This is the story of Mr. and Mrs. Sheldon and their seven children. They built Aurora's first house and cleared land for its first farm. As you read, think about the problems people might face in building a community.

AURORA
Means Dawn

by Scott Russell Sanders

illustrated by Jill Kastner

When Mr. and Mrs. Sheldon reached Ohio in 1800 with seven children, two oxen, and a bulging wagon, they were greeted by a bone-rattling thunderstorm. The younger children wailed. The older children spoke of returning to Connecticut.

The oxen pretended to be four-legged boulders and would budge neither forward nor backward, for all of Mr. Sheldon's thwacking. Lightning toppled so many oaks and elms across the wagon track that even a dozen agreeable oxen would have done them no good, in any case.

They camped. More precisely, they spent the night squatting in mud beneath the wagon, trying to keep dry.

Every few minutes, Mrs. Sheldon would count the children, touching each head in turn, to make sure none of the seven had vanished in the deluge.

Mrs. Sheldon remarked to her husband that there had never been any storms even remotely like this one back in Connecticut. "Nor any cheap land," he replied. "No land's cheap if you perish before setting eyes on it," she said. A boom of thunder ended talk.

They fell asleep to the roar of rain.

Next morning, it was hard to tell just where the wagon track had been, there were so many trees down.

Husband and wife tried cutting their way forward.

After chopping up and dragging aside only a few felled trees, and with half the morning gone, they decided Mr. Sheldon should go fetch help from Aurora, their destination.

On the land-company map they had carried from the East, Aurora was advertised as a village, with mill and store and clustered cabins. But the actual place turned out to consist of a surveyor's post topped by a red streamer.

So Mr. Sheldon walked to the next village shown on the map—Hudson, which fortunately did exist, and by morning he'd found eight men who agreed to help him clear the road.

Their axes flashed for hours in the sunlight. It took them until late afternoon to reach the wagon.

With the track cleared, the oxen still could not move the wagon through the mud until all nine men and one woman and every child except the toddler and the baby put their shoulders to the wheels.

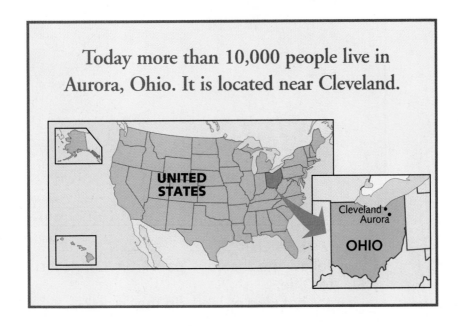

They reached Aurora at dusk, making out the surveyor's post in the lantern light. The men from Hudson insisted on returning that night to their own homes. Ax blades glinted on their shoulders as they disappeared from the circle of the campfire.

Huddled together like a basketful of kittens, the children slept in the hollow of a sycamore tree. Mr. and Mrs. Sheldon carried the lantern in circles around the sycamore, gazing at this forest that would become their farm. Aurora meant dawn; they knew that. And their family was the dawn of dawn, the first glimmering in this new place.

The next settlers did not come for three years.

Today more than 10,000 people live in Aurora, Ohio. It is located near Cleveland.

UNITED STATES

Cleveland•
Aurora•

OHIO

Communities Are in Different Places

Link to Our World

What makes the place where you live different from other places?

Focus on the Main Idea

Read to find out some of the things that make places different.

Preview Vocabulary

physical feature
landform
mountain range
valley
plateau
plain
peninsula
coast
climate
desert
human-made feature

The Sheldon family knew little about Aurora. The land-company map showed a mill, a store, and some cabins. But when the family got there, they found only a post topped by a red streamer. The place called Aurora was nothing more than a clearing in a forest.

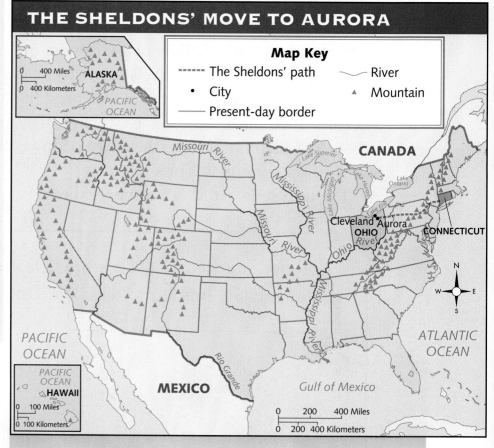

THE SHELDONS' MOVE TO AURORA

Map Key
------ The Sheldons' path
• City
—— Present-day border
⁀ River
▲ Mountain

MOVEMENT
Follow the Sheldons' path from Connecticut to Ohio.
■ What kind of land did they cross?

What Makes Places Different?

All places on the Earth have features, or things that are special about them. You can describe a place by talking about its features. The features of any one place make it different from other places.

The Sheldons first arrived in Ohio during a terrible thunderstorm. They had never seen storms like this back in Connecticut. The kind of weather a place has is one of its physical features. A **physical feature** is something found in nature, such as weather and plant life. Land and water are also physical features. People build communities in places with many different physical features.

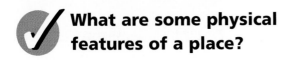 **What are some physical features of a place?**

A family hiking through a meadow in Yosemite National Park

Highlands and Lowlands

People build cities or towns on many **landforms**, or land that has different shapes. Some are built in the highlands, which rise above the land around them. Some are in the lowlands, where the land is lower and often flatter.

Mountains are one kind of highland. There are many mountains in the United States. The two largest **mountain ranges**, or groups of mountains, are the Rocky Mountains and the Appalachian Mountains. **Valleys** are the lowlands between hills and mountain ranges.

The Rocky Mountains are in the western part of our country. The Appalachians are in the eastern part. These mountain ranges are different from each other. The Rocky Mountains are very high, and their tops are mostly pointed. The Appalachians are lower, and their tops are rounded. That is because the Appalachians are older. Over many, many years wind and rain have worn down their tops.

Mountain range

Valley

Pointed tops of the Rocky Mountains

Rounded tops of the Appalachians

Plains

Plateaus

Hills are highlands, too. However, hills are not as high as mountains. **Plateaus** (pla•TOHZ) are also highlands. They have steep sides like some mountains, but their tops are flat.

Plains are lowlands. They are flat or gently rolling. In the middle of our country, between the Rocky Mountains and the Appalachians, much of the land is plains. Because this area is so large, the western part of it is called the Great Plains.

 What are some kinds of landforms?

Waterways and Bodies of Water

Many communities in the United States are built near flowing waterways or bodies of water. They may be built on peninsulas. A **peninsula** is a piece of land that has water almost all the way around it. Communities are also built on **coasts**—the land next to oceans—or on the shores of lakes, or along rivers.

Many cities and towns are built along rivers that start high in the Rocky or Appalachian mountains. These rivers flow down toward the middle of the country and into the Mississippi River. The Mississippi River is the longest river in the United States. It flows into the Gulf of Mexico, a part of the Atlantic Ocean.

Other cities and towns are built along rivers that also start in the mountains but flow west or east toward the ocean coasts. These rivers flow into the Pacific Ocean on the west coast or the Atlantic Ocean on the east coast.

Peninsula

↑ The Yampa River winds through Dinosaur National Monument in Colorado.

← Waves crash against the rocky coastline of the Big Sur area in California.

Many communities in the United States are built on the ocean coasts. Others are built on the shores of the country's five largest lakes. These lakes are called the Great Lakes because of their size. They are Lakes Superior, Michigan, Huron, Erie, and Ontario. The Great Lakes lie between the United States and Canada.

 Along what kinds of waterways and bodies of water do people build communities?

Climate and Plant Life

The climate and plant life are physical features of a place, too. **Climate** means the kinds of weather a place has in each season year after year. How hot or cold it gets and how much rain or snow falls are all part of a place's climate.

Because of its size, the United States has many climates. They may be hot, warm, mild, cool, or cold, as well as wet or dry. People live in all these different climates.

These photographs show two places that have different climates. What is the climate where you live?

Once you know the climate of a place, you can understand its plant life. Places with hot, dry climates, such as **deserts**, have some kinds of plants that do not grow in cold, wet climates. Some grasses can grow in cool, dry climates as well as in warm, wet climates. Most trees need a lot of rain, so only places with wet climates have thick forests.

 **What is climate?**

Grasses that grow in the desert do not need much rain.

LEARNING FROM DIAGRAMS
In what ways are a peninsula and an island the same and different?

mountain

hill

plateau

lake

valley

river

plain

coast

peninsula

island

ocean

What People Add to a Place

When you describe a place, you might also talk about the features that people have added to it. These are its **human-made features**. The house and farm that the Sheldons built were among Aurora's earliest human-made features. The post topped by a red streamer was the first!

Today Aurora is a city that has many human-made features. Its buildings, houses, bridges, and roads are features it did not have when the Sheldon family moved there. The roads now join Aurora to many other communities. Each of these communities has features that make it different from all other places, just as Aurora is.

 **What is one kind of human-made feature?**

The library in Aurora, Ohio, is visited by both children and adults.

LESSON 1 REVIEW

Check Understanding

1. **Recall the Facts** How is a human-made feature different from a physical feature?
2. **Focus on the Main Idea** What are some things that make places different from one another?

Think Critically

3. **Think More About It** What physical features might make a place good for building a community?

Show What You Know

 **Map Activity** Draw a map of the city or town where you live. Be sure to show at least one physical feature and one human-made feature. Explain the map to a classmate.

S·K·I·L·L·S

How To

Read a
Landform Map

Why Is This Skill Important?

Have you ever visited a friend or family member who lived in another part of the United States? Did you know anything about the place before you got there?

The Sheldon family knew very little about Aurora before they got there. The map that the land company gave them showed only a mill, a store, and some cabins.

Some maps show streets and roads to help you get where you need to go. Other maps show you other features. The landform map of the United States tells you about the shape of the land. It tells you where the mountains and hills are. It tells you if the land is a plateau or a plain.

Understand the Process

Follow the numbered steps in the next column. They will help you read the map and understand the landforms of the United States.

1. Find the purple box in the map key. What is shown with the color purple? The key tells you that mountains are colored purple on the map. Where are the Appalachian Mountains located?

2. Look at the map key again. What things are shown with the colors brown, yellow, and green? The key tells you what each color stands for on the map. Brown stands for plateaus. Yellow stands for hills. Green stands for plains.

3. Which city is on higher ground, Salt Lake City or New Orleans?

4. Which cities are on the plains?

5. On what kind of land is Phoenix?

Think and Apply

Look at the landforms shown on the map for your state. Write a paragraph that describes the landforms of your state to someone who has never been there.

LANDFORM MAP OF THE UNITED STATES

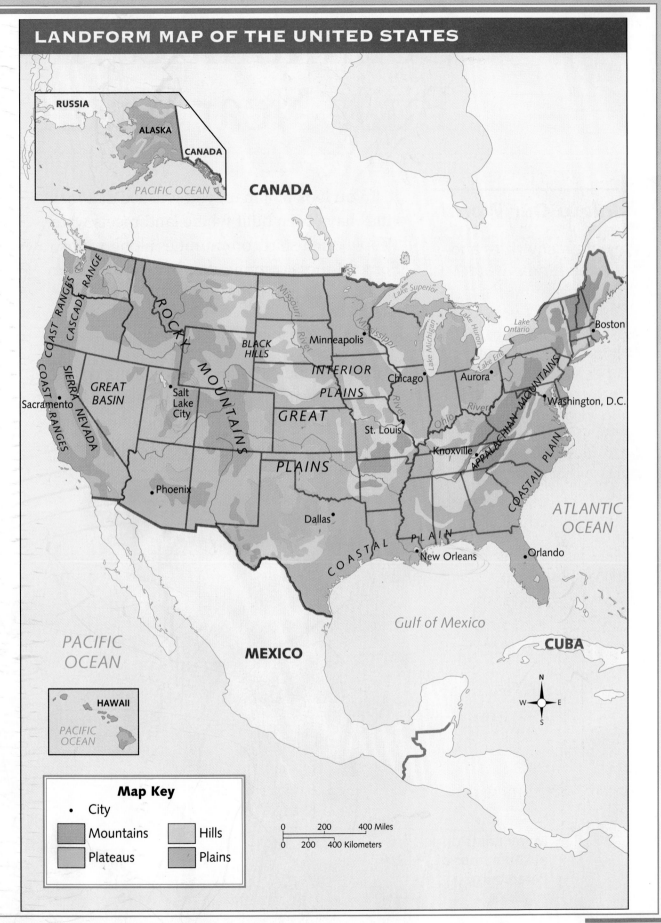

RUSSIA

ALASKA

CANADA

PACIFIC OCEAN

CANADA

COAST RANGES

CASCADE RANGE

ROCKY MOUNTAINS

BLACK HILLS

Missouri River

Lake Superior

Minneapolis

INTERIOR PLAINS

Chicago

Lake Michigan

Lake Huron

Lake Erie

Lake Ontario

Boston

SIERRA NEVADA

COAST RANGES

GREAT BASIN

Sacramento

Salt Lake City

GREAT

PLAINS

St. Louis

Aurora

Ohio River

Mississippi River

APPALACHIAN MOUNTAINS

Washington, D.C.

Knoxville

COASTAL PLAIN

ATLANTIC OCEAN

Phoenix

Dallas

COASTAL

PLAIN

New Orleans

Orlando

PACIFIC OCEAN

MEXICO

Gulf of Mexico

CUBA

N
W   E
S

HAWAII

PACIFIC OCEAN

Map Key

- • City
- Mountains
- Plateaus
- Hills
- Plains

0   200   400 Miles

0   200   400 Kilometers

Communities Are Built Near Water

Link to Our World

Why are many cities and towns built near water?

Focus on the Main Idea
Read to find out why land next to water is often a good place to build a community.

Preview Vocabulary
port
harbor
trade center
rapids

If you look at a map, you will see that many cities have been built where land meets water. People often start communities along waterways. Some of these communities have grown from small towns into large cities.

Bodies of Water

People build cities and towns along coasts where the water is deep, often where rivers run into oceans or lakes. A community next to deep water may become a great **port**, a place where ships can dock.

Many boats dock at the harbor of Petersburg, Alaska.

All port cities have harbors. A **harbor** is a protected place where ships can stay safe from high waves and strong winds. Nature makes some harbors. People make others.

Roads cross the land and come together at the ports. Roads help people and goods get to the ships that sail on the water.

Long ago, goods were bought and sold at ports where ships docked. Wood that came into port was made into furniture there, and then the furniture was shipped out. Iron that came in was made into steel, and then the steel was shipped out.

Many large cities grew from ocean ports. Port cities and harbors are all along the coasts of our country. They are on the west coast next to the Pacific Ocean. They are also on the east coast next to the Atlantic Ocean. Port cities can also be found along the shores of the Great Lakes.

 Why is land next to a body of water a good place to build a community?

Boston and San Francisco

San Francisco and Boston are port cities on peninsulas. Boston's sheltered harbor on the Atlantic coast makes the city a busy seaport. San Francisco is on the northern tip of a peninsula. In 1849 it became a supply center for gold miners. Today both Boston and San Francisco are large and important cities.

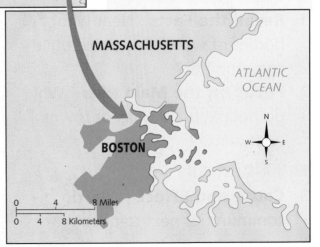

Waterways

People have built many cities and towns along waterways, too. Flowing water makes it easy to move heavy loads. It takes many railroad cars and a lot of fuel to move a huge load of coal over land. The same amount of coal can be moved over water on one ship using less fuel.

Many settlements that were built along deep waterways became trade centers. **Trade centers** are communities where buying and selling goods is the main work.

Places next to waterfalls and rapids are also good for building cities and towns. **Rapids** are the parts of rivers where the water runs very fast, often over rocks. Tumbling water can be very powerful. Long ago, people used rapids to turn huge waterwheels. Waterwheels turned millstones to make flour and ran machines in factories.

When people traveled by boat along rivers, they had to stop and carry their goods around waterfalls and rapids. Sometimes they decided not to travel any farther. Instead, they stayed and built towns where they had stopped.

 Why is land next to a waterway a good place to build a community?

Tugboat and barge on the Mississippi River

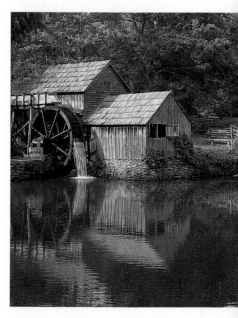

Waterwheel at Mabry Mill on the Blue Ridge Parkway, Virginia

LESSON 2 REVIEW

Check Understanding

1. **Recall the Facts** Near what bodies of water do people build communities?

2. **Focus on the Main Idea** Why do people build cities or towns near water?

Think Critically

3. **Cause and Effect** Why do communities next to deep water often grow into large port cities or trade centers?

Show What You Know

 **Creative-Writing Activity** Write a four-line poem about a city or town built near water. The lines do not have to rhyme. Read your poem out loud to other class members.

How To

Follow a Diagram

Why Is This Skill Important?

Knowing how to follow the steps in a diagram can help you understand how something works. You can also use a diagram to explain to another person how something works.

Understand the Process

Long ago, people built flour mills next to waterfalls and rapids. The fast-moving water turned a waterwheel outside the mill. Follow the numbers on the diagram below and the steps in the next column to find out what happened inside a mill.

Step 1. The waterwheel turned other wheels inside the mill.

Step 2. The wheels inside the mill turned a grinding stone.

Step 3. The stone ground the wheat into flour.

Step 4. The flour was put into sacks to be sold.

Think and Apply

A diagram can show you how to do something you have never done before. You can also use a diagram to show someone else how to do something. Draw a diagram that shows how something in your classroom works. For example, you could choose a pencil sharpener or a three-ring notebook. Then list the steps and explain the diagram to a classmate.

Communities Are Built Where People Meet

People start communities for different reasons. Sometimes communities grow at places where people meet each other or where roads cross.

Routes and Crossroads

A **route** is a path from one place to another. A route can be a river, a road, a railroad, or even a hiking trail.

Link to Our World

Where do people meet in your town?

Focus on the Main Idea

Read to find out why cities and towns are built at the places where people meet.

Preview Vocabulary

route
crossroads
ferry
ford

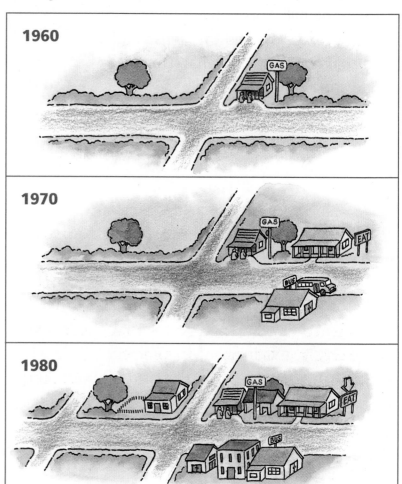

These drawings show how over the years a community can change and grow.

Today

Compare this drawing with the others. Many changes have taken place at this crossroads, but some things have also stayed the same. What are the things that have not changed?

Some cities and towns started at a **crossroads**, a place where two routes cross. Perhaps a trader built a store there to sell supplies to travelers. Then a restaurant or hotel was built to feed the travelers and give them a place to rest. Before long, people settled at the crossroads instead of going on. Those who stayed built houses, churches, and schools. Soon they had a town. Some of these towns grew into cities.

 What is the place called where two routes meet?

Crossing Points

When a land route meets a river, travelers need a way to cross the river. They may use a bridge, a ferry, or a ford. A bridge is a road built over a waterway. A **ferry** is a boat that carries people and goods across a waterway. A **ford** is a shallow place in a waterway that can be crossed by walking, riding, or driving.

Places on both sides of a bridge, a ferry, or a ford are good for building cities or towns. Many famous cities began as crossing points at rivers.

Do you know this song?

> "London Bridge is falling down,
> Falling down, falling down,
> London Bridge is falling down,
> My fair lady!"

The song is about a bridge that was in the city of London, England, for hundreds of years. London Bridge crossed the Thames (TEMZ) River at a place where the water is deep. Ships from the sea sailed up the river to the bridge. Wagons from farms and mills used the bridge to cross the river.

A ferry crossing the bay in Seattle, Washington

What?

London Bridge

London Bridge helped the city of London grow. Today the old bridge is thousands of miles from London. Business people in the United States bought it as a tourist attraction and moved it to Lake Havasu City, Arizona!

This black-and-white drawing shows London Bridge in the 1660s. You can see that homes and shops were built right on the bridge. This bridge has been rebuilt many times.

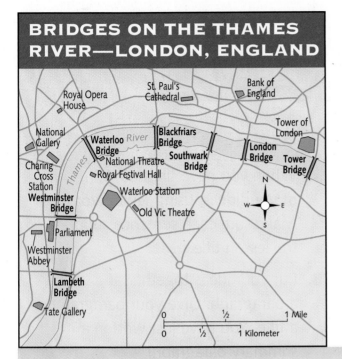

BRIDGES ON THE THAMES RIVER—LONDON, ENGLAND

Royal Opera House
St. Paul's Cathedral
Bank of England
National Gallery
Waterloo Bridge
River
Blackfriars Bridge
Tower of London
Charing Cross Station
National Theatre
Southwark Bridge
London Bridge
Tower Bridge
Thames
Royal Festival Hall
Westminster Bridge
Waterloo Station
Old Vic Theatre
N W E S
Parliament
Westminster Abbey
Lambeth Bridge
Tate Gallery
0   ½   1 Mile
0   ½   1 Kilometer

HUMAN–ENVIRONMENT INTERACTIONS
■ Why do you think there are now many bridges that cross the Thames River?

Farmers long ago went to London Bridge with grains, wool, butter, and pigs to trade for cloth or leather goods carried there by ships. Sometimes the farmers needed to see a doctor, so doctors went to live near London Bridge. Soon many people settled close to the bridge and built a city. Today more than 9 million people live in and around London.

 Why is a crossing point a good place to build a city?

LESSON 3 REVIEW

Check Understanding

1. **Recall the Facts**   What are some ways travelers can cross rivers?
2. **Focus on the Main Idea**   Why are crossing points good places to start communities?

Think Critically

3. **Personally Speaking**   What might be good and bad about living near a crossing point? Would you want to live there?

Show What You Know

 **Research and Writing Activity**   There are many kinds of bridges. Some bridges go over large bodies of water, while others go over deep valleys between mountains. There are railroad bridges that trains use and footbridges that you might walk across.

Choose one bridge in or near your community and find out more about it. You may need to use books or talk to people to get your information. Write three paragraphs. In your paragraphs tell when and why the bridge was built. Also write about the kind of waterway or landform it crosses. Share your report with your classmates.

How To

Write a Summary

Why Is This Skill Important?

A summary gives the main ideas of a story, but uses fewer words. To write a summary, you include only the main ideas and leave out the details.

Understand the Process

1. Choose a lesson from this unit, and write down the lesson title. Then, for each paragraph of the lesson, write one sentence telling the main idea. Each main idea should support the lesson title. Look at the example below for Lesson 3.

2. When you have finished, join some of your ideas, using fewer words. Make sure each sentence supports the lesson title.

3. Put your ideas together and write a paragraph. Give your paragraph a title. You have just written a summary paragraph!

Think and Apply

Read a magazine article or a story. Then write a summary paragraph. Read your summary to a classmate.

REMEMBER WHAT YOU HAVE READ

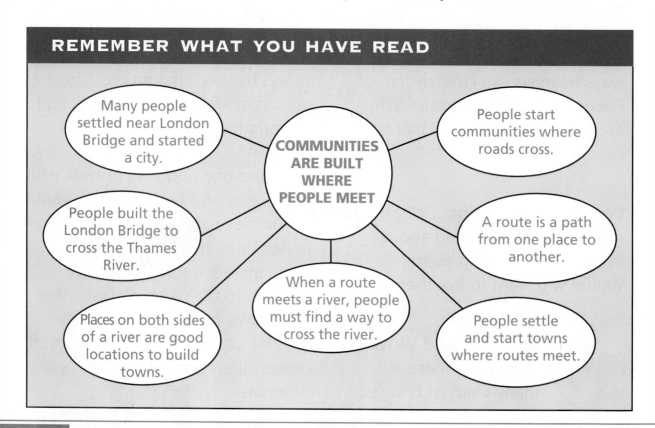

Many people settled near London Bridge and started a city.

People start communities where roads cross.

COMMUNITIES ARE BUILT WHERE PEOPLE MEET

People built the London Bridge to cross the Thames River.

A route is a path from one place to another.

Places on both sides of a river are good locations to build towns.

When a route meets a river, people must find a way to cross the river.

People settle and start towns where routes meet.

Why Did People Build Cahokia and St. Louis?

Link to Our World

What is it about a place that makes people want to build communities there?

Focus on the Main Idea

Read to find out why two groups of people chose to build their communities near the same place.

Preview Vocabulary

riverbank
branch
gateway
manufacture

Sometimes people living at different times built communities near the same places. This happened at Cahokia and St. Louis, Missouri, two cities along the Mississippi River.

Cahokia Long Ago

Nearly 1,500 years ago Native Americans built a city that today we call Cahokia (kuh•HOH•kee•uh). They built Cahokia at the place where the Missouri River flows into the Mississippi River, in the middle of what is now the United States. This settlement was built before people came from Europe.

Cahokia was built on the **riverbank**, the land beside the river. The rich soil along the riverbank was good for growing corn, beans, and squash.

Long ago, as this painting shows, Native Americans lived and worked in their community of Cahokia.

97

The Mississippi River and its branches were very important to the people of Cahokia. A **branch** is a smaller river that flows into a larger one. The people traveled on these rivers in boats, moving themselves, their crops, and other goods. Along the way they met other Indian people and traded goods and ideas with them.

Cahokia soon became a trade center, where people bought and sold many goods. In its markets people could buy tools, jewelry, and supplies. With all this trade Cahokia grew and grew. Soon it became a city where about 40,000 people lived.

THE MISSISSIPPI RIVER AND ITS BRANCHES

LOCATION
■ What rivers are west of the Mississippi River?

Then something happened to Cahokia. No one is sure just what happened or when it happened. Whatever it was, the Cahokians left their city and did not return.

 Why were the branches of the Mississippi River important?

The Mississippi River area before and during a flood

What?

Floods

Some people think that a great flood destroyed the city of Cahokia hundreds of years ago. Today floods are still a problem for people who live in the area.

St. Louis Long Ago

Other people came to live along the river near where Cahokia once stood. Iowa and Osage (oh•SAYJ) Indians each built settlements. Their settlements were much smaller than Cahokia.

To get what they could not grow or make, the Iowa and Osage Indians traded with other people. They traveled the waterways just as the Cahokians had done, trading food and furs for other items. At first the Iowa and Osage people traded with other Indians. Later they also traded with people who had come from Europe.

In 1764 a European boy named René Auguste Chouteau (ruh•NAY ah•GŌŌST shoo•TOH) arrived at this place. He was 14 years old. He and his stepfather built a small trading post on the riverbank, across the Mississippi River from where Cahokia had once stood.

René Auguste Chouteau lived most of his life near the trading post he and his stepfather built.

Indians and Europeans from up and down the river came to Chouteau's trading post to trade goods with one another. They traded all kinds of items. There were pots, pans, metal tools, blankets, food, and other supplies.

With all this trading, more people came to live and work near Chouteau's trading post. They formed a community, and the settlement grew and grew. People called the settlement St. Louis to honor a past king of France. As Cahokia had done earlier, St. Louis grew to be a great city at the place where the Missouri River flows into the Mississippi.

 Why was the location of Chouteau's trading post important?

Early settlers spent many hours making butter with a churn like this. ➔

← Soup's on! This kettle heated many meals long ago.

A sharp knife could turn a piece of wood into a bowl and a spoon like the ones shown here. ➔

This photograph, taken in the 1850s, shows settlers on their way west.

Why St. Louis Grew

Over the years, things changed in St. Louis. Hotels were built. Churches, stores, banks, and houses were also built for the people living and working there.

In the 1800s thousands of people came to St. Louis on their way to settle in the West. They stopped in St. Louis to buy wagons and supplies. The city became a **gateway**, or entrance, to the West.

Soon people arrived to build factories and **manufacture**, or make, all kinds of goods. They manufactured shoes, cereal, and farm supplies. They shipped these goods on steamboats to other cities along the Mississippi River and its branches. St. Louis became a trade center and a manufacturing center, and it grew bigger.

As time passed, bridges were built across the Mississippi River. Trains and trucks from St. Louis could now reach new towns over land. More factories and bridges were built, and St. Louis grew even more. Later, airports were added. Airplanes could reach cities all over the world. And the city kept growing!

Better land and air routes let people live and work away from the river. Many of the buildings along the riverfront became empty and started to fall apart. The leaders of St. Louis decided to make some changes.

When?

Building of the First Steel Arch Bridge to Cross the Mississippi River

The Eads Bridge at St. Louis, Missouri, was the bridge people said could not be built. They thought the river was too deep and too strong. However, James Buchanan Eads did not agree. In 1867 he and his workers started building the bridge. At last the bridge was opened on July 4, 1874. People from many countries came to see the bridge and to ask Eads to build bridges for them.

The Gateway Arch welcomes people to the city of St. Louis.

One person had the idea of making a park. Another person wanted to build a museum. Neither idea seemed just right. Then someone said that something should be built that would stand for St. Louis. A young artist from Michigan sent in a drawing of a tall, slim arch made of stainless steel. The idea seemed perfect!

Today the Gateway Arch is a symbol of St. Louis's past. The arch stands over the place where young Chouteau and his stepfather built their trading post long ago. The Gateway Arch is also a symbol for today. People still think of St. Louis as a gateway to the West for business and trade.

Who?

Eero Saarinen
1910–1961

The designer of the Gateway Arch was 12 years old when he won a prize for his design, or plan, for a building. This was just the first of many prizes Eero Saarinen (AIR•oh SAR•uh•nuhn) won as an architect, or building designer. Sadly, Saarinen did not live to see the arch built. Today anyone who visits St. Louis can see it reaching high into the sky.

Flowing past the Gateway Arch is the Mississippi River. The mighty river is as important to St. Louis today as it ever was. Many people live along its banks, farm on land near it, and use it to move themselves and their goods, just as people did long, long ago.

 What does the Gateway Arch stand for?

LESSON 4 REVIEW

Check Understanding

1. **Recall the Facts** What waterways were important for people in both Cahokia and St. Louis?

2. **Focus on the Main Idea** Why might people who lived at different times choose to build their communities near the same place?

Think Critically

3. **Explore Viewpoints** When cities grow, it often means there will be new jobs for people. It can also mean that the land will become crowded or dirty. Choose one worker from your community, and tell what that person might say about the growth of your community.

Show What You Know

 Art Activity Choose a landmark in your community or state that stands for something from the past. Make a model, and display it for the class. Explain what it stands for.

How To

Find Intermediate Directions on a Map

Why Is This Skill Important?

You use directions when you want to tell someone where you have been or where you are going. North, south, east, and west are cardinal directions. They are the most important. There are also four "in-between" directions. Northeast, southeast, southwest, and northwest are **intermediate directions**. Each one is midway between two cardinal directions.

Understand the Process

Find St. Louis on the map. It is the center point of a large compass rose. Put your finger on St. Louis, and trace the compass rose line toward North. Now slowly move your finger toward East. The part of the country between North and East on this map is the land northeast of St. Louis. Keep moving your finger toward South to find the land that is southeast of St. Louis. Move your finger toward West to find the land southwest of St. Louis, and toward North again to find the land northwest of St. Louis.

Think and Apply

Use the map to help you answer these questions.

1. From St. Louis, in what direction is Orlando?

2. If you went from New York to El Paso, in which direction would you go?

3. If you traveled northwest from St. Louis, what city would you reach?

THE UNITED STATES AND INTERMEDIATE DIRECTIONS

North

Northwest   Northeast   New York

West   St. Louis   East

Seattle

Los Angeles

Southwest   Southeast

El Paso

South   Orlando

Communities Are Built Near Resources

Link to Our World

Why do you think cities and towns are built near resources?

Focus on the Main Idea
Read to find out why people build communities in places near fuels, mineral supplies, and water.

Preview Vocabulary
crop
natural resource
growing season
mineral
fuel
ghost town

The first settlers leaving St. Louis headed west across the Great Plains. The wind made the tall grasses ripple like ocean waves. The settlers were glad to finish their journey—just as sailors are glad to reach land after a long voyage.

On the Land

While most people kept moving across the vast plains, a few settled along the way and began to farm the land. Some farmers raised chickens, hogs, and cows. Others grew **crops**, or plants used by people for food or other needs.

Although these farms were different from one another, they all needed the same natural resources. A **natural resource** is something found in nature that people can use. Trees, water, animals, and soil are examples of natural resources.

This worker is picking peppers on a farm near Waupaca, Wisconsin.

Crops will not grow if the weath[er] too cold for them. That is why farm[ers] in places with cold climates plant i[n] the spring, when the cold winter weather is over.

The months in which crops can grow are called the **growing seas[on].** Growing seasons depend on the climate of a place. In places with lo[ng,] cold winters, the growing season is short. In places with short, warm winters, the growing season is long[.]

In the top photograph Holstein cows graze near a watering hole. The children in the bottom photograph are feeding the animals on a Wisconsin farm.

FARM PRODUCTS OF NEBRASKA

MINNESOTA

SOUTH DAKOTA

WYOMING

IOWA

Scottsbluff •

Norfolk •

North Platte

Omaha •

★ Lincoln

Hastings •

COLORADO

KANSAS

MISSOURI

Map Key
- 🐄 Cattle
- 🌽 Corn
- ✖ Hay
- 🐖 Hogs
- Potatoes
- 🐔 Poultry
- 🐑 Sheep
- Soybeans
- Wheat
- • City
- ★ State capital

0   50   100 Miles
0   50   100 Kilometers

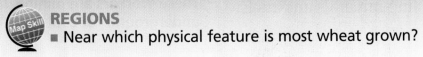

REGIONS
■ Near which physical feature is most wheat grown?

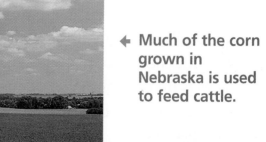

← Much of the corn grown in Nebraska is used to feed cattle.

Farmers sell their goods in Omaha and shop in the city's stores.

In places where there were plenty of resources for farming, cities and towns grew up nearby. Omaha, Nebraska, is a city on the plains. The rich soil is good for farming, and around Omaha, corn grows well.

 How do resources help people decide where to start farms?

Inside the Earth

Some communities grew up in places where natural resources were found deep in the Earth. Towns started quickly in places where minerals and fuels were found. A **mineral**, such as silver, gold, or iron, is a resource found inside the Earth. Minerals can be used to make metal tools, glass, or jewelry. Some kinds of **fuels**, such as coal or oil, are also found inside the Earth. Fuels can be burned for heat and for power to make machines work.

People dug mines and oil wells to get the resources from the Earth. They found that they could earn a lot of money from selling minerals and fuels.

These workers are mining underground for coal.

So they built communities near these resources, even in places with physical features that made their lives hard. They even built in places with very cold or very hot climates if resources they wanted could be found there.

A lot of people must work to get minerals and fuels out of the ground. Then more people must work to get these materials ready to be sold and used. People are needed to sell clothes and food to the workers and to provide them with other services. With all these people moving in, many towns near places with underground resources grew fast.

Oil wells share the land with office buildings near the busy port city of Long Beach, California.

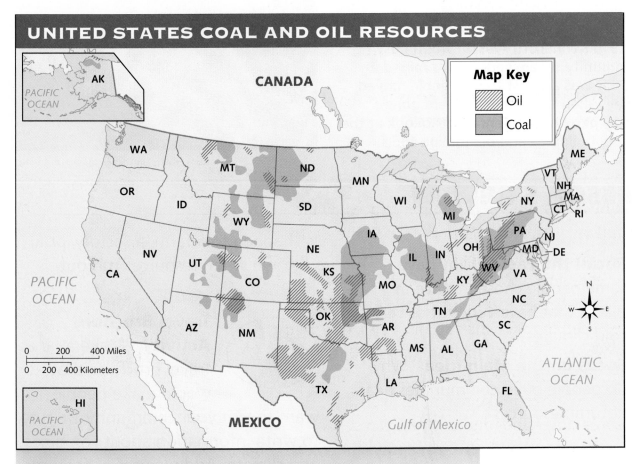

UNITED STATES COAL AND OIL RESOURCES

Map Key
Oil
Coal

HUMAN–ENVIRONMENT INTERACTIONS
■ Name a state in the northeastern part of the United States where both coal and oil are found.

Some towns grew into cities. Others did not grow at all. When the minerals and fuels ran out in these places, the people left. These towns became **ghost towns**, with buildings but no people. Today some ghost towns have come back to life—at least a little. People like to visit the old buildings to find out what life was like for the people who lived there.

 How can the location of minerals help people decide where to build communities?

In 1916 Kennecott, Alaska, was a busy community where copper was mined. By 1938 it was a ghost town. People moved away when the resources were gone. Today people visit Kennecott to look at the empty buildings and old mining tools.

LESSON 5 REVIEW

Check Understanding

1. **Recall the Facts** Why have some people chosen to live in places that have very hot or very cold climates?

2. **Focus on the Main Idea** Why do people build communities near natural resources?

Think Critically

3. **Cause and Effect** Explain some of the things that might happen to a farm, a factory, or a town when resources run out.

Show What You Know

 **Travel Brochure Activity** Make a travel brochure that would make people want to visit your community. Be sure to write information about resources and climate. Add pictures of features people would like about your community. Display your brochure.

Communities Are Built for Government

Link to Our World

Why would location be an important reason for building a city or town?

Focus on the Main Idea

Read to find out why location was important in building Washington, D.C., and other places of government.

Preview Vocabulary

capital city
capitol
state capital
county
county seat

The early leaders of the United States decided it was time to build a new city where the country's laws would be made. The people of Virginia and Maryland gave the country some land along the Potomac River on which to build the new city.

The Story of Washington, D.C.

George Washington rode out on his horse to look at the land along the Potomac River. The new nation was going to build a **capital city** where the leaders of the country could meet and work. President Washington wanted to find a good place to build this city.

Each day from the middle of October until the end of October in 1791 he rode along the riverbank. It was hard to choose just the right place to build the nation's capital. George Washington talked with Thomas Jefferson about the problem. He talked with other leaders, too. At last a good place was chosen. Washington, D.C., was soon to be built.

A painting of George Washington, the first President of the United States

The United States Capitol building as it looked in 1800

The Capitol building as it looks today

George Washington chose an area of low wetlands and woods for the new capital. But he did not choose the place so much for its physical features as for its good location. It was halfway between the states of Vermont and Georgia. In 1791 this was right in the middle of the United States.

Building the capital city in the middle of the nation had its good points and bad points. A good point was that lawmakers from all over the country could more easily get to the capital. A bad point was that the place was a swamp! The first lawmakers would not stay there in the summer because of the heat and the mosquitoes. The hot, swampy place for the capital was not perfect, but its location was.

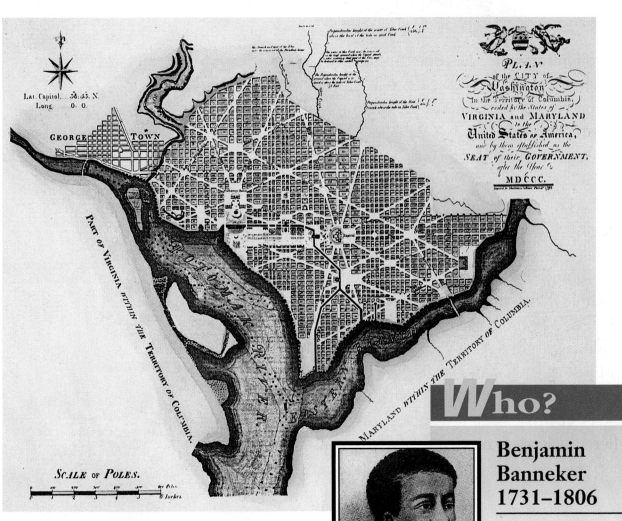

From this drawing by Pierre L'Enfant, the city of Washington, D.C., began to take shape.

Who?

Benjamin Banneker 1731–1806

This picture of Benjamin Banneker was drawn when he was a young man. Thomas Jefferson knew that Banneker had many skills. So Jefferson told George Washington that Banneker would be a good person to help lay out the streets of Washington, D.C.

Two former clock makers, Andrew Ellicott and Benjamin Banneker, measured the land. An engineer, Pierre L'Enfant (pee•AIR lahn•FAHN), used their measurements to plan the city's streets and buildings. The first thing built was the **capitol**, the building where lawmakers meet. Where you find a capitol building, you will find a capital city.

 Why was the capital city located in the middle of the nation?

State Capitals and County Seats

The United States has one capital city for the whole country. But there are 50 state capitals, one for each of the 50 states in our country. A **state capital** is a city where lawmakers meet to make laws for a state.

A city does not have to be the biggest in the state to be the state capital. In fact, none of the five largest cities in the United States is a state capital. Houston is not the capital of Texas, even though it is the largest city in Texas. Austin is the capital.

Just as a part of the United States is called a state, a part of a state is called a **county**. And just as each state has its own state capital, each county has its own county seat. A **county seat** is a city or town where the leaders meet.

Like every other state capital, Austin, Texas, has its own capitol building.

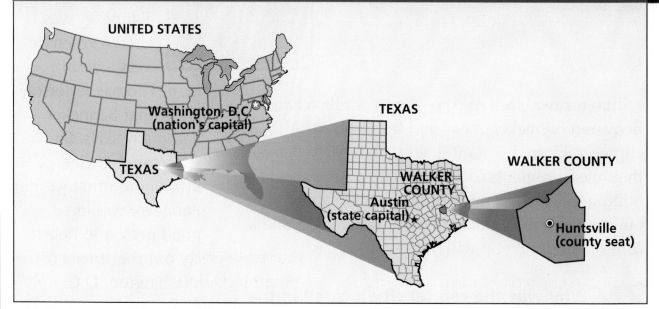

STATE CAPITALS AND COUNTY SEATS

UNITED STATES

Washington, D.C. (nation's capital)

TEXAS

TEXAS

WALKER COUNTY

WALKER COUNTY

Austin (state capital)

Huntsville (county seat)

LEARNING FROM DIAGRAMS
What do these places have in common?

Many state capitals and county seats were chosen for the same reason Washington, D.C., was built where it is. Being located in the middle of a state or a county makes the city or town easier for lawmakers and others to get to.

 Where are many state capitals and county seats located? Why?

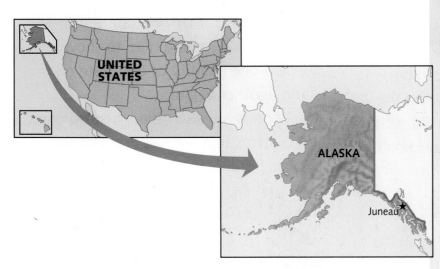

UNITED STATES

ALASKA

Juneau

Juneau, Alaska

Not all state capitals were chosen because they are easy to get to. One of the hardest state capitals to reach is Juneau (JOO•noh), Alaska, because no roads lead to it. Lawmakers get to Alaska's state capital by airplane or boat. The capital was built there because it was near a resource—gold.

LESSON 6 REVIEW

Check Understanding

1. **Recall the Facts** Where do people meet to make laws for a country and for a state?
2. **Focus on the Main Idea** Why is location important for places of government?

Think Critically

3. **Personally Speaking** Do you think the nation's capital should be moved to what is today the middle of the United States? Why or why not?

Show What You Know

 **Collage Activity** Use pictures from magazines and newspapers to make a collage about your state or county. Be sure to show something about the capital city or the county seat. Display your collage on a class bulletin board.

How To

Find State Capitals and Borders

Why Is This Skill Important?

Look at the map of the United States. It shows the shapes of states and the locations of state capitals.

You can use this map to find the location and shape of your state. You can also use it to find the location of your state's capital.

Understand the Process

The symbol of a star tells you that a city is a state capital. Find the state capital symbol in the map key. Then look at the map. What is the state capital of Texas?

The symbol of a star with a circle around it is used to show the nation's capital. Find the nation's capital symbol in the map key. Now look at the map. Where is Washington, D.C., located?

This map also shows national and state borders. **Borders** are the lines that are drawn on a map to show where one country or one state ends and another begins.

Borders are also called **boundaries**. The states that are just north of the Texas border are New Mexico, Oklahoma, and Arkansas. Which states are on the eastern border of Texas?

Think and Apply

Use the map key to help you answer these questions.

1. What is your state capital?

2. What states are your neighbors to the north, south, east, and west? What are the capitals of each of those states?

STATES AND THEIR CAPITALS

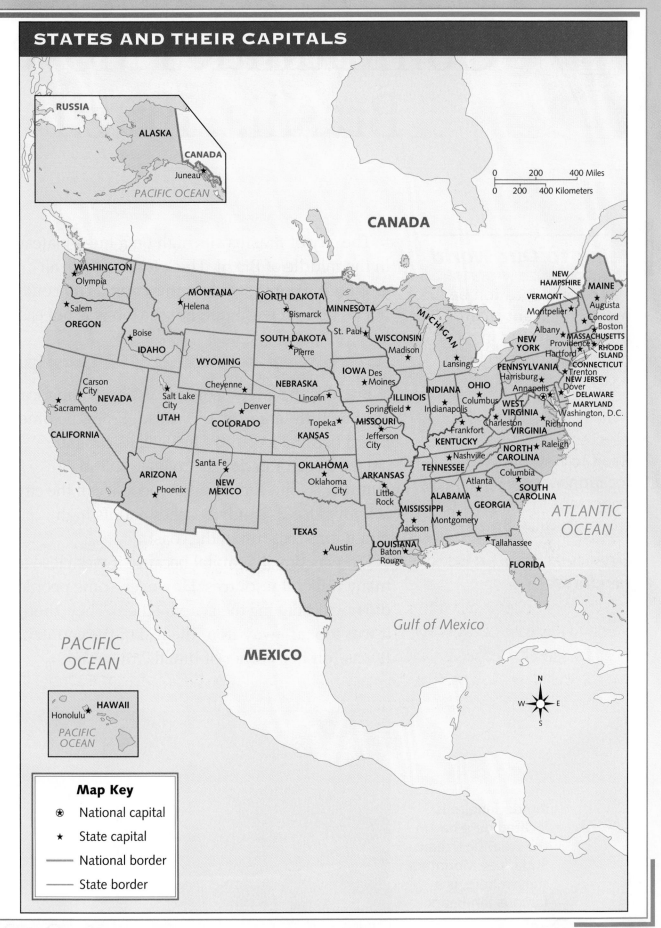

RUSSIA

ALASKA

CANADA

Juneau

PACIFIC OCEAN

0   200   400 Miles
0   200   400 Kilometers

CANADA

WASHINGTON
★ Olympia
★ Salem
OREGON

MONTANA
★ Helena

NORTH DAKOTA
★ Bismarck

MINNESOTA
St. Paul ★

MICHIGAN

NEW
HAMPSHIRE
VERMONT
★ Montpelier

MAINE
★ Augusta
★ Concord
★ Boston

★ Boise
IDAHO

SOUTH DAKOTA
★ Pierre

WISCONSIN
★ Madison

★ Lansing

Albany ★
NEW
YORK

MASSACHUSETTS
★ Providence
Hartford RHODE
ISLAND
CONNECTICUT

WYOMING

NEBRASKA

IOWA Des
★ Moines

PENNSYLVANIA
Harrisburg ★

★ Trenton
NEW JERSEY

Carson
City ★
NEVADA
★ Sacramento

★ Cheyenne

Salt Lake
City ★
UTAH

★ Denver

COLORADO

★ Lincoln

ILLINOIS
★ Springfield

INDIANA

Indianapolis ★

OHIO

Columbus ★

WEST
VIRGINIA
★ Charleston

Annapolis ★ Dover
DELAWARE
MARYLAND
⊛ Washington, D.C.
★ Richmond

Topeka ★
KANSAS

MISSOURI
★ Jefferson
City

Frankfort ★
KENTUCKY

VIRGINIA

CALIFORNIA

ARIZONA
★ Phoenix

Santa Fe ★
NEW
MEXICO

OKLAHOMA
★ Oklahoma
City

ARKANSAS
★ Little
Rock

TENNESSEE
★ Nashville

NORTH
CAROLINA

★ Raleigh

Columbia
★ SOUTH
CAROLINA

ALABAMA

Atlanta ★

GEORGIA

ATLANTIC
OCEAN

TEXAS

★ Austin

MISSISSIPPI

Jackson ★

★ Montgomery

★ Tallahassee

LOUISIANA
Baton ★
Rouge

FLORIDA

Gulf of Mexico

PACIFIC
OCEAN

MEXICO

N
W   E
S

HAWAII
Honolulu ★
PACIFIC
OCEAN

Map Key

⊛ National capital

★ State capital

─ National border

─ State border

Communities Move— Brasília, Brazil

Link to Our World

Why would location be more important than physical features in deciding where to build a city?

Focus on the Main Idea
Read to find out why location was so important in building the city of Brasília, Brazil.

Preview Vocabulary
rain forest

The city of Brasília sits high on a huge plateau in the middle of Brazil. Thick forest grows all around it. People said that this capital city could not be built. It was built, but the job was not easy.

A Problem with the Old Capital

Brazil is the largest country in South America and the fifth-largest in the world. From the time Brazil became a country in 1822, its capital city had been Rio de Janeiro (REE•oh DAY zhuh•NAIR•oh). Rio, as many people call the city, is known for its sandy beaches and its high mountains that run to the coast.

Rio was Brazil's capital because it was close to many mineral resources. However, some people did not like having their capital there. They thought it was too far away from the rest of the country. It was "off in a corner of Brazil," they said.

Rio de Janeiro is located on a bay in the Atlantic Ocean. Sugarloaf Mountain, shown here, is a famous landmark.

Leaders in Brazil thought of the same things leaders in the United States did when they decided where to build Washington, D.C. The new capital of Brazil, too, needed to be close to the center of the country. But the leaders in Brazil had another reason for moving the capital. They wanted more people to move away from the coast, inland, where there were few people. For these reasons, the government leaders of Brazil decided to move the capital.

 Why did Brazil's leaders want to move the capital city?

A City Called Brasília

Brazil covers almost half the continent of South America. A huge **rain forest**, or thick forest that has a hot, wet climate, covers much of the land. The Amazon River flows through this rain forest. The Amazon is Brazil's longest river and the second-longest in the world. Only the Nile River in Africa is longer.

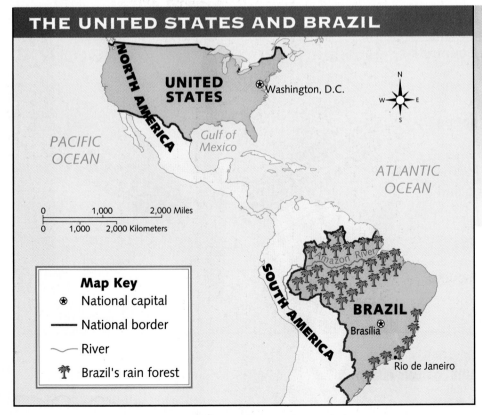

THE UNITED STATES AND BRAZIL

NORTH AMERICA

UNITED STATES

⊛ Washington, D.C.

PACIFIC OCEAN

Gulf of Mexico

N
W   E
S

ATLANTIC OCEAN

SOUTH AMERICA

Amazon River

BRAZIL
⊛
Brasília

Rio de Janeiro

0   1,000   2,000 Miles
0   1,000   2,000 Kilometers

Map Key
⊛ National capital
— National border
⌒ River
🌴 Brazil's rain forest

PLACE
Map Skill
Find Brasília, Brazil, and Washington, D.C., on the map.
■ What things are the same about these two capitals? What things are different?

The place the government leaders chose to build the new capital was on a plateau rising from the rain forest. They chose this place for its location, not for its physical features. There were no roads. And because it was so hard to travel through the rain forest, everything that was needed to build the new city had to be taken there by airplane.

Like Washington, D.C., Brasília was carefully planned. A city planner named Lúcio Costa designed every detail of the city—every street and even every park bench. Costa laid out the city in the shape of an airplane. The "body" is 4 miles (6 km) long. The "wings" stretch 12 miles (19 km) across. Costa put houses and businesses along the wings and government buildings along the body. He put the most important buildings, where the government leaders meet, at the "nose" of the airplane.

Twenty-six people sent in ideas for Brasília's city plan. Lúcio Costa's plan took first place.

CITY PLAN FOR BRASÍLIA

1. **Buildings for government leaders from other countries**

2. **Schools**

3. **Police station and shops**

4. **Railroad station**

5. **Apartment buildings and houses**

6. **Government buildings**

7. **Art and science museums**

LEARNING FROM DIAGRAMS
What is located at the "tail" of this city plan?

Brasília has been called a city of the future. Its buildings look as if they could be from some future time.

It took less than 10 years to build Brazil's new capital city. In 1960 the government began meeting there instead of in Rio de Janeiro. Today more than a million people live in Brasília.

 Why did people think Brasília could not be built?

This church in Brasília is made of concrete, sand, and glass. What does its shape make you think of?

LESSON 7 REVIEW

Check Understanding

1. **Recall the Facts**   Why did the people of Brazil want to move the capital city?
2. **Focus on the Main Idea**   Why was the location of Brasília more important than the area's physical features?

Think Critically

3. **Past to Present**   How was the building of Brasília like the building of Washington, D.C.? How was it different?

Show What You Know

Poster Activity
Make a poster that shows a plan for a city you would like to build. First, decide where you will build the city. What physical features or bodies of water will it be near? Why? Next, draw your city plan and label the important places on it. Share your poster with your classmates. Explain why you chose to build your city where you did.

MAKING SOCIAL STUDIES REAL

CHANGES IN THE LAND

The people of La Conchita, California, thought they had built their community in a good place. However, something that they did not plan on happened to the land. For days and days heavy rain soaked the ground. When more rain fell, the ground could not hold the extra water. Tons of mud began to slide down slowly from rain-soaked hills.

When the mudslide reached the community, it pushed buildings over. It also blocked roads, pulled down bridges, and covered up crops. The people who lost their homes did not know what to do. Should they try to build new homes in the same location? Or should they look for a new place to live? Some people decided to start over in the same place. Others packed up and went to new places. A change in the land had changed their lives forever.

BUILDING CITIZENSHIP

Sometimes things that happen in nature—such as mudslides, hurricanes, and earthquakes—cause great changes in people's lives. Would you know what to do if any of these things happened in your community? Make a list of the steps you would take and the items you would need. Compare your list with a classmate's list.

STORY CLOTH

Follow the pictures shown in this story cloth to help you review the things you read about in Unit 2.

Summarize the Main Ideas

1. People often build communities near water.

2. Communities sometimes start at the places where people meet.

3. Different groups of people may build communities near the same place.

4. Some people build towns so they will be near resources.

5. The leaders of a country think about location before they build places of government.

Write a Paragraph Choose any of the events shown in the story cloth, and write a paragraph. Your paragraph should describe, or tell, what you think is happening. In your paragraph, write details and give examples that will make it clear to the reader what you are writing about.

COOPERATIVE LEARNING WORKSHOP

Remember

- Share your ideas.
- Cooperate with others to plan your work.
- Take responsibility for your work.
- Show your group's work to the class.
- Discuss what you learned by working together.

Activity 1

Draw a Map

Work with a group of classmates to decide where the most important meeting places are in your school. Draw a map that shows these meeting places. Put a map key on your map to explain the colors or symbols you used. Give your map a title that tells what the map is about.

Activity 2

Use a Computer

Use a computer to make a database of the questions your group would like to ask people about the places where they live. In the database, list questions about the different physical features and human-made features that make up their community or town.

Activity 3

Simulation

Role-play a scene about the Sheldon family. Decide who will play the parts of Mr. and Mrs. Sheldon, the children, and the people of Hudson. Your scene should be about what happened to the Sheldon family and about where they chose to build their house and farm. Make a list of the vocabulary words you learned in this unit. Use these words as you act out your scene for the class.

CONNECT MAIN IDEAS

Use this graphic organizer to show how the unit's main ideas are connected. First, copy the organizer onto a separate sheet of paper. Then, complete it by writing one main idea for each lesson.

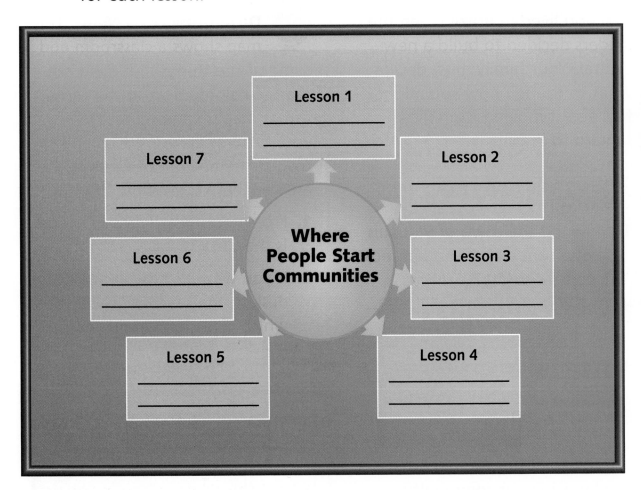

USE VOCABULARY

Sometimes the name of a city or town tells where it is located. What vocabulary words from this unit are in the names of the cities listed on the right? Write a sentence to show the meaning of each vocabulary word.

1. Port Jefferson, New York

2. Safety Harbor, Florida

3. Bonners Ferry, Idaho

4. Friday Harbor, Washington

5. Port Arthur, Texas

REVIEW

WRITE MORE ABOUT IT

Write a Diary Entry Imagine that you lived in Brazil when the leaders decided to build a new capital. Your family must decide what to do. Tell how you might feel about moving from Rio de Janeiro to Brasília.

CHECK UNDERSTANDING

1. How did the town of St. Louis grow from a small trading post into a large city?

2. Why are waterways important for trade?

3. What are crossroads?

THINK CRITICALLY

1. **Link to You** Name two places in your community where people meet.

2. **Think More About It** Waterways are sometimes called river highways. What do you think that means?

3. **Personally Speaking** What would you tell settlers who are going to start a new community?

APPLY SKILLS

How to Find Intermediate Directions on a Map This map shows a classroom and some of the things in it. Find the orange-colored desk in the center of the map. Imagine that this is your desk. Then use the compass rose at the bottom of the map to answer these questions.

1. From your desk, what direction is the clock?

2. If you wanted to walk from your desk to the teacher's desk, in which direction would you go?

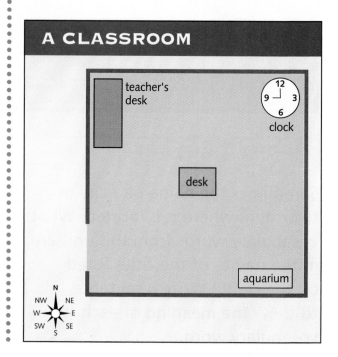

A CLASSROOM

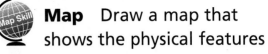

How to Find State Capitals and Borders

The map below shows the state of Idaho. It shows the state capital and some of the county names. Use the map to answer these questions.

1. What is the name of the state capital?

2. In which county is the capital?

3. Which counties border the state capital's county?

How to Read a Landform Map

Draw a map that shows the physical features and human-made features outside your school. Use colors to stand for the different things, such as green for trees and blue for lakes.

How to Write a Summary

Choose one of the lessons in this unit to read again. Use what you have learned to write a summary paragraph of the lesson.

How to Follow a Diagram

Suppose that you need to explain to someone how to wash dishes or check out a library book. Write a list of steps that explain how. Then draw a diagram to show the steps.

READ MORE ABOUT IT

Going West by Jean Van Leeuwan. Dial. Hannah and her family leave their home to travel west, where they will start a new life.

Natural Wonders of America by David M. Brownstone and Irene M. Franck. Atheneum. Read about the features of places in the United States and Canada.

Our Home Is the Sea by Riki Levinson. Dutton. A boat in the Hong Kong harbor is home to this Chinese family.

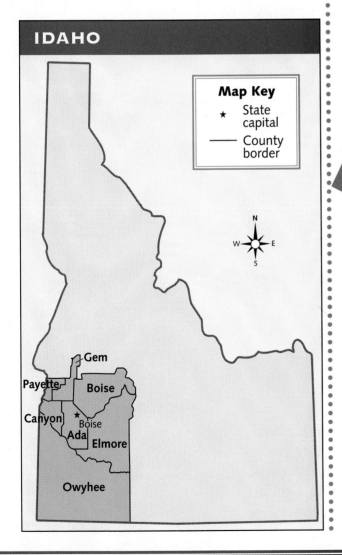

IDAHO

Map Key
★ State capital
— County border

Gem
Payette
Boise
Canyon
★ Boise
Ada
Elmore
Owyhee

The Many People of a Community

People move from one community to another and from one country to another. ➤

Large communities include groups of people who share a culture or cultures. ➤

Communities are made up of many groups of people. People whose ancestors came from countries all over the world live in communities across the United States. They have brought with them the languages, customs, foods, literature, art, beliefs, and celebrations of those countries. People who have come from all over the world make the United States an interesting place to live.

◆ Children in Los Angeles celebrate the Vietnamese New Year.

Language, customs, religion, food, literature, art, and music are important parts of a culture. ➔

People of many cultures can live together in one country, community, or neighborhood. ➔

GRANDFATHER'S JOURNEY

SET the SCENE
with Literature

This is the story of a man who leaves Japan, his home country, and moves to the United States. After many years he returns to Japan and marries his girlfriend. They then decide to live in the United States. Whether the man is in Japan or in the United States, he is homesick for the other place. As you read, think about what it would be like to move to a country where the culture is different from your own.

by ALLEN SAY

My grandfather was a young man when he left his home in Japan and went to see the world.

He wore European clothes for the first time and began his journey on a steamship. The Pacific Ocean astonished him.

For three weeks he did not see land. When land finally appeared it was the New World.

He explored North America by train and riverboat, and often walked for days on end.

Deserts with rocks like enormous sculptures amazed him.

The endless farm fields reminded him of the ocean he had crossed.

Huge cities of factories and tall buildings bewildered and yet excited him.

He marveled at the towering mountains and rivers as clear as the sky.

He met many people along the way. He shook hands with black men and white men, with yellow men and red men.

The more he traveled, the more he longed to see new places, and never thought of returning home.

Of all the places he visited, he liked California best. He loved the strong sunlight there, the Sierra Mountains, the lonely seacoast.

After a time, he returned to his village in Japan to marry his childhood sweetheart. Then he brought his bride to the new country.

They made their home by the San Francisco Bay and had a baby girl.

As his daughter grew, my grandfather began to think about his own childhood. He thought about his old friends.

He remembered the mountains and rivers of his home. He surrounded himself with songbirds, but he could not forget.

Finally, when his daughter was nearly grown, he could wait no more. He took his family and returned to his homeland.

Once again he saw the mountains and rivers of his childhood. They were just as he had remembered them.

Once again he exchanged stories and laughed with his old friends.

But the village was not a place for a daughter from San Francisco. So my grandfather bought a house in a large city nearby.

There, the young woman fell in love, married, and sometime later I was born.

When I was a small boy, my favorite weekend was a visit to my grandfather's house. He told me many stories about California.

He raised warblers and silvereyes, but he could not forget the mountains and rivers of California. So he planned a trip.

But a war began. Bombs fell from the sky and scattered our lives like leaves in a storm.

When the war ended, there was nothing left of the city and of the house where my grandparents had lived.

So they returned to the village where they had been children. But my grandfather never kept another songbird.

The last time I saw him, my grandfather said that he longed to see California one more time. He never did.

And when I was nearly grown, I left home and went to see California for myself.

After a time, I came to love the land my grandfather had loved, and I stayed on and on until I had a daughter of my own.

But I also miss the mountains and rivers of my childhood. I miss my old friends. So I return now and then, when I can not still the longing in my heart.

The funny thing is, the moment I am in one country, I am homesick for the other.

I think I know my grandfather now. I miss him very much.

People from Many Places

Link to Our World

What parts of the world have people in your community come from?

Focus on the Main Idea

Find out why people from many places come to live in a community.

Preview Vocabulary

opportunity
religion
immigrant

People move from one place in the world to another for many reasons. Sometimes, as in *Grandfather's Journey,* a person moves to a new country for adventure. Allen Say's grandfather traveled all over the United States. He found the country beautiful and exciting. But adventure is not the only reason people move to new places.

People Move for Many Reasons

Many people who move from one part of the world to another are looking for opportunity. **Opportunity** means the chance to find a job, get an education, or have a better way of life. People hope to find opportunities in their new country.

Sometimes people move because they are not allowed to follow their religion in their home country. **Religion** is what a person believes about God or a set of gods. So people may move to a country where they can be free to worship in their own way.

Some people move because a war is making life very difficult. They need safety. Still other people move because of hunger in their country. They are looking for a country where there is more to eat.

During the late 1800s and early 1900s, millions of Europeans arrived at Ellis Island, in New York Harbor.

 Why do people move from one country to another?

Many People Move to the United States

People have moved to the United States from countries all over the world. People who move from one country to live in another country are called **immigrants**.

From 1881 until 1920 almost 24 million immigrants came to the United States. While immigrants came from all over the world, the greatest number of them were from Europe. They traveled here on ships to Ellis Island, in New York Harbor. Many immigrants made New York City their new home. Some looked for opportunities in other cities along the East Coast. Other immigrants traveled to the middle of the United States and worked as farmers.

These immigrants are walking on a pier, perhaps thinking about the new life ahead of them.

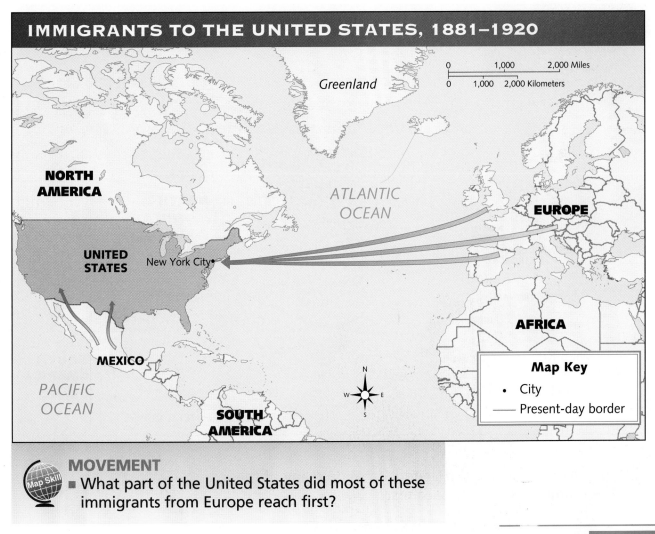

IMMIGRANTS TO THE UNITED STATES, 1881–1920

Greenland

0   1,000   2,000 Miles
0   1,000   2,000 Kilometers

NORTH AMERICA

ATLANTIC OCEAN

EUROPE

UNITED STATES

New York City•

AFRICA

MEXICO

Map Key
• City
— Present-day border

PACIFIC OCEAN

SOUTH AMERICA

MOVEMENT
■ What part of the United States did most of these immigrants from Europe reach first?

Today, immigrants still come from Europe. Others come from Africa. However, greater numbers are now coming to the United States from Mexico and Central and South America. Others come from countries on islands in the Caribbean Sea, between Florida and South America. Large groups of immigrants also come from China, the Philippines, Vietnam, India, and other countries in Asia.

 What is an immigrant?

The Statue of Liberty

As their ships entered New York Harbor, many immigrants from Europe saw the Statue of Liberty. It is one of the largest statues ever built.

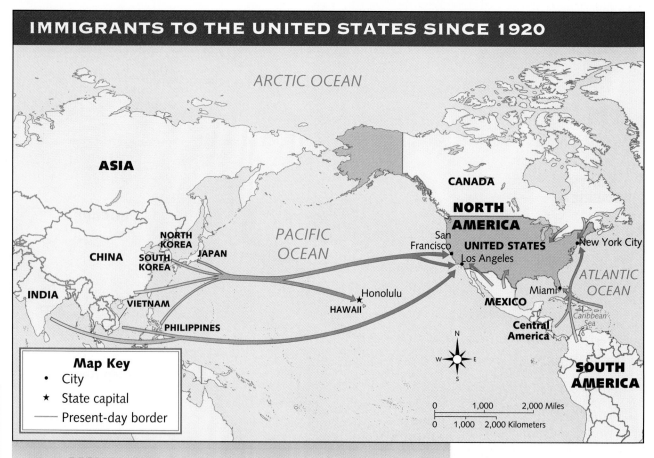

IMMIGRANTS TO THE UNITED STATES SINCE 1920

ARCTIC OCEAN

ASIA

NORTH KOREA

CHINA   SOUTH KOREA   JAPAN

INDIA

VIETNAM

PHILIPPINES

PACIFIC OCEAN

CANADA

NORTH AMERICA

San Francisco   UNITED STATES   New York City
Los Angeles

Honolulu
★
HAWAII

MEXICO   Miami

ATLANTIC OCEAN

Caribbean Sea

Central America

SOUTH AMERICA

Map Key
- City
- ★ State capital
- — Present-day border

N
W   E
S

0   1,000   2,000 Miles
0   1,000   2,000 Kilometers

MOVEMENT
■ Which places in the United States do many of these immigrants today reach first?

A City of Many Cultures

Like the characters in *Grandfather's Journey*, many immigrants feel homesick for their country. To feel homesick is to feel sad about missing one's family, language, and customs.

Often people move to neighborhoods or communities where others from their home country have lived for a long time. These communities help new immigrants learn about their new country. They also help new immigrants not to miss their home country so much. In these communities the immigrants can speak their own language and follow their own customs. Los Angeles, California, is one city that has several neighborhoods in which many of the people have immigrated from other countries.

Chinatown in Los Angeles

Where?

Los Angeles, California

Los Angeles is a large city in southern California that was built along the Pacific coast. More than half of the people who live in Los Angeles and the area around it have moved from other parts of the United States or from other countries. People moved to Los Angeles to find good jobs, to get away from problems in their countries, or to enjoy the mild climate. Los Angeles can be divided into several main sections. One of these sections is known as East Los Angeles.

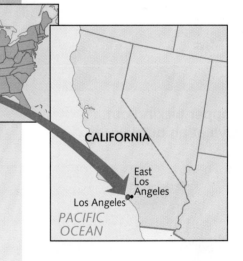

⬆ A shopper picking out a papaya at an outdoor market

⬆ A woman at an outdoor market making tortillas

⬆ **Many people shop at this grocery store in East Los Angeles.**

One of the largest neighborhoods in Los Angeles is called East Los Angeles. The people who live here call it the *barrio* (BAHR•ee•oh), a Spanish word for *neighborhood*. Many of the people are immigrants from Mexico and Central and South America or are the children and grandchildren of these immigrants.

In East Los Angeles, outdoor markets and grocery stores sell the fruits, vegetables, meats, and breads that people from these countries like to eat. If you shop there, you might think you are in a marketplace in Mexico or in Central or South America.

There are many neighborhoods in Los Angeles where other groups of people share their cultures, too. These pictures show some of these groups.

 What is the Spanish word for *neighborhood*?

↑ People of many cultures enjoy a meal at this restaurant in Los Angeles.

← A Korean festival in Los Angeles, California

LESSON 1 REVIEW

Check Understanding

1. **Recall the Facts** Why do immigrants often move to certain neighborhoods in their new countries?

2. **Focus on the Main Idea** Why do some communities include many different groups of people?

Think Critically

3. **Explore Viewpoints** What do you think would be the hardest thing to learn if you moved to another country? What do you think would be the easiest? What things do you think are difficult to learn for new immigrants who have come to the United States? Why?

Show What You Know

 **"Packing for a Journey" Activity** Work in groups of four. On a sheet of paper, one person should draw a large suitcase shape. Take turns writing or drawing in it things you would take if you were moving to another country. Talk about why these things are important to you. Then share with the class what your group has "packed."

How To

Read a Table

Why Is This Skill Important?

Lists of facts are often shown in a table. A **table** is a way to organize information. There are many kinds of tables that people use every day to help them understand information and numbers more easily. For example, people who work in some stores use a table to find out how much sales tax to charge. Bus riders use a table to find out what time their bus will come. Knowing how to use a table will help you compare things more easily.

Understand the Process

You have been reading about the many people who live in the United States. Suppose you want to compare the populations of several cities. **Population** is the number of people who live in a place. You could use a table like the one shown here.

Look at the table. It has two columns and six rows. Columns go up and down, and rows go across. If you want to find the population of a city, find its name in the first column. Then read the number that appears in the same row as the city's name. What is the population of Dayton?

Think and Apply

Use the table below to help you answer these questions.

1. Which city has the largest population?

2. Compare the populations of Spring and Danville. How can you find out how many more people live in Danville than in Spring?

3. List the six cities in order from smallest population to largest population.

4. What tables do you use? Work in a small group to brainstorm three tables you might use when you are not in school. Share your list with the other groups.

POPULATIONS OF CITIES	
CITY	**POPULATION**
Charlotte, North Carolina	395,934
Danville, Virginia	53,056
Dayton, Ohio	182,044
Gary, Indiana	116,646
Spring, Texas	33,111
Twin Falls, Idaho	27,591

Culture in Harlem

Link to Our World

What kinds of stories, poems, art, and music are part of your community?

Focus on the Main Idea

Find out about the culture in a New York City neighborhood called Harlem.

Preview Vocabulary

literature
heritage

New York City is another community that is made up of many neighborhoods. In several neighborhoods in New York City, people live together and share a culture. One of those neighborhoods is Harlem. Many of the people of Harlem did not move there from other countries, but came from other parts of the United States.

The South Moves North

During the early 1900s many African Americans who lived in the South decided to move to the North to find jobs. They left small farms in the South to find opportunities in large cities like New York City, Detroit, and Chicago. Many of them found work in factories.

This African American family moved from the rural South to Chicago.

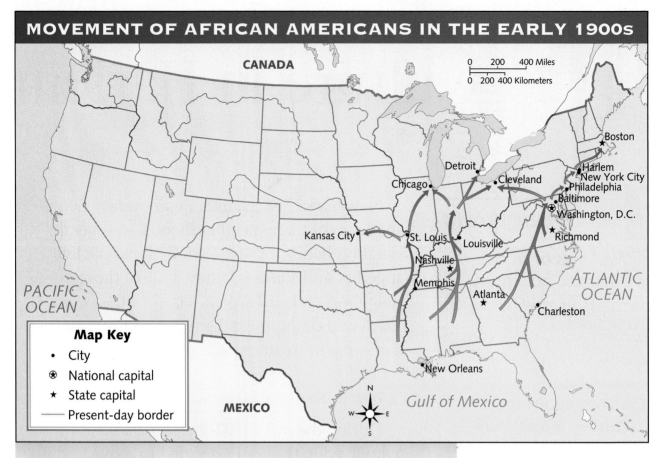

MOVEMENT OF AFRICAN AMERICANS IN THE EARLY 1900s

CANADA

0   200   400 Miles
0   200 400 Kilometers

Detroit

Chicago
Cleveland

Boston

Harlem
New York City
Philadelphia
Baltimore
Washington, D.C.

Kansas City
St. Louis
Louisville
Richmond

Nashville

Memphis

Atlanta

PACIFIC OCEAN

ATLANTIC OCEAN

Charleston

Map Key
- • City
- ⊛ National capital
- ★ State capital
- — Present-day border

MEXICO

New Orleans

Gulf of Mexico

N
W   E
S

MOVEMENT
- What do the arrows show you about where African Americans moved in the early 1900s?

The New York City neighborhood known as Harlem soon became one of the largest African American neighborhoods in the country. A writer, Loften Mitchell, described Harlem in the 1900s.

66 The small town of black Harlem . . . was crowded with togetherness, love, human warmth, and neighborliness. 99

In Harlem, African Americans created an exciting place to live. They were proud of themselves and their culture. This pride began to show in the stories and poems people wrote. It also began to show in the art they made and in the music they played.

In the 1930s a family takes a Sunday afternoon walk in Harlem.

 Why did many African Americans leave the South and move to cities in the North?

Children in art classes
in Harlem in the 1930s.

Literature and Art in Harlem

During the 1920s and 1930s, Harlem became
well-known for its literature and art. **Literature**
includes books, poetry, stories, and plays written by
people to share ideas. Like language and customs,
literature and art are also part of a culture.

Langston Hughes and Zora Neale Hurston were
two writers who lived and worked in Harlem
during the 1920s and 1930s. They wrote about the
experiences of African Americans in a new way.
They used the language that people use every day to
make their poems and stories sound natural and true.
Their writing showed that they were proud of their
African heritage. **Heritage** is the culture left to
someone by his or her ancestors.

Many other artists in Harlem were also proud of
their African heritage. They created paintings and
other works of art that showed what it was like to be
African American.

Zora Neale Hurston

 **What is literature?**

A photo from the 1920s shows King Oliver's Creole Jazz Band

Jazz Comes to Harlem

Another important part of Harlem's culture in the 1920s and 1930s was its music. People from all over New York City went to Harlem to hear a new kind of music called jazz. It had been started by African Americans in other parts of the United States. But this new kind of music quickly became an important part of Harlem's culture.

Jazz bands played in restaurants and jazz clubs in Harlem. The music was fun to listen to because jazz musicians would often make up music while they were playing or singing. A song might begin one way and end very differently.

Jazz is a style of music that began in the United States. Jazz is enjoyed by people all over the world.

Today, people of many cultures live in Harlem. But it is still a neighborhood where African Americans celebrate and enjoy their culture through art, literature, and music.

 What form of music became popular in Harlem?

Who?

Judith Jamison (1944)

Judith Jamison has been a ballet dancer since she was a child. In the 1970s she became a dancer with the famous Alvin Ailey American Dance Theater in New York City. Many dances were created especially for her. Ms. Jamison is now the artistic director of a dance company. She also teaches dance and creates dances for others to perform. She is the dancer in the center of this photograph.

LESSON 2 REVIEW

Check Understanding

1. **Recall the Facts** Name two important writers from Harlem.
2. **Focus on the Main Idea** What were some parts of Harlem culture in the 1920s and 1930s?

Think Critically

3. **Personally Speaking** Think about the importance of music in your own life. What does music express about culture? How does music make you feel?

Show What You Know

 **Poster Activity** Choose a jazz musician, and make a poster to advertise that person's next performance. Include words and details that will interest others. Show the type of instrument the musician plays. Try to find a recording by the musician to share with the class. Many libraries have records, tapes, and CDs that you can borrow.

People express their heritage and culture in many ways. Poetry is one way. Poetry is a kind of literature that tells a lot about something in just a few words. Sometimes it rhymes, but it does not have to. A poet chooses words that show how something sounds, looks, smells, tastes, or feels.

Two of the poets whose poems are on these pages, Langston Hughes and Claude McKay, lived and worked in Harlem in the 1930s. Their work helped encourage many poets who came after them. As you read each poem, think about what the poet is saying about his or her African American heritage and culture.

Color

by Langston Hughes

Langston Hughes

Wear it
Like a banner
For the proud—
Not like a shroud.
Wear it
Like a song
Soaring high—
Not moan or cry.

shroud
a covering

The Tropics in New York

by Claude McKay

Bananas ripe and green, and ginger-root,
　　Cocoa in pods and alligator pears,
And tangerines and mangoes and grape fruit,
　　Fit for the highest prize at parish fairs,

Set in the window, bringing memories
　　Of fruit-trees laden by low-singing rills,
And dewy dawns, and mystical blue skies
　　In benediction over nun-like hills.

rills streams

mystical having
secret meaning

benediction
blessing

My eyes grew dim, and I could no more gaze;
　　A wave of longing through my body swept,
And, hungry for the old, familiar ways,
　　I turned aside and bowed my head and wept.

Claude McKay

Knoxville, Tennessee

by Nikki Giovanni

I always like summer
best
you can eat fresh corn
from daddy's garden
and okra
and greens
and cabbage
and lots of
barbecue
and buttermilk
and homemade ice-cream
at the church picnic
and listen to
gospel music
outside
at the church
homecoming
and go to the mountains with
your grandmother
and go barefooted
and be warm
all the time
not only when you go to bed
and sleep

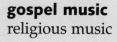

Nikki Giovanni

okra a vegetable

gospel music religious music

Margaret Walker

Lineage

by Margaret Walker

My grandmothers were strong.
They followed plows and bent to toil.
They moved through fields sowing seed.
They touched earth and grain grew.
They were full of sturdiness and singing.
My grandmothers were strong.

toil work hard

sturdiness strength

Sonia Sanchez

Haiku

by Sonia Sanchez

i have looked into
my father's eyes and seen an
african sunset.

Literature Review

1. What does each poet say about African American life?

2. In "The Tropics in New York," the poet describes his memories of the place where he grew up—Jamaica. Jamaica is a small island in the Caribbean Sea. How is the poem like the story told in *Grandfather's Journey*?

3. Choose one of these poems, and illustrate it in your own way. Your picture should show what you think the poet was saying in the poem.

How To

Understand Point of View

Why Is This Skill Important?

In *Grandfather's Journey,* artist Allen Say uses words and pictures to tell the story of his grandfather's life. Say's pictures also tell you about his point of view. A person's **point of view** is the way he or she feels about something. If you know what to look for in a picture, you can understand what the artist is saying to you.

Understand the Process

There are many ways a painter can show his or her point of view. Look at the painting of Langston Hughes on page 157, and ask yourself the following questions.

- Who is the person in the painting? What is the person doing? What feeling does the person's face show?
- What colors did the artist use? Are the colors bright or dull? How do these colors make you feel?

- Has the artist painted the person to look close up or far away?
- If you could touch the painting, how might it feel?

Think and Apply

Look once again at the painting, and answer the questions below.

1. The artist could have shown Langston Hughes in many ways. Why do you think he chose to show Langston Hughes with his chin in his hand?

2. What does the artist want you to think Langston Hughes was like? How does the artist feel about Langston Hughes?

3. A painting can show you how things were at a certain time in history. What does this painting tell you about the person's culture or heritage?

Winold Reiss painted this picture of Langston Hughes in 1925.

Holiday Customs and Traditions

Link to Our World

How do you celebrate your favorite holiday?

Focus on the Main Idea

Find out how a holiday can be celebrated in many different ways.

Preview Vocabulary

holiday
tradition

People all over the world celebrate holidays. A **holiday** is a special day for remembering a person or an event that has importance for the people in a community. The Fourth of July and Thanksgiving are holidays that celebrate the beginning of this country. They are important holidays to people in the United States, but not to people who live in other countries.

The United States is home to people from many cultures. Each group celebrates its own holidays with special customs. Here are some ways that people celebrate the New Year's holiday in the United States.

Aya

Mikesha and her mother

Suc

Chet

A Japanese Tradition

Aya was born in the United States, but her parents came from Japan. They still follow many Japanese traditions. **Traditions** are customs, or ways of doing things, that are passed on from parents to children. In Japan the New Year's holiday is called *Oshogatsu* (oh•shoh•GAHT•soo). It is one of the most important holidays of the year there.

There are many traditions for the Japanese celebration of the New Year. One of the most important is to begin the New Year with everything in order. First, Aya and her family clean the house. Then, they try to pay back any money they have borrowed. Next, they take the time to solve any personal problems they might have. Last, the family puts on new clothes and visits friends, and together they eat a special soup called *ozoni* (oh•ZOH•nee). Japanese people say this soup will bring them a long, good life.

All of the foods eaten on *Oshogatsu* have a special meaning. Snapper, a kind of fish, is eaten for happiness. *Soba* (SOH•bah) noodles are for long life. *Mochi* (MOH•chee), which is made of sweet rice balls, is for wealth. *Kuro mame* (KOO•roh MAH•meh), black beans, are for good luck.

Aya holds a tray of foods she and her family eat to celebrate *Oshogatsu*.

 What traditions are important to Japanese people for the New Year's holiday?

A Vietnamese Custom

In another part of the United States lives Suc (SOOK), whose parents moved to this country from Vietnam. Suc and his family call their New Year's celebration *Tet*. Like Aya's family, the members of Suc's family clean their house, pay back money they have borrowed, and wear new clothes. But the foods they make are very different. Suc and his family eat special rice cakes called *banh day* (BYN ZAY) and *banh chung* (BYN CHUHNG). Each child receives a small red envelope with money inside. Suc likes that part the best!

 What do Vietnamese people call the New Year's holiday?

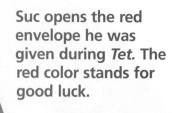

Suc opens the red envelope he was given during *Tet.* The red color stands for good luck.

An African American Celebration

Mikesha (my•KEE•sha) and her family celebrate Kwanzaa (KWAHN•zuh), a festival that honors their African American heritage. It lasts for one week and ends on New Year's Day. Each day during the celebration, Mikesha lights a candle in the *kinara* (KIN•ah•ruh), a candle holder with places for seven candles, and thinks about that day's special meaning. She looks forward to the *karamu* (KAR•uh•muh), the big feast that takes place on New Year's Day. During Kwanzaa, Mikesha hears many words in Swahili, a language of her African ancestors.

 **What is Kwanzaa?**

During Kwanzaa, Mikesha and her mother prepare food, give gifts, and light the candles in the *kinara.*

Celebrating at Times Square

Chet and his family live in New York City. They celebrate the New Year with hundreds of thousands of other people they do not know. They ride the subway to Times Square, a traditional gathering place to celebrate the holiday. There they wait in a huge crowd for the big clock on the top of a building to say it is midnight. When it does, the New Year has begun, and the crowd cheers and sings "Auld Lang Syne," which means "good old times." This song was written more than 200 years ago in Scotland by a poet named Robert Burns.

> "Should auld acquaintance be forgot,
> And never brought to mind?
> Should auld acquaintance be forgot
> And days of auld lang syne?"

Chet wears a party hat and blows on a noisemaker to celebrate the New Year at Times Square in New York City.

New Year's is a time to remember old times and old friends and to get ready for the new ones. People feel ready for a fresh start and a chance to do things differently. Everywhere people live, they celebrate the New Year, but they do it in their own special ways.

 Why do many people celebrate the New Year's holiday at Times Square?

These people in Times Square are waiting for the clock to strike midnight so they can welcome in the New Year.

LESSON 4 REVIEW

Check Understanding

1. **Recall the Facts**   What do the Japanese call the celebration of their New Year?
2. **Focus on the Main Idea**   What are some of the many ways people in the United States celebrate the New Year?

Think Critically

3. **Think More About It**   Why do you think many people in the United States sing a song to celebrate the New Year's holiday?

Show What You Know

 **Write a Report**
Choose one holiday that your family might celebrate. Make a list of some of the traditions that you follow. Then pick one tradition to write a report about. You might choose a special food, a piece of clothing, a song, or an activity that goes with the holiday. If you wish, you can make drawings or find pictures to go with your report. Share your report with your classmates.

How To

Follow a Sequence of Events

Why Is This Skill Important?

When Allen Say decided to write about his grandfather, he had to think about the best way to tell his story. He wanted to make it easy for everyone to understand. So he decided to tell about his grandfather's life in sequence. **Sequence** is the order in which things happen. Say begins the story when his grandfather is a young man. He ends the story when his grandfather has died. Understanding the sequence of events can help you remember what happened.

Remember What You Have Read

In Lesson 4 you learned about Aya and her family and how they celebrate *Oshogatsu*. What sequence do they follow as they celebrate the New Year?

Understand the Process

To follow a sequence, you can look for certain clues. Some authors use word clues like *first, then, next,* and *last.* These words help put events in sequence. Another way to understand a sequence of events is to look for

dates. Dates will often give clues to the sequence you are reading in a social studies book.

Look at the second paragraph on page 159. Find the words that tell what Aya and her family do to celebrate *Oshogatsu.* What do they do first? What is the last thing they do? How can you tell?

Think and Apply

Choose three activities that you do in the same sequence every day. Write a paragraph that tells about them. Write the sentences in sequence. Use the words *first, then, next,* and *last.* Read your paragraph to a partner so he or she can draw a time line for your day.

Aya helps clean her family's house.

Different Countries, Different Cultures

Link to Our World

Compare the way you live with the way a person your age in another country lives.

Focus on the Main Idea
Find out how life in India is like life in the United States and how it is different.

Preview Vocabulary
folktale

In *Grandfather's Journey* the author's grandfather traveled back and forth between two countries—Japan and the United States. He enjoyed the beautiful physical features of the United States. Landforms like the mountains and coasts amazed him. But he also discovered that many interesting people lived in the United States. He met many people from different cultures.

Traveling is one of the ways people learn about other countries in the world. If you could travel to India, you would learn that it is an interesting country. Like the United States, India is filled with beautiful places and many groups of people who have different cultures.

People in Bombay, India

People and Places

The United States and India are located in very different parts of the Earth. The United States is on the continent of North America, in the Western Hemisphere. India is located on the other side of the world, in the Eastern Hemisphere. It is on the continent of Asia.

Both the United States and India are made up of states. There are 50 states in the United States. In India there are 25 states. In both places each state has features that make it different from other states, as well as features that make it similar.

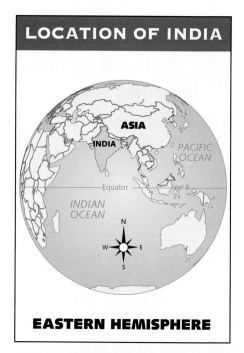

LOCATION OF INDIA

ASIA

INDIA

PACIFIC OCEAN

Equator

INDIAN OCEAN

EASTERN HEMISPHERE

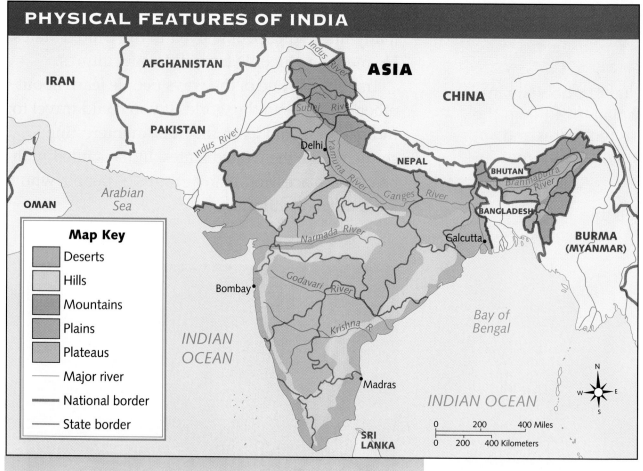

PHYSICAL FEATURES OF INDIA

AFGHANISTAN

IRAN

ASIA

CHINA

PAKISTAN

Indus River

Sutlej River

Delhi

Yamuna River

NEPAL

BHUTAN

Brahmaputra River

Arabian Sea

OMAN

Ganges River

BANGLADESH

BURMA (MYANMAR)

Calcutta

Narmada River

Map Key

Deserts

Hills

Mountains

Plains

Plateaus

Major river

National border

State border

Bombay

Godavari River

Krishna R.

Madras

INDIAN OCEAN

Bay of Bengal

INDIAN OCEAN

0   200   400 Miles
0   200   400 Kilometers

SRI LANKA

PLACE

Map Skill

Compare this map with the Landform Map of the United States on page 87.

■ How are the two countries alike and different?

Like the United States, India also has many different landforms. There are mountains, hills, plains, and coasts. And, as in the United States, many rivers flow through India.

 On which continent is India located?

Many People, Many Languages

Many people live in India. The table on this page shows the five countries with the most people. You can use the table to compare the population of India with the population of the United States.

LEARNING FROM TABLES
Look at the table below. Which country has more people, the United States or India?

POPULATIONS OF COUNTRIES	
COUNTRY	POPULATION
China	1,192,000,000
India	911,600,000
United States	260,800,000
Indonesia	199,700,000
Brazil	155,300,000

← Many cities in India are crowded.

↟ The sign on this shop is in two different alphabets.

As in the United States, many different groups of people live in India. People in each group have their own culture and may have their own language. One of the largest groups in India is the Hindus (HIN•dooz). Most of these people speak a language called Hindi (HIN•dee). But if you travel all over India, you can hear people speak many languages, including English.

Different languages are often written using different alphabets. So signs on shops and public buildings in India may be printed in three or more alphabets.

 What is one of the largest groups of people in India?

Children in an outdoor classroom in India ➜

Literature

Like language, literature is an important part of any culture. One example of literature is the **folktale**, a traditional story that often teaches a lesson. "The Jackal's Tale" is an Indian folktale that tells what happens to a jackal who pretends he is something he is not.

The Jackal's Tale

Once there was a clever jackal who always wanted to be something special. He tried hard to be noticed by the other animals in the forest, but nothing worked. Then one day he tripped and fell into a large bucket of blue powder. When he came out, his dull fur was a bright blue.

"At last!" the jackal thought to himself. "There is something different about me." But when he ran into the other animals, they looked at him in fear. They were frightened by the strange color of his fur and ran away.

The jackal called to them and said, "Do not be afraid. I was sent here to be your king." The other animals thought about what he said. They decided to welcome him. Not only that, they spoiled him. They brought him the best pieces of food to eat. They built a comfortable shelter where he could sleep in peace. Many days passed, and the jackal thought he was happy.

Then one night the jackal was awakened by the howls of a pack of jackals nearby. He suddenly felt very sad. He missed his old friends very much. Before he could think more about it, the blue jackal pointed his nose into the air and howled.

All at once, the other animals realized that the blue jackal was really just a jackal. He was not their king after all. They chased him back into the forest and threw pieces of food at him.

The lesson is that it is impossible to fool all the people all the time. Sooner or later, your true colors will show through and people will know you as you really are!

 What is the important lesson taught by "The Jackal's Tale"?

The small balls of *chapati* are pushed flat with the hands and then cooked on a griddle, a flat metal pan. ➜

⬆ Curry was used to make this dish of shrimp madras.

Food, Clothing, and Music

In neighborhoods all over the United States, people of many cultures eat different kinds of food. This is also true in India. Many Indians eat foods made with curry. Curry is a mixture of spices. Some Indian cooks grind their own mixture of spices every day. They use the curry to flavor their foods.

People in India make many different kinds of bread, too. One kind, *chapati* (chuh•PAH•tee), is made from little balls of dough. Another kind of bread, *roti* (ROH•tee), is hollow. It is made by frying balls of dough in oil. The balls puff up like doughnuts.

All over India you can see people wearing different kinds of clothing. In some places in India, women and girls wear a long piece of cloth that is wrapped around the body. This is a kind of dress called a *sari* (SAHR•ee). Often a piece of the same cloth is used to make a veil or a head covering. Saris are cool and comfortable, but it is not easy to run and play games in them.

In the cities, many Indian men wear suits and ties to work. The woman shown here is wearing a *sari*.

⬆ When Indian dancers perform, they wear colorful costumes.

Some adults and children wear loose cotton shirts and pants. Clothing for both boys and girls often has beautiful patterns and bright colors.

Music is another important part of India's many cultures. Indian musicians play mostly drums and instruments with strings. One stringed instrument is called a *sitar* (SIH•tar). It looks like a guitar but has many more strings. At festivals Indian dancers perform to music. When they dance, they use their arms, hands, and fingers to tell stories.

 What makes the people of India different from one another?

The sitar was first played about 800 years ago. It is a stringed instrument made from a vegetable called a gourd. It can have as many as 19 strings.

← Musicians also play *tablas*, or drums.

The Belur Hindu Temple in Karnataka, a state in southwestern India

Religion

In India there are two main religions—Hinduism and Islam. About 550 million Indian people are Hindus. They follow Hinduism, one of the oldest religions in the world. Hindu temples can be found all over India.

About 76 million Indian people are Muslims. They follow the religion of Islam. Muslims worship in mosques (MAHSKS). Many mosques, too, can be found all over India.

Although most people in India are either Muslim or Hindu, there are other religious groups as well. The table below shows how many people in India are members of each religious group. The table also shows how many people in the United States are members of these groups.

LEARNING FROM TABLES
In which country do the largest number of Hindus live?

POPULATIONS OF RELIGIOUS GROUPS		
RELIGIOUS GROUPS	INDIA	UNITED STATES
Hindus	549,700,000	340,000
Muslims	75,600,000	3,332,000
Christians	16,200,000	132,000,000
Sikhs	13,100,000	350,000
Buddhists	4,700,000	590,000
Jews	4,500	5,981,000

The Jama Mosque in Delhi, India

People of many cultures live in the United States and in India. The languages and literature of the people are important parts of each culture. The foods they eat, the clothing they wear, the music they play, and the religion they follow are also important to the people of each culture.

 What are the two main religions in India?

The Taj Mahal

More than 300 years ago, about 20,000 workers built one of the world's most beautiful buildings, the Taj Mahal (TAHJ muh•HAHL). Shah Jahan, one of India's rulers, ordered workers to build the Taj Mahal in memory of his wife. It is made of white marble and stands in a beautiful garden. The workers started the Taj Mahal in 1632 and finished it 22 years later.

LESSON 5 REVIEW

Check Understanding

1. **Recall the Facts** What foods do people in India eat?
2. **Focus on the Main Idea** In what ways are the United States and India alike? In what ways are they different?

Think Critically

3. **Think More About It** What is good about living in a country that has people of many cultures?

Show What You Know

 **Collage Activity** Choose a country you would like to know more about. Cut out magazine pictures or draw your own pictures that show the people, food, music, art, literature, and religion of that country. Share your collage with the class. Tell how the country's culture seems similar to and different from the cultures in the United States.

How To

Use a Product Map

Why Is This Skill Important?

Sometimes it is easier to learn something if you can picture it. By learning to interpret, or explain, symbols on a map, you can understand information more easily.

Understand the Process

Many people in India make their living in agriculture. **Agriculture** is the raising of crops and farm animals. The map on page 175 shows the location of the most important crops and farm animals raised in India. Each symbol stands for a different product raised on Indian farms. These symbols are explained in the map key.

Farms cover more than half the land in India. Only China grows more rice than India. Find the symbol for rice. In what part of India is the most rice grown? There are more cattle in India than in any other country in the world. These cows are not raised for meat, but to provide milk. Look at the map key. Where are the most cattle raised? What other animals are raised in India?

 Think and Apply

1. Look on the map to find where cotton is grown. What areas of India raise the most cotton?

2. Find the symbol for wheat. Near what city is wheat grown?

3. What symbols stand for things that are not planted? Are these products found mostly in the west or in the east? Why?

4. Compare this map to the physical features map of India on page 166. On what kind of land is tea grown?

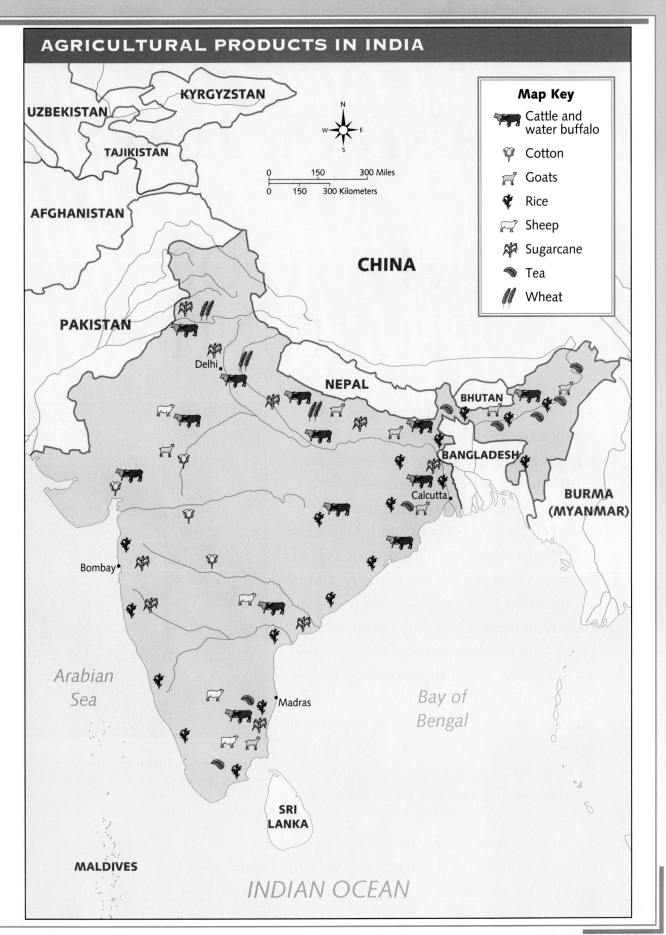

AGRICULTURAL PRODUCTS IN INDIA

Map Key
- Cattle and water buffalo
- Cotton
- Goats
- Rice
- Sheep
- Sugarcane
- Tea
- Wheat

0   150   300 Miles
0   150   300 Kilometers

UZBEKISTAN

KYRGYZSTAN

TAJIKISTAN

AFGHANISTAN

PAKISTAN

CHINA

Delhi

NEPAL

BHUTAN

BANGLADESH

BURMA (MYANMAR)

Calcutta

Bombay

Arabian Sea

Madras

Bay of Bengal

SRI LANKA

MALDIVES

INDIAN OCEAN

ISLAND OF TEARS OR ISLAND OF OPPORTUNITY?

In 1892 tiny Ellis Island in New York Harbor became the first stop in the United States for millions of immigrants. They went there to be checked before being allowed to live in this country.

Immigrants started in a baggage room and then walked up a long staircase. At the top of the stairs, they came to a huge room called the Great Hall. It spread out before them as far as they could see. Rows and rows of people stood in lines separated by metal pipes or wooden benches. There doctors examined the immigrants, and government workers asked them about their past. At any one time an immigrant could hear people answering questions in more than 30 languages.

There were restaurants, a hospital, a post office, laundries, and courtrooms on Ellis Island. It was like a small city.

Immigrants climbing stairs to the Great Hall

Bad Memories of Ellis Island

People who went through Ellis Island have had different feelings about their experience. Vera Clark was seven years old when she came from Barbados. She remembers what it was like when she got to the Great Hall. "We were like in cages . . . It was just one human mass of people who couldn't understand each other . . . it was just horrible."

Good Memories of Ellis Island

Other immigrants have different memories. Lillian Kaiz was also seven when she came from Russia. She remembers, "I ate my first hot dog and my first banana there. . . . The first night they were celebrating Christmas. They had a movie. I had never seen one."

Ellis Island Today

By 1954 fewer immigrants passed through Ellis Island. Its buildings began to fall apart, and it was finally closed. Today the buildings on Ellis Island have been rebuilt as an immigration museum. There people can walk up the stairs to the Great Hall and imagine they hear the voices of their ancestors.

COMPARE VIEWPOINTS

1. What is Vera Clark's memory of Ellis Island?
2. What is Lillian Kaiz's memory of Ellis Island?
3. How are their viewpoints different?
4. Do you think their experiences changed their feelings about the United States? Explain.

THINK –AND– APPLY

With a group, think of a place in your community that most of you have visited.

BUILDING CITIZENSHIP

How many students had a good time there? How many did not enjoy the place? Talk about why people can visit the same place but have different feelings about it.

Ellis Island as it looks today

STORY CLOTH

Follow the pictures shown in this story cloth to help you review the things you read about in Unit 3.

Summarize the Main Ideas

1. People move from one community to another and from one country to another.

2. Large communities include groups who share a culture or cultures.

3. Language, customs, religion, food, literature, art, and music are important parts of a culture.

4. People of many cultures can live together in one country, community, or neighborhood.

Create a Mural Celebrate the different cultures of the world by creating a class mural. Cover a bulletin board with paper. Then use paints, brushes, and other art materials to draw a mural of people from many different cultures. Show different parts of each culture, such as food, clothing, art, musical instruments, and language. Include as many details as you can. Invite other classes to see the mural.

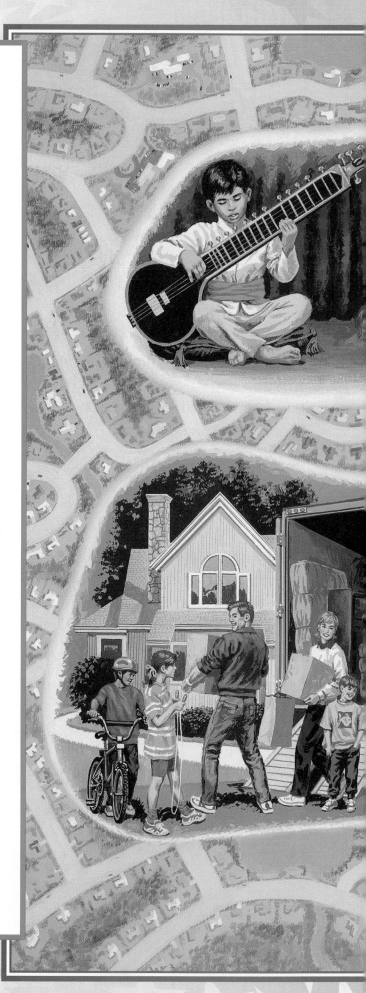

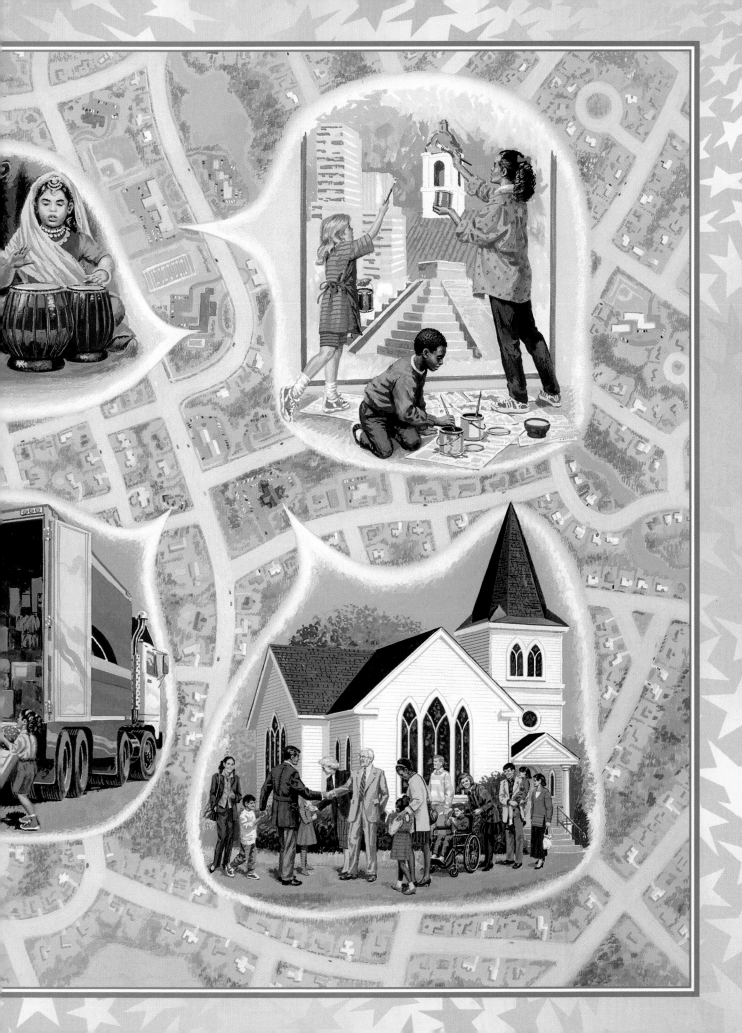

COOPERATIVE LEARNING WORKSHOP

Remember
- Share your ideas.
- Cooperate with others to plan your work.
- Take responsibility for your work.
- Show your group's work to the class.
- Discuss what you learned by working together.

Activity 1

Use a Computer

Use a computer to make a database of the customs and traditions of people in five different countries. Include favorite foods, literature, religion, music, art, clothing, and family customs. Use the database to tell other groups about the people you studied.

Activity 2

Simulation

Write a play about a family that moves to the United States from another country. Tell where the family is from and what customs they follow. Explain why they left their country to start a new life. Then decide who will play the parts of the family members. Finally, act out the play for the other groups.

Activity 3

Make a Collection

Collect magazine and newspaper pictures and articles that describe different cultures. For example, you might find pictures of musical instruments, special foods, and people practicing customs and traditions. Work together to decide how to put the pictures in a scrapbook. You might organize them by the cultures they show.

CONNECT MAIN IDEAS

Use this graphic organizer to show how the unit's main ideas are connected. First, copy the organizer onto a separate sheet of paper. Then, fill in the blanks by writing two details from the unit that support each main idea.

People move from one community to another and from one country to another.

1. _____ 2. _____

Large communities include groups of people who share a culture or cultures.

1. _____ 2. _____

Language, customs, food, literature, art, and music are important parts of a culture.

1. _____ 2. _____

People of many cultures can live together in one country, community, or neighborhood.

1. _____ 2. _____

USE VOCABULARY

Choose five of the vocabulary words below. Use these words to tell a story about yourself or your community.

heritage	**literature**
holiday	**opportunity**
immigrant	**tradition**

WRITE MORE ABOUT IT

Write a Story Write two paragraphs that tell a story about your favorite holiday. In the first paragraph, tell why the holiday is special to you. In the second paragraph, explain how you and your family celebrate the holiday.

CHECK UNDERSTANDING

1. What are two reasons people move from one community to another?

2. What makes up the culture of a people?

3. How does the celebration of the New Year in the United States show that there are many cultures in this country?

THINK CRITICALLY

1. **Past to Present** How have immigrants who came to the United States in the past made a difference in the country today?

2. **Think More About It** Why is it important to learn about cultures that are different from yours?

3. **Personally Speaking** If you could live anywhere in the world, where would you live? Explain.

APPLY SKILLS

How to Read a Table Use the information in the table in the next column to answer the questions about the populations of several cities.

POPULATIONS OF CITIES

CITY	POPULATION
Austin, Texas	465,622
Flint, Michigan	140,761
Macon, Georgia	106,612
Oak Park, Illinois	53,648
Tallahassee, Florida	124,773

1. How many people live in Macon?

2. List the cities in order from the smallest to the largest.

How to Follow a Sequence of Events Word clues can help you put events in the right order. Some word clues to look for are *then, next,* and *last.* On another sheet of paper, number the sentences below in the right sequence.

1. _____ Then, she went to high school in Baltimore, Maryland.

2. _____ Zora Neale Hurston was born in Florida but moved away.

3. _____ After college she began writing books.

4. _____ Next, she went to college and became interested in African American traditions.

How to Use a Product Map

The map below gives you information about fuel and farm products in Texas. Use the symbols on the map to help you answer these questions.

1. Are more cattle raised in the southeastern or southwestern part of Texas?

2. On what type of land is rice grown?

3. What kind of animal is raised near San Antonio?

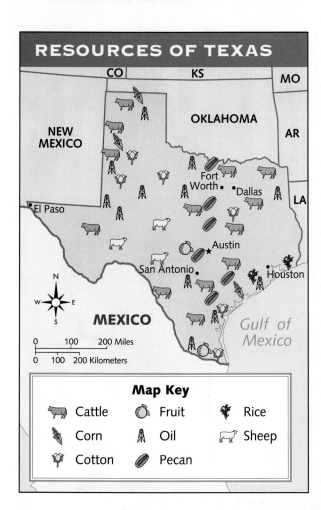

RESOURCES OF TEXAS

Map Key

- Cattle
- Corn
- Cotton
- Fruit
- Oil
- Pecan
- Rice
- Sheep

How to Understand Point of View

Look at this painting of the girl and her cat. Think about ways to understand the artist's point of view. Then answer these questions.

© 1995, Board of Trustees, National Gallery of Art, Washington, DC

Woman with a Cat by Auguste Renoir

1. What is the girl doing?

2. What is the artist trying to tell you about this girl?

READ MORE ABOUT IT

Klara's New World by Jeanette Winter. Knopf. Klara and her family leave Sweden to come to America to find a better life.

Lights on the River by Jane Resh Thomas. Hyperion. Teresa and her family work in the United States but miss their friends in Mexico.

People Working Together

People work together to make products and provide services. ➡

People choose the products or services they will buy. ➡

People in communities live together. They have fun together. They also help one another and work together to get things done.

◀ Children and young adults work together at a car wash to raise money.

People trade with each other. ▶

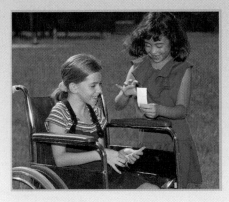

Products and services get to market in different ways. ▶

REUBEN and the FIRE

BY MERLE GOOD

ILLUSTRATED BY P. BUCKLEY MOSS

This is a story about a boy who lives in an Amish (AH•mish) community. The Amish are a group of people who share religious beliefs. They live and work together in their own communities. The Amish depend on each other for meeting most of their needs. For some things, however, they get help from people outside of their community. The story begins when Reuben and his friends see that a neighbor's barn is on fire.

Reuben had never run so hard. It looked like the smoke was coming from his homeplace.

"I hope it's not our barn," he gasped to the twins as he ran, trying to see over the tops of the crops.

They saw the billowing smoke as they came over the ridge. The roof of a barn was burning.

"It's Abner Fisher's place," Sam said. The three of them stopped, staring at the frightening scene.

"We better go home and tell our parents," Sam said.

"Glad it's not our place," Reuben replied.

The twins nodded. "Yeah, but I feel sorry for Abner's family," Sam said.

Annie was hurrying out of the barn as Reuben came running around the corner. She looked upset.

"Can I go along over to the fire?" he asked.

"Better get a fork and a shovel if you're going," she said. "But be quick."

Annie Reuben's oldest sister

It was hot and scary close to the fire.
Neighbors were letting out the cows and horses.

"Can I help?" Reuben asked Abner.

"There are five little puppies in the milk house,"
Abner's oldest son answered. "See if someone can
help you move them to the house. But be careful."

The fire was still at the other end of the big barn.
Sam and Ben drove up with their father just in time
to help Reuben carry the pups to the back porch of
the house.

They could feel the heat of the fire as they ran,
big eyes and droopy ears in their arms.

Ben Sam's twin

Reuben had never seen so many fire trucks. They came from everywhere, lights flashing red.

At first, everyone was afraid the house would burn too, but the firemen quickly sprayed water on it.

It was past midnight when Reuben crawled into bed. Dawdi had waited for them and wanted to hear all about the fire.

Dawdi (DAW•dee) Grandfather

At first Reuben couldn't sleep, his mind full of flashing lights and smoke. Then Mamm looked in on him and rubbed his forehead and his arm to help him relax. She was good that way.

Reuben dreamed that the puppies ran away on the fire truck.

Next morning Reuben could hardly stay awake during the milking. "Don't walk with your eyes closed," his sister Barbie complained.

At breakfast Datt announced the bad news. Reuben would have to stay home and bale the hay with Annie and Nancy.

Mamm Mother

Datt Father

"Cleaning up after a fire is no place for a young boy," Datt said. "Maybe you can go along to the barnraising tomorrow."

Mamm baked all day, with Barbie and Mary helping. A lot of food was needed for the barnraising. Reuben drove the horses and Annie and Nancy stacked the bales.

A barnraising is like a holiday. It seemed to Reuben that everyone was there. His cousins from the southern end even came.

Ben and Sam brought their hammers, but they never got to use them. All the boys could do was watch and run errands if they were asked.

Big Henry Stoltzfus was the boss. Reuben liked him. By lunch the rafters were all in place. And the roof was going on before milking time.

"I'd like to be a carpenter like Big Henry," Sam said.

Ben laughed. "You better start growing."

Abner walked up to Datt and Reuben as they were leaving. He had one of the little pups in his arm. "Thanks for your help," he smiled. He looked tired.

"Gladly," Datt said. "We'll be back tomorrow if you can use us."

Abner smiled again. "Reuben, this puppy needs a home." Reuben couldn't believe it. He looked at Datt, afraid he'd say no. But his father nodded with a smile.

People in an Amish Community Work Together

Link to Our World

How do you work with others in your community, school, and home?

Focus on the Main Idea
Read to find out how people in the Amish community work together to meet their needs.

Preview Vocabulary
basic needs
rural
service
product

The community Reuben lives in has an uncommon way of life. But the Amish, like people in every other community, work together to meet the same basic needs. Those **basic needs** are food, clothing, and shelter.

The Amish Way of Life

The Amish religion began in Europe. The name *Amish* comes from one of the early leaders, Jacob Ammann. The first Amish group to move to the United States came from Switzerland in the early 1700s. They came here to find a place where they could follow their religion. Because the Amish like to live simply, they did not settle in big cities. Instead, they started their own communities in rural areas. A **rural** area is out in the countryside, away from cities and towns.

Because of their beliefs, the Amish live just as their ancestors did more than 200 years ago. They are sometimes called the Plain People. The women and girls wear long dresses, aprons, and caps. The men and boys wear straw hats in the summer and black cloth hats in the winter. Their pants are held up by suspenders instead of belts.

Amish children enjoy playing games.

AMISH COMMUNITIES IN THE UNITED STATES

Map Key
- Amish community

LOCATION
- In which states are most Amish communities located?

Most Amish people are farmers. They grow most of their own food. They use horses instead of tractors to pull their plows.

Amish homes have no electricity. The Amish do not own or use computers, televisions, or radios. They use lanterns to provide light for reading or sewing at night. They live this way so that they can spend time with one another. The Amish want to keep their way of life from changing.

The Amish do not own or drive cars. Instead, they drive buggies or small wagons pulled by horses.

Why are the Amish sometimes called the Plain People?

This picture shows
a barn raising in an
Amish community.

A Barn Is Built

In "Reuben and the Fire," Reuben and his family
and friends help a neighbor build a new barn after
the old one burns down. Helping each other is an
important part of Amish community life. If one
Amish family has a problem, the rest of the Amish
community helps the family solve it. They say, "It is
better for a group to work together than for a person
to labor alone."

When a family in an Amish community needs a
new barn, the people get together for a barn raising.
As you learned in the story, men, women, and
children from the community gather early in the
morning with materials and tools. They work all day
long. By the time it is dark, they have built a new
barn. While the men and boys are building, the
women and girls are cooking and serving meals. No
one is ever paid money for working at a barn raising.
People do it to help each other. After the barn is
finished, families in the community may even fill
the new barn with their own hay.

The Amish build their own homes and barns. They also make their own clothing. Many of the things they need, they make by hand. By working together, they can meet the basic needs of their families and community.

What is a barn raising?

Amish People Depend on the Outside World

The Amish help each other meet their needs. But sometimes the Amish must get help from other places. In "Reuben and the Fire," firefighters from other communities help put out the barn fire. These firefighters provide a service. A **service** is something one person does for another. Police officers and teachers provide services. So do carpenters and plumbers. The Amish have no doctors in their communities. When a doctor's help is needed, the Amish must get this service from outside their community.

People outside the Amish community use Amish services, too. Some Amish men work as carpenters or blacksmiths. Blacksmiths work with iron to make horseshoes and tools.

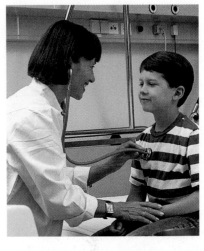

This doctor provides a service by helping people keep healthy.

← Car-repair people provide a service by fixing cars.

This Amish blacksmith provides a service by making things from iron. →

A quilt is made by sewing together small pieces of cloth. Amish women and girls make and sell quilts to earn money. They will save the money, then use it to buy the items they need.

Besides providing services, the Amish make products to sell to people outside the community. A **product** is something that people make or grow, often to sell.

Quilts are one kind of product Amish people make. Quilts are used as covers on beds. Often they have interesting and beautiful designs. Amish women and girls work in groups to sew the quilts. Then they sell them to people from other communities. Other products the Amish sell are cheese, vegetables, jellies and jams, and tools made from wood.

The Amish buy products from outside their community that they cannot make themselves. They buy fuel for their lanterns and materials for building new barns and homes. They buy cloth for making clothes and quilts. They also buy shoes.

Amish children wear clothes that have been made by hand. But they buy athletic shoes because athletic shoes last longer than handmade shoes.

The Amish have their own way of life. But the Amish are like people in other communities, too. They need to buy products they cannot make and services they cannot provide. To be able to do this, they sell their own products and services to others.

 What are some products and services the Amish buy from other communities?

The Amish sell their products to people from other communities.

Stores in any community offer products for people to buy.

LESSON 1 REVIEW

Check Understanding

1. **Recall the Facts** Why are products and services important to people?
2. **Focus on the Main Idea** In what ways do Amish people help each other in their own communities?

Think Critically

3. **Think More About It** What products and services are important to you and your family or community? Why?

Show What You Know

 **Quilting Activity**
Fold a sheet of paper into three parts, first the long way and then the short way. Now unfold it. You will have nine boxes like the squares of a quilt. In each box, draw a picture that shows something about the Amish way of life. Use your textbook or another book for ideas. Add your "Amish quilt" to a classroom display, and talk about your drawings.

How To

Read Graphs

Why Is This Skill Important?

Sometimes you need to compare sets of numbers. A graph can make it easier. There are several kinds of graphs. Two of them are shown on this page. A **pictograph** is a graph that uses small pictures to show amounts of things. A **bar graph** uses bars of different heights to show amounts of things.

Understand the Process

Compare the two graphs. Each has a title that tells you what it is about. The pictograph has a key to explain what the pictures stand for. The bar graph has labels that explain what the different bars mean.

Use the graphs to answer these questions.

1. Were more quilts sold on Wednesday or on Saturday?

2. On what day were the most quilts sold? How many were sold that day?

3. How many quilts were sold in all?

Think and Apply

Think of something you would like to show in a graph. Then gather the information and make a pictograph and a bar graph. Share your graphs with your classmates.

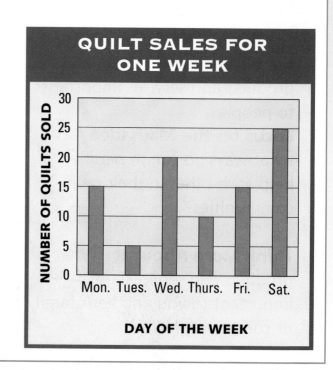

QUILT SALES FOR ONE WEEK

DAY OF THE WEEK	NUMBER OF QUILTS SOLD
Monday	🔲🔲🔲
Tuesday	🔲
Wednesday	🔲🔲🔲🔲
Thursday	🔲🔲
Friday	🔲🔲🔲
Saturday	🔲🔲🔲🔲🔲

🔲 = 5 quilts

People Work Together to Make a Product

Link to Our World

How are most products made?

Focus on the Main Idea

Read to find out how people work together to make products.

Preview Vocabulary

technology
producer
raw materials
marketing
human resources
wage
industry

The Amish people work together to make their products by hand, one at a time. But most of the products you use every day are manufactured, or made by machines.

Working Together in a Factory

Many of the products you use are made by machines, not by hand. Workers in factories use machines to make great numbers of products at one time. The use of machines, tools, and materials to make products faster and more easily is called **technology**.

In one community in Illinois, a factory makes a certain product—bicycle helmets. The people who make a product are called **producers**. In that factory, work is done in steps to produce the helmets.

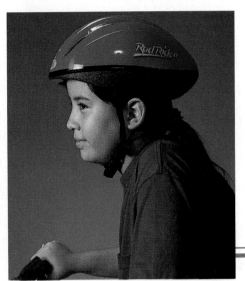

Products like crayons and bicycle helmets are made in factories.

Rantoul, Illinois, is the location of this Bell bicycle helmet factory.

1. Designing the Product

A group works together in the factory to design the helmet. Some people work on computers, and some work on paper. They use drawings and models to decide what the helmet should be like. Designers talk to scientists to find out whether there is a new technology they might use in producing the helmets. They make a few sample helmets by hand and test their safety. In some factories designers do these tests on computers without making samples first.

Testing the helmet for safety

2. Getting the Materials

When all the safety tests have been passed, the raw materials for making the helmets must be bought. **Raw materials** are the resources needed to make a product. Raw materials such as oil are needed to make helmets. Oil is needed to make the plastics used in helmet manufacturing. These materials are shipped to the factory from places around the world.

Holding black foam pellets that will become an inner shell

3. Making the Product

Workers use raw materials to make each part of the helmets. They use machines to make the shell, or outside, of the helmet. They use other machines to produce the straps. Some workers make the same part all the time. Other workers assemble, or put together, all the different parts.

Using machines to make the outer shell

4. Marketing the Product

Marketing means planning how to sell a product to the community. The people who work in marketing decide where to sell the helmets. They also talk about how to get people to buy them.

 How are most products made today?

Adding the thin plastic shell

Attaching chin straps to the helmet

The many workers at Bell are proud of the product they help manufacture.

The label is designed to help people remember the manufacturer's name.

Using Resources

It takes more than raw materials to make a helmet or another product. A factory uses other kinds of resources, too. One of its most important resources is its people. **Human resources** are the people who work for a company. It takes many people working together to produce what a factory makes.

Another important resource that is needed to make the helmets is money. Money is needed to pay for the factory. It is also needed to buy the machines and raw materials to make the helmets.

Money is needed to pay the workers, too. The workers are paid **wages** for the work they do. The people who own the factory must have enough money for all the resources they need. They must have this money before the first helmet can be made.

 **What are human resources?**

Industries

You have just read about how one factory produces bicycle helmets. There are more than 50 companies around the world that manufacture these helmets. The many companies that make bicycle helmets belong to an industry. An **industry** is made up of all the companies that make the same product or provide the same service.

The clothing industry produces the clothes you wear every day.

The bicycle helmet industry is just one industry that is needed by people who ride bicycles. They also need the bicycle and bicycle tire industries. The shipping industry is important, too. Shipping companies move products from where they are made to where they are sold. Communities all over the world depend on both service and product industries to meet their needs.

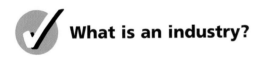 **What is an industry?**

LESSON 2 REVIEW

Check Understanding

1. **Recall the Facts** What kinds of resources are needed to manufacture a product?

2. **Focus on the Main Idea** How do people work together to make products in a factory?

Think Critically

3. **Cause and Effect** How do you think the making of products in factories has changed the way people live and work?

Show What You Know

Writing Activity Think about a product you would like to make. What resources would you need to make your product? Write a how-to paragraph that tells each of the steps you would follow in manufacturing the product. Work with your classmates to turn your idea into a real product.

How To

Read a Cross-Section Diagram

Why Is This Skill Important?

Have you ever picked up something and wondered what it looked like inside? If you could see a cross section of it, you would know. A **cross section** is a drawing or photo that shows what an object would look like if it were cut open. Looking at a cross section can help you understand how an object is made or how it works.

Understand the Process

A cross-section drawing often has a title that tells you what you are looking at. It also has labels to explain what is shown. If you pick up a bicycle helmet like the one in the drawing below, you cannot see every part of the helmet. You cannot see what is inside it.

BICYCLE HELMET

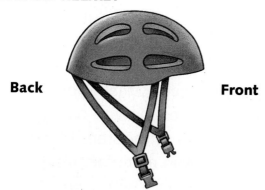

Back   Front

However, if you cut the bicycle helmet apart, you can look at it in a different way. Look at the drawing below of the cross section of a bicycle helmet. Then answer the questions.

1. What material is on the outside of the helmet?

2. What does this cross section tell you about the material on the inside of the helmet?

3. What are some other reasons you might want to look at a cross-section drawing?

CROSS SECTION OF A BICYCLE HELMET

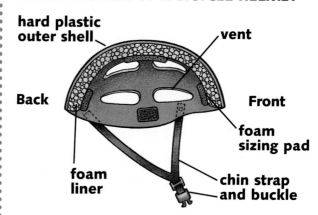

hard plastic outer shell — vent
Back — Front
foam liner — foam sizing pad — chin strap and buckle

Think and Apply

Do you think that studying cross-section drawings of products can help people decide which product to buy? Write a paragraph to explain your answer.

People Buy Products and Services

Link to Our World

What makes a person decide to buy one product or service rather than another?

Focus on the Main Idea
Read to find out how people decide to buy a product or service.

Preview Vocabulary
consumer
price
competition
supply
demand
advertisement
invention

People work together to make products and provide services. In communities everywhere, people buy those products and services every day.

Deciding What to Buy

The person who buys a product or a service is called a **consumer**. A consumer has to think about many things before buying. Suppose you were a consumer looking for new bicycle equipment. How would you decide what to buy?

Since people cannot have everything they want, they have to decide what things they need, what things they want the most, and what things they can do without. Suppose you want to buy both a jacket and a bicycle helmet, but you have enough money for only one. You might decide that safety is more important than a new jacket. Then you would choose to buy the helmet and wear your old jacket.

These consumers have saved enough money to buy a bicycle helmet. Now they must decide if the helmet is worth the price.

207

When many companies are in competition, prices may be lower.

Another thing consumers keep in mind is price. The **price** is the amount of money needed to buy a product or service. Factories decide the price they will charge the stores for the helmets they ship to them. Then the stores decide the price they will charge the consumers.

Setting a price for a product or a service is not simple. The price of a product can depend on competition. Companies that produce and sell the same product are in **competition** with one another. Each one tries to sell more of the product. There are several companies in the United States that make and sell bicycle helmets. Each one wants consumers to buy its helmets rather than those made by the other companies. So each company tries to make the best product and keep its prices as low as possible.

Stores often put different companies' products side by side so that consumers can decide which one to buy. Many times consumers choose the product with the lowest price.

When stores are in competition, each tries to sell the same products at the lowest prices.

When the supply of a product is too high, stores often lower the price to raise **demand** for the product.

Competition takes place between stores, too. Two stores may sell the same product, but their prices may be different. A consumer who compares prices may choose to buy the product from the store that has the lower price.

The price of a product can also depend on supply and demand. **Supply** is the amount of a product or service there is to be sold. If there are many helmets waiting to be bought, the supply is high. If there are few helmets, the supply is low. **Demand** is the wish that people have for a product or a service. If there are many people who will pay for bicycle helmets, then the demand is high. If there are few people who will buy helmets, then the demand is low.

 What can competition do to price?

Advertisements Affect Choices

You might want to buy a certain bicycle helmet because of its low price. However, there are other things to keep in mind. For example, you want to make sure that a helmet will protect your head in an accident. You might also want to know how much it weighs or what colors it comes in.

Where could you find this kind of information? You might look at advertisements on television or in magazines and newspapers. An **advertisement** is information that a producer provides about its products or services. Advertisements try to get consumers to buy a product or service.

Some advertisements are written for consumers your age. They use words, colors, and music that young people like. However, bright colors and music should not help you decide which helmet is the best one to buy. Consumers need to be careful. They should get more information than an advertisement gives.

 **What is an advertisement?**

What information does this bicycle helmet advertisement give you? Would it make you want to buy the helmet?

Information about several bicycle helmets is shown in this table. How can using a table make it easier for you to decide which helmet to buy?

COMPARING BICYCLE HELMETS				
BRAND	PRICE	WEIGHT (in ounces)	CRASH-TEST RESULTS	APPEARANCE
A	$30.00	8	very good	good
B	$25.00	8	good	very good
C	$40.00	10	very good	excellent
D	$30.00	12	excellent	good

Raising Demand

What fits in your hand and tells you the time, the temperature, and the distance you have gone? A bicycle computer can do all these things!

When bicycle riders learned about this invention, demand for it grew very fast. An **invention** is something that has been made for the first time. Many bicycle riders wanted to own a bicycle computer. The demand was so great that manufacturers could not make enough products for all the people who wanted to buy them.

The demand for products is always changing. New inventions and advertisements can cause greater demand. Two other things that can raise demand are new laws and better products.

Many people in communities have strong feelings about bicycle safety. They work with community leaders to pass laws that say bicycle riders must wear helmets. These laws have caused a demand for helmets. As more communities pass these laws, more people will buy helmets. Producers will have to make more helmets to keep up with the demand from consumers.

This computer is easily snapped on and off a bicycle.

Demand is also raised when new materials or new technology makes a product better. Early bicycle helmets were made of thick foam and heavy plastic. They looked ugly and did not fit well. Then designers and scientists came up with new materials to make helmets lighter and safer. These changes even made helmets cost less and look better! More bicycle riders are now wearing helmets, and many riders who wore the old kind have bought new ones.

 How do inventions create demand?

ho?

Jeremy Hall (1979)

When Jeremy Hall was thirteen years old, he got some sad news. His new friend had been killed in a bicycle accident. His friend was not wearing a helmet. Jeremy knew that a helmet might have saved his friend's life. So he decided there should be a law about wearing bicycle helmets. First Jeremy helped get a bicycle helmet law passed in his county in Maryland. Jeremy then went to Washington, D.C., to talk to lawmakers about bicycle safety. Jeremy hopes to get a law passed that will say that every bicycle rider in the United States must wear a helmet.

LESSON 3 REVIEW

Check Understanding

1. **Recall the Facts** What is a consumer?
2. **Focus on the Main Idea** How do people decide which product or service to buy?

Think Critically

3. **Personally Speaking** Do you think advertisements help consumers make good choices? Why or why not?

Show What You Know

 **Poster Activity** Invent a product that you think will change the way people live or work. Then make a poster that advertises your invention. Use bright colors and interesting words to persuade someone to buy your product. Share your poster with the class.

Tell Fact from Opinion

Why Is This Skill Important?

Learning how to tell fact from opinion will help you make good decisions. It will help you decide everything from which product to buy to what to eat or drink.

Understand the Process

Advertisements use both facts and opinions. **Facts** are statements that are true. You can prove that a fact is correct. **Opinions** tell you what someone believes or thinks. Read this advertisement about a drink that is sold to bicycle riders.

1. Look at the first sentence. Could you prove that this statement is true? Yes, you could taste Power Punch to prove whether or not it has an orange flavor. This is a fact.

2. Now look at the second sentence. The advertisement says the drink tastes great. Is this something you could prove true or false? You might think the drink tastes great, but one of your friends might not. Is this sentence a fact or an opinion?

3. Sometimes people think that their opinions are facts. Why is it important for people to learn to tell fact from opinion?

Think and Apply

Watch a television advertisement for a product that is made for someone your age. Make a list of the facts in the advertisement. Also make a list of the opinions. Were there more facts or more opinions? Did the advertisement make you want to buy the product? Why or why not?

Power Punch is an orange-flavored drink. This drink tastes great! It was invented by a bicycle rider and studied by scientists for three years. Power Punch will make you ride faster than ever. Power Punch is sold in bottles you can carry on your bike or in your backpack. Try Power Punch today!

Saturday Sancocho

Instead of using money to buy a product or service, people sometimes *barter,* or trade, with one another. In this story you will meet Maria Lili and her grandparents. They live in a small town in South America. They want to make their special chicken sancocho (sahn•KOH•choh), a kind of stew. But they have no money for shopping. Find out how Maria Lili and her grandmother use their extra eggs to get what they need for their meal.

by Leyla Torres

cilantro
(sih•LAHN•troh)
a flavoring made
from the leaves of
a plant

Every Saturday, Maria Lili looked forward to making chicken sancocho with her grandparents Mama Ana and Papa Angelino. Just the thought of stew simmering on the stove and filling the house with the aroma of cilantro made her mouth water. But one Saturday morning Papa Angelino announced, "There is no money for sancocho. Not even a penny to buy the vegetables, let alone a chicken. All we have is a dozen eggs."

"Then we will use the eggs to make sancocho," replied Mama Ana.

"Egg sancocho! Everyone knows sancocho is not prepared with eggs," said Maria Lili.

Smiling, Mama Ana removed her apron and asked Maria Lili to take two baskets and place the eggs in one of them.

"Come, my dear, we are going to the market."
And off they went.

At the market square they walked from stall to stall. First they found Don Eugenio and his son, Sebastian. Mama Ana persuaded Don Eugenio to accept six eggs for a bunch of green plantains. It did not take much bargaining; Sebastian was one of Maria Lili's classmates.

The next stop was the stall of Doña Carmen. She was not interested in the eggs, but Mama Ana managed to trade nine plantains for four pounds of thick cassava.

At first Don Mateo was not in the mood for bartering. It took some time for Mama Ana to convince him to take two pounds of cassava for six ears of corn. She gave him a couple of eggs as well. "So he doesn't pout," Mama Ana whispered, making sure the corn was fresh.

plantains
(PLAN•tuhnz) the bananalike fruits of a plant grown in warm countries for food

cassava
(kuh•SAH•vuh) the root of a plant grown in warm countries for food

Doña Dolores wanted all the corn for just eight carrots.

"All my corn? No, dear lady, your carrots are not that big," Mama Ana said. Doña Dolores settled for three ears of corn, and agreed that it was a fair exchange.

Under the noonday sun, Mama Ana and Maria Lili traded their remaining eggs for onions and tomatoes; tomatoes for cilantro; cilantro for garlic and garlic for cumin, always keeping some for themselves. But they still needed one more ingredient.

"The chicken. What about the chicken?" asked Maria Lili. "How are we going to get it?"

"I have an idea," said Mama Ana, wiping her brow. "Let's divide the vegetables equally between the two baskets."

Mama Ana offered one of the baskets to Doña Petrona in exchange for a large, red-feathered chicken.

"Impossible," Doña Petrona said, sniffing. "I'll give you this one instead." She showed Mama Ana a smaller one.

"No, it's much too skinny," said Mama Ana, frowning.

They haggled until Mama Ana added two more carrots and some cumin to the basket. Doña Petrona accepted the offer, handing Maria Lili a nice, potbellied chicken. It was not the largest one, but it was good enough for a wholesome stew.

haggled
(HA•guhld) argued over price

cumin
(KYOO•mihn) a spice made from seeds

As Mama Ana and Maria Lili were leaving the marketplace, they passed Don Fernando's stall. He had always admired Mama Ana's hand-knit bags and suggested they trade the one Maria Lili was carrying for one of his wooden ladles. With a wink, he also handed her a colorful spinning top.

Papa Angelino plucked the chicken while Mama Ana boiled the water and peeled the vegetables. Maria Lili chopped the onions and the cilantro. This was a teary job.

That afternoon, no later than usual, they sat down to enjoy their chicken sancocho. Maria Lili ate slowly, blowing gently on each spoonful. The stew was delicious.

Literature Review

1. How did Maria Lili and Mama Ana get the things they needed to make the sancocho?

2. In bartering, why should the traded items be worth about the same amount? What would happen if you tried to trade a dozen eggs for a computer?

3. Think of a time when you traded something for another thing. What happened during your trade? Write a paragraph that explains what you traded and how you traded it. In your paragraph, also explain what made you decide to make a trade. Share your paragraph with your classmates.

How To

Use a Map Grid

Why Is This Skill Important?

One way to find a location is to use a map that has a grid. A **grid** is a set of lines the same distance apart that cross one another to form boxes. Learning to use a map grid will make it easier for you to quickly find locations on a map.

Understand the Process

Look at the grid below. You can see that a grid divides a space into boxes. Find the row labels—the letters along the left side of this grid. Now look for the column labels—the numbers at the top of this grid.

Find the box that is blue, and put your finger on it. Now slide your finger to the left side of the grid. You will see that the blue box is located in row C.

Now put your finger on the blue box again. Slide your finger to the top of the grid. You will see that the blue box is in column 2. To describe the location of the blue box, you would say that it is at C–2. What is the location of the red box?

Now look at the map of a South American market. It has a grid. Use the map and its grid to answer these questions. Give a letter and a number when you are asked for a location.

1. The market stalls are located in different parts of the grid. What stall can you find at C–2?

2. Where is the store?

3. Where can you find carrots?

4. What do you see in the box at D–3?

5. Where is the bridge to the market?

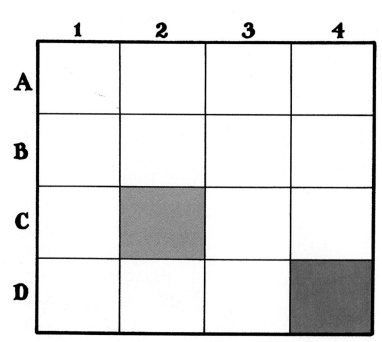

Think and Apply

Draw a map that shows a place you know. You might draw your neighborhood, your school, or your classroom. Add a grid so people can find places on your map.

Now share your map with a classmate or a family member. Ask that person to use a letter and a number to give the location of something on the map.

South American Market

LESSON

5

The World Is a Marketplace

L ink to Our World

How do people in your community buy products from other countries?

Focus on the Main Idea
Read to find out how products all over the world get to market.

Preview Vocabulary
international trade
communication links
export
import

In "Saturday Sancocho" you read about a grandmother and granddaughter who took eggs to market. There they were able to barter the eggs for other products. In places all over the world, people take products and services to market.

International Trade

Products get to market in many ways. Sometimes people take products to market by carrying them on their backs or on their heads. In some places people use donkeys, goats or even elephants. Many products are brought to market in wagons, vans, trucks, trains, airplanes, or ships. Some products travel just a few miles to market. Others may travel thousands of miles to markets all over the world.

People carry products to market in different ways.

This painting shows European, African, and Asian traders in the early 1600s.

GRAPES FROM CHILE

Today products from many countries can be bought in supermarkets.

Ships, airplanes, and other types of transportation make it possible for people all over the world to trade with one another. Trade between people in different countries is called **international trade**.

People in different parts of the world have traded with one another for a very long time. Hundreds of years ago traders left their countries and traveled to new lands. They looked for things that they could not find or produce in their own countries. They also looked for new trade routes that would make their long trips easier and faster. These traders traveled by sailing ship or by riding on large animals. The journeys took many months or even years. The traders returned home with new ideas as well as new products.

 How is international trade today different from trade long ago?

The products being loaded onto this airplane will arrive at a marketplace in just one day.

An order for a product can be sent anywhere in the world by using a fax machine.

Trading Becomes Easier and Faster

Today faster transportation and new technology make trade between people in different nations as easy as trade between people who live in the same community. People living in different parts of the world can trade by using communication links. **Communication links** are machines that let people who are far apart communicate with one another. People use computers, telephones, and fax machines to buy and sell thousands of products and services. Today a person can pick up a telephone and order a product from someone on the other side of the Earth. With modern transportation the product can arrive in a few days or weeks instead of in months or years.

 How do communication links help trade?

Countries Depend on One Another

You have seen that bicycle helmet factories need raw materials like oil. Many resources come from other countries and are exported to the United States. To **export** is to send a product or resource out of one country to another country.

Many countries import bicycle helmets made in the United States. To **import** is to bring a product or resource into a country from another country.

Most bicycle helmets are made in the United States, Australia, Canada, China, Great Britain, Italy, South Korea, and Taiwan. These countries supply the rest of the world with bicycle helmets.

Some products are sent from one country to another by airplane. However, most large products, such as bicycles, are carried on huge container ships. These ships can carry thousands of tons of products from one port to another.

....

LEARNING FROM CROSS-SECTION DIAGRAMS
What parts of this container ship are used to load and unload cargo?

CONTAINER SHIP

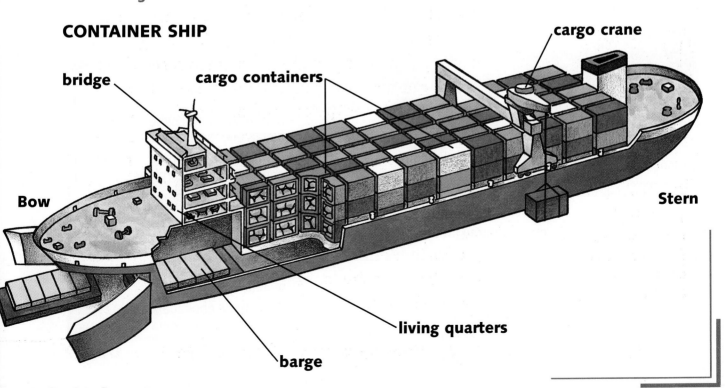

cargo crane

bridge

cargo containers

Bow

Stern

living quarters

barge

The United States exports many kinds of products. At the same time, products made in other countries are imported into the United States. Think of all the things you use every day that were made in places far, far away. Look at the labels in your clothing. You may read "Made in Hong Kong." The shoes you wear may have been made in Spain, Italy, or Korea. Your toys may have come from Mexico, China, or Japan.

LEARNING FROM TABLES
Which countries export natural resources? Which countries export manufactured products?

MAJOR IMPORTS AND EXPORTS		
COUNTRY	MAJOR IMPORTS	MAJOR EXPORTS
Brazil	oil, chemicals, coal	coffee, iron ore, soybeans, sugar, shoes
France	oil, iron and steel products, chemicals	clothing, machinery, chemicals, cars, airplanes
India	oil, chemicals, fertilizer, machinery	gems, jewelry, clothing, cotton fabric
Saudi Arabia	manufactured products, food, cars	oil
South Africa	car parts, machinery, chemicals	gold, diamonds, minerals, metals
United States	oil, machinery, cars	machinery, chemicals, airplanes, grains, cars

Countries depend on one another for the products their people must have. The world is a huge marketplace that can supply things that people want and need.

 How is an export different from an import?

LESSON 5 REVIEW

Check Understanding

1. **Recall the Facts** What is trade between countries called?

2. **Focus on the Main Idea** What are some of the ways products from all over the world get to market?

Think Critically

3. **Explore Viewpoints** In what ways do you think trade brings people around the world together? How could trade cause them to disagree?

Show What You Know

 **Map Activity** Make a list of products that you and your family use that were made in other countries. Then draw a simple map of the world, and label the continents. Create a symbol that represents each product. Draw each symbol in the country where the product was made. Then draw arrows from the country where each product was made to your home in the United States. Explain your map to a classmate.

"Togetherness" Is Good Business

They call themselves the Umoja (uh•MOH•juh) Children. *Umoja* is a Swahili word that means "unity, or togetherness." The Umoja Children of Baltimore, Maryland, have made more than $150,000 in just two years selling their greeting cards.

How did all of this start? The young people in this group wanted to raise money for their church. So they went to summer school to learn about business. They hired artists to design the cards, and they wrote the words themselves.

Some of the cards have Christmas greetings. Other cards show Kwanzaa scenes. The Umoja Children sell cards door to door, but most of their business is done by mail order.

"It's a lot of fun, and it's a learning experience," said Nicole Seivers, at work on a computer. The Umoja Children's business continues to grow and grow!

UMOJA CHILDREN INC.

THINK AND APPLY

Does your school need new computer equipment or playground equipment? You and a group of classmates might be able to earn money to help buy it. Think of some products you could make and sell. Then make a plan for one of those products. Decide which group members will design and make the product. Also decide which group members will advertise and sell the product. Present your plan to the rest of the class.

STORY CLOTH

Follow the pictures in this story cloth to help you review what you read about in Unit 4.

Summarize the Main Ideas

1. People work together to make products and provide services.

2. People choose the products and services they will buy.

3. People trade with each other.

4. Products and services get to market in different ways.

Write a Paragraph Choose one of the summary statements above. Then find the picture in the story cloth that goes with it. Write a paragraph to explain the picture. In your paragraph, tell what the picture shows about the summary statement.

Make a Bulletin Board Display Work with your classmates to make a bulletin board display that shows the steps in a manufacturing process. First, decide which process you will illustrate. Second, get information about the subject from newspapers, books, or industry brochures. Third, organize the information and put it on the bulletin board. Last, invite other classes to see the display.

COOPERATIVE LEARNING WORKSHOP

Remember
- Share your ideas.
- Cooperate with others to plan your work.
- Take responsibility for your work.
- Show your group's work to the class.
- Discuss what you learned by working together.

Activity 1

Make an Advertisement

Make an advertisement that shows an important resource that your community has. Show the advertisement to other groups. Look at their advertisements. Then talk with the other members of your group about how you might make your advertisement better.

Activity 2

Make a Museum

With a group, collect pictures or make drawings showing how products were manufactured long ago. Then collect pictures or make drawings showing how the same products are made today. Add your pictures to a bulletin board display. Put them in pairs showing the old and the new product. Share your display with other classes.

Activity 3

Conduct a Survey

Write a list of questions you can ask people about their favorite restaurants. You might ask about favorite foods and drinks at the restaurants. Or you might ask about the prices of the food. Make copies of your list, and give them to classmates, friends, and parents or other adult family members. Have them answer each question and return the list to you. After you have the answers, show them in a chart. Display your chart so everyone can see it.

CONNECT MAIN IDEAS

Use this graphic organizer to show how the unit's main ideas are connected. First, copy the organizer onto a separate sheet of paper. Then, complete it by writing one detail for each main idea.

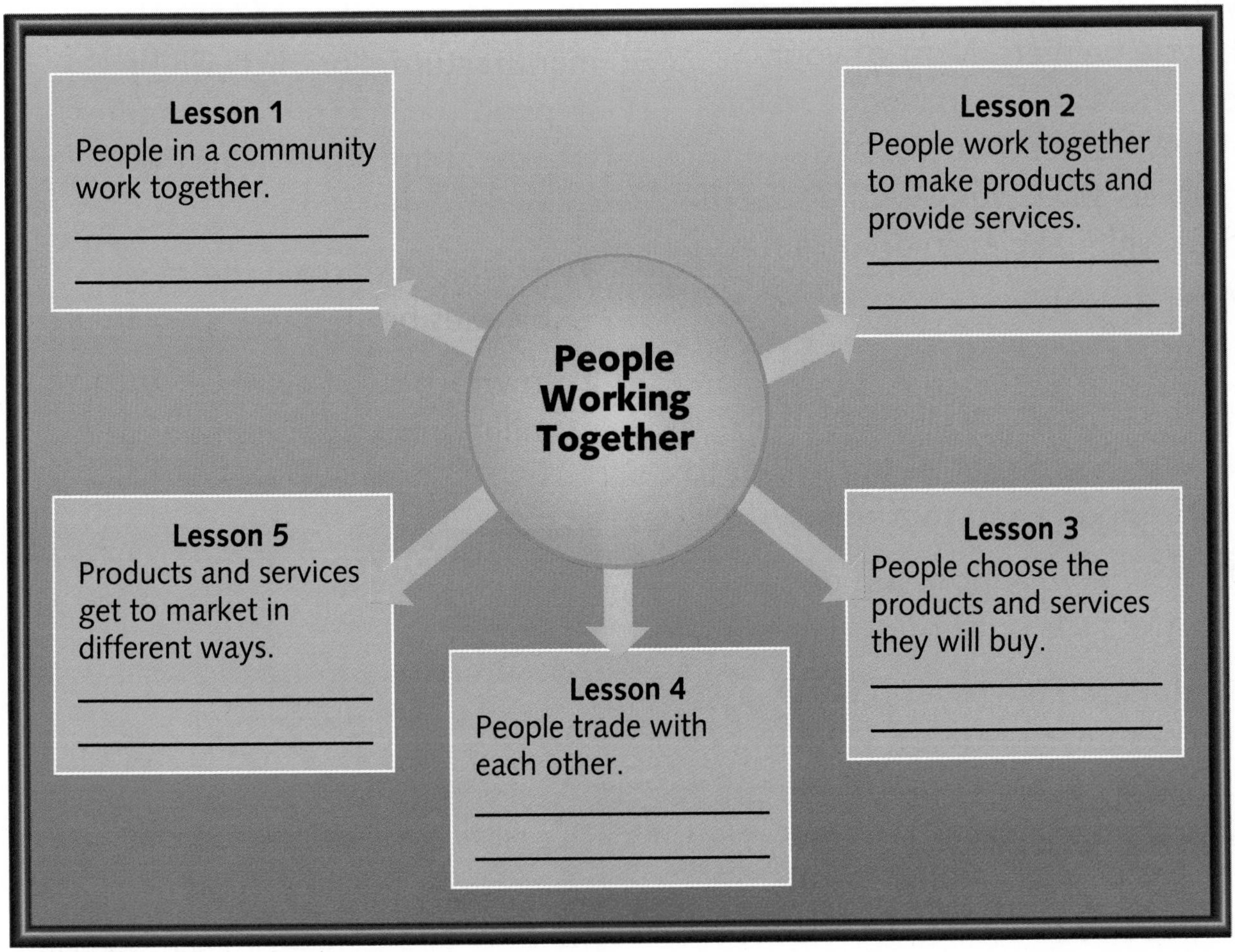

Lesson 1
People in a community work together.

_____
_____

Lesson 2
People work together to make products and provide services.

_____
_____

People Working Together

Lesson 5
Products and services get to market in different ways.

_____
_____

Lesson 3
People choose the products and services they will buy.

_____
_____

Lesson 4
People trade with each other.

_____
_____

USE VOCABULARY

Think of a time you bought or received a special item. Write a paragraph about that time. In your paragraph, use four of the vocabulary words shown here.

**advertisement   basic needs   consumer   demand
invention   price   rural   technology   wage**

WRITE MORE ABOUT IT

Write a Speech Imagine that your class has received a box of bicycle helmets. Most of your classmates want to wear a helmet. A few do not. You know that helmets save lives. Write a speech that will make everyone want to wear a helmet.

CHECK UNDERSTANDING

1. Why are resources important to producers and consumers?

2. How does supply and demand affect the price of products?

3. How can advertising affect a consumer's choice?

THINK CRITICALLY

1. **Past to Present** How does a large population affect demand for raw materials and products?

2. **Think More About It** In what way has new technology helped people trade with others?

3. **Personally Speaking** Tell three ways technology has made your life easier or better.

APPLY SKILLS

How to Read Graphs This graph shows the number of bicycles that manufacturers predict will be shipped to United States markets. Use the graph to answer the following questions.

1. In which year will the most bicycles be shipped?

2. In which two years will 20 million bicycles be shipped?

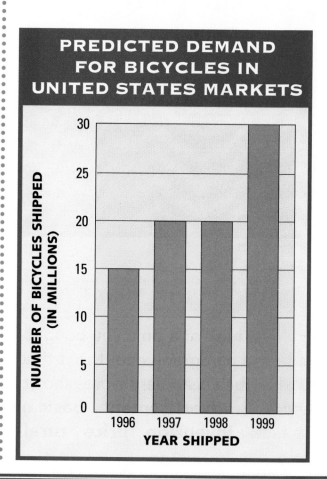

PREDICTED DEMAND FOR BICYCLES IN UNITED STATES MARKETS

NUMBER OF BICYCLES SHIPPED (IN MILLIONS)

YEAR SHIPPED

How to Read a Cross-Section Diagram

Look at this cross section of a cargo airplane. Use the cross section to answer the following questions.

1. Where is the flight deck located?

2. In what part of the plane is most of the cargo stored?

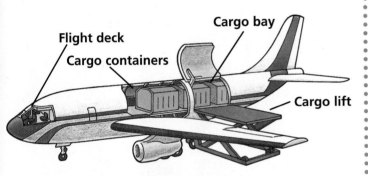

Flight deck

Cargo containers

Cargo bay

Cargo lift

CARGO AIRPLANE

How to Tell Fact from Opinion

Imagine that you just bought a bicycle helmet. Now your classmates need to buy helmets, and they want to know why you bought the one you did. Write a list of reasons you think they should buy the same kind of helmet you have. Some of the reasons should be facts, and some should be opinions. Share your list with two classmates. Ask them to tell you which statements are facts and which are opinions.

How to Use a Map Grid

Draw a map of your classroom. On the map, draw a map grid. Along one side, label the rows by using letters. At the top, label the columns by using numbers.

Hide an object someplace in the room. On your map, mark the location of the object. Then give your map to a classmate, and see if he or she can find the object. Is your classmate able to find the hidden object by using the map? If you had to draw the map grid again, what changes would you make?

READ MORE ABOUT IT

Market Days: From Market to Market Around the World by Madhur Jaffrey. BridgeWater. Read about six different marketplaces around the world.

Saturday Market by Patricia Grossman. Lothrop, Lee & Shepard. In this book you will have a chance to visit a busy market in Mexico.

Stephen Biesty's Incredible Cross-Sections by Richard Platt, illustrated by Steven Biesty. Dorling Kindersley. Take a look inside some amazing things!

Living Together in a Community, State, and Nation

People in communities work together to solve their problems. →

Rules and laws are for the common good of a community. →

People in a community work together. They share many of the same needs and problems. But sometimes people disagree. How can people work and live together peacefully? In this unit, you will read about the ways governments help people in communities solve problems and get along with one another.

← The school day begins with a pledge to the flag.

The parts of a government work together for the common good. ↓

Displaying a flag is one way citizens show pride in their country. →

City Green

by DyAnne DiSalvo-Ryan

In this story, a wrecking ball is used to tear down an old apartment building in Marcy's neighborhood. All that is left is an empty lot covered with trash and broken glass. Find out how Marcy, her neighbors, and the city government work together to turn an ugly, empty lot into a place that everyone can enjoy.

Miss Rosa and I go to see Mr. Bennett. He used to work for the city. "I seem to remember a program," he says, "that lets people rent empty lots."

That's how Miss Rosa and I form a group of people from our block. We pass around a petition that says: WE WANT TO LEASE THIS LOT. In less than a week we have plenty of names.

"Sign with us?" I ask Old Man Hammer.

"I'm not signin' nothin'," he says. "And nothin' is what's gonna happen."

But something did.

The next week, a bunch of us take a bus to city hall. We walk up the steps to the proper office and hand the woman our list. She checks her files and types some notes and makes some copies. "That will be one dollar, please."

We rent the lot from the city that day. It was just as simple as that.

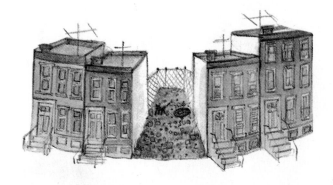

Saturday morning I'm up with the sun and looking at this lot. My mama looks out too. "Marcy," she says, and hugs me close. "Today I'm helping you and Rosa."

After shopping, Mama empties her grocery bags and folds them flat to carry under her arm. "Come on, Mrs. B.," Mama tells her friend. "We're going to clear this lot."

Then what do you know but my brother comes along. My brother is tall and strong. At first, he scratches his neck and shakes his head just like Old Man Hammer. But Mama smiles and says, "None of that here!" So all day long he piles junk in those bags and carries them to the curb.

Now, this time of day is early. Neighbors pass by and see what we're doing. Most say, "We want to help too." They have a little time to spare. Then this one calls that one and that one calls another.

"Come on and help," I call to Old Man Hammer.

"I'm not helpin' nobody," he hollers. "You're all wastin' your time."

Sour grapes my mama'd say, and sour grapes is right.

Just before supper, when we are good and hungry, my mama looks around this lot. "Marcy," she says, "you're making something happen here."

Next day the city drops off tools like rakes and brooms, and a Dumpster for trash. Now there's even more neighbors to help. Miss Rosa, my brother, and I say "Good morning" to Old Man Hammer, but Old Man Hammer just waves like he's swatting a fly.

"Why is Old Man Hammer so mean and cranky these days?" my brother asks.

"Maybe he's really sad," I tell him. "Maybe he misses his building."

"That rotten old building?" My brother shrugs. "He should be happy the city tore down that mess."

"Give him time," Miss Rosa says. "Good things take time."

Mr. Bennett brings wood—old slats he's saved— and nails in a cup. "I knew all along I saved them for something," he says. "This wood's good wood."

Then Mr. Rocco from two houses down comes, carrying two cans of paint. "I'll never use these," he says. "The color's too bright. But here, this lot could use some brightening up."

Well, anyone can tell with all the excitement that something is going on. And everyone has an idea about what to plant—strawberries, carrots, lettuce, and more. Tulips and daisies, petunias, and more! Sonny turns the dirt over with a snow shovel. Even Leslie's baby tries to dig with a spoon.

For lunch, Miss Rosa brings milk and jelly and bread and spreads a beach towel where the junk is cleared. By the end of the day a fence is built and painted as bright as the sun.

Later, Mama kisses my cheek and closes my bedroom door. By the streetlights I see Old Man Hammer come down his steps to open the gate and walk to the back of this lot. He bends down quick, sprinkling something from his pocket and covering it over with dirt.

In the morning I tell my brother. "Oh, Marcy," he says. "You're dreaming. You're wishing too hard."

But I know what I saw, and I tell my mama, "Old Man Hammer's planted some seeds."

Right after breakfast, I walk to the back of this lot. And there it is—a tiny raised bed of soil. It is neat and tidy, just like the rows we've planted. Now I know for sure that Old Man Hammer planted something. So I pat the soil for good luck and make a little fence to keep the seeds safe.

Every day I go for a look inside our garden lot. Other neighbors stop in too. One day Mrs. Wells comes by. "This is right where my grandmother's bedroom used to be," she says. "That's why I planted my flowers there."

I feel sad when I hear that. With all the digging and planting and weeding and watering, I'd forgotten about the building that had been on this lot. Old Man Hammer had lived there too. I go to the back, where he planted his seeds. I wonder if this was the place where his room used to be.

I look down. Beside my feet, some tiny stems are sprouting. Old Man Hammer's seeds have grown! I run to his stoop. "Come with me!" I beg, tugging at his hand. "You'll want to see."

I walk him past the hollyhocks, the daisies, the peppers, the rows of lettuce. I show him the strawberries that I planted. When Old Man Hammer sees his little garden bed, his sour grapes turn sweet. "Marcy, child." He shakes his head. "This lot was good for nothin'. Now it's nothin' but good," he says.

Soon summertime comes, and this lot really grows. It fills with vegetables, herbs, and flowers. And way in the back, taller than anything else, is a beautiful patch of yellow sunflowers. Old Man Hammer comes every day. He sits in the sun, eats his lunch, and sometimes comes back with supper.

Nobody knows how the sunflowers came—not Leslie, my brother, or Miss Rosa. Not Mr. Bennett, or Sonny, or anyone else. But Old Man Hammer just sits there smiling at me. We know whose flowers they are.

People Make Communities Good Places to Live

Link to Our World

What can you do to help solve a problem in your community?

Focus on the Main Idea
Read to find out how people in a community can work together to solve problems.

Preview Vocabulary
petition
council
government service
tax

In *City Green* you read about Marcy and her neighbors. They saw a problem in their community. There was an ugly and dangerous empty lot near their apartments. Like people in communities everywhere, Marcy and her neighbors discovered that the problem could be solved. They could cooperate, or work together, to turn the lot into a garden.

City Government Helps People

To solve their problem, Marcy and her neighbors first found out how to cooperate with their city government. They learned that they could rent the lot from the city. So Marcy and Miss Rosa wrote a petition asking to rent the lot. A **petition** is a written request for government action that people sign. By signing the petition, people show that they support the request for action.

Marcy and many of her neighbors signed the petition and took it to city hall. City hall is the building where people in city government work.

These students are asking people to sign a petition. The petition asks for a law that says bicycle riders must wear helmets.

After paying a dollar for rent, Marcy and her neighbors agreed to take responsibility for the empty lot. They would begin by cleaning it up.

In communities everywhere, people work with their local government to solve problems. In some small communities, all the citizens are invited to attend town meetings. At a town meeting, citizens discuss problems in their community and ways to solve them. However, many towns and cities are much too large for all their citizens to fit into one room. So most towns and cities are run by a council instead of by town meetings. A city or town **council** is a group of people who have been chosen by citizens to meet and solve problems. In many communities a council and a mayor make laws for everyone to follow.

These citizens are taking part in a town meeting in Francestown, New Hampshire. About 1,200 people live in this community.

This mayor and city council are holding a meeting in Austin, Texas. More than 465,000 people live in this city.

Young citizens listening to a story-teller in a library

Firefighters provide an important government service.

City and town governments provide many services to their citizens. A **government service** is a service that is provided for all the citizens of a community. Fire and police protection are government services. Most city governments also provide libraries, street and traffic signs, sewers, and water for their citizens.

City governments can provide services like these because the community's citizens pay taxes. A **tax** can be money paid to a government to run a city. People also pay taxes to run their county, state, and national governments. The government uses taxes to pay wages to the workers who provide services. The government also uses taxes to build new buildings and to buy equipment, such as police cars and fire engines.

 How do city governments pay for government services?

Leaders Help Solve Problems

In *City Green* the people in Marcy's neighborhood worked together to solve a problem. But before people start working on a project, a leader usually brings them together. Marcy was a leader of her group because she told her neighbors how they could solve a problem. She and Miss Rosa organized many people in their neighborhood to make a garden from an empty lot.

In communities all over the United States, leaders help make things happen. Wilma Mankiller is a leader who helped solve problems in Cherokee communities. For many years she was the Chief of the Cherokee Nation. Her office was located in Tahlequah (TAL•uh•qwaw), Oklahoma. One of the many communities she worked with was Bell, Oklahoma. Bell is a rural community where about 350 people live. Most of its citizens are Cherokee, like Wilma Mankiller.

Where?

Tahlequah, Oklahoma

The community of Tahlequah is located in the northeastern part of Oklahoma. This area of Oklahoma, known as the Ozark Plateau, has many fast-moving streams and steep river valleys. Southeast of Tahlequah is the Cherokee Heritage Center, a place where people can learn about Cherokee history and culture. This group of buildings includes the Cherokee National Museum and the Tsa-La-Gi Ancient Cherokee Village.

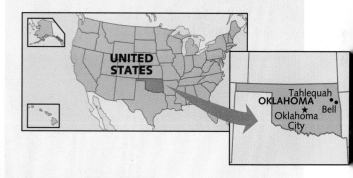

Wilma Mankiller

Lack of running water was one of the biggest problems in Bell. Most people who lived in Bell had to carry water in barrels from other communities to their homes. The community needed a pipeline that would bring in running water.

Wilma Mankiller began to solve the problems by getting the people of Bell together. She held meetings where people could share ideas. She helped the citizens find other leaders in their community who could be in charge of building the pipeline. She found out how to ask the United States government for money to help pay for the pipeline. When the United States government and the citizens of Bell disagreed, Wilma Mankiller helped everyone find a way to make things work.

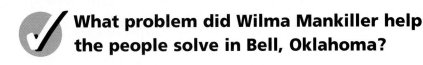

What problem did Wilma Mankiller help the people solve in Bell, Oklahoma?

Wilma Mankiller leads meetings where people can share their ideas for solving problems.

Success Means Working Together

Wilma Mankiller knew that the Cherokees had a tradition of working together. She helped organize people in the community, but she did not do the work herself. The United States government did not do the work, either. Volunteers from Bell built the pipeline. Wilma Mankiller thought all along that the Cherokees could solve this problem with a little help. She was right.

In *City Green* Marcy also knew that the people in her neighborhood needed only a little help to solve their problem. Leaders like Marcy and Wilma Mankiller help organize people in a community. Then the people must do the work together.

These citizens are working together to decide where in their community to build a park.

 **Who built the new pipeline in Bell, Oklahoma?**

LESSON 1 REVIEW

Check Understanding

1. **Recall the Facts** How can a leader help a community get what its citizens need or want?
2. **Focus on the Main Idea** How do people in communities cooperate to solve problems?

Think Critically

3. **Cause and Effect** What would happen if community leaders could not first bring people together? Explain your answer.

Show What You Know

 Petition-Writing Activity Work in a small group. Write a petition to your teacher or principal that clearly describes a problem at your school and tells a way to solve it. Then get signatures from other students who agree with your plan. Share your petition with the teacher or principal. Work as leaders to carry out your group's solution.

Resolve Conflicts

Why Is This Skill Important?

Conflicts can make people take sides in every country, every community, and every home. A **conflict** is a disagreement. In a conflict, people or groups do not agree because they have different needs, wants, or ways of thinking. Learning how to handle conflicts will help you get along with others. You can use this skill all your life.

Remember What You Have Read

People in a conflict sometimes know one another very well and sometimes only a little. Conflicts can be upsetting or scary. **Conflict resolution** is a way to solve disagreements among people or groups. Conflict resolution can lead to changes that help people understand one another better.

Understand the Process

You can take the following positive steps when there is a conflict. Remember that these steps may not work every time, so you may need to try more than one way to end your conflict.

- **Walk away.** Just walk away. Let time pass before you say or do anything. Later, people may not have such strong feelings. Then they may be able to think more calmly about what to say or do.

- **Laugh about it.** Use humor. Make things seem less serious. People who can find something to smile about may be able to work together to solve the problem.

- **Compromise.** Cannot walk away from a conflict or laugh it away? If so, try to compromise with the other person. **Compromise** (KAHM•pruh•myz) means that to end a conflict each person gives up some of the things he or she wants. Also, both persons get some of the things they want or need.

- **Choose someone who can help.** Cannot compromise? Choose a mediator to help. A **mediator** is a person who works to help both sides settle their disagreement. A good mediator does not favor one side. Sometimes the mediator has a new, helpful point of view.

Think and Apply

Describe the steps taken to resolve conflicts at your school. Talk with classmates. How do you think these conflicts might have been resolved earlier?

Rules and Laws in a Community

Link to Our World

What rules and laws help resolve conflicts in your community?

Focus on the Main Idea

Read to find out how rules and laws helped people in communities resolve conflicts long ago.

Preview Vocabulary

vote
Constitution
election

Rules and laws help people in a community cooperate. In *City Green* you read how Marcy and her neighbors learned how to rent the empty lot from the city. By following those rules, they were able to solve their problem peacefully. As they do today, rules and laws also helped people cooperate a long time ago.

Native Americans Made Laws

Before the first Europeans settled in North America, native peoples lived here. In the 1500s there were five Iroquois (IR•uh•kwoy) tribes. They had many conflicts with one another. They disagreed over which tribes should be allowed to use the best land for hunting and farming. They often fought wars with one another because of their disagreements. One wise Iroquois leader named Dekanawida (deh•kahn•uh•WIH•duh) believed that if the tribes did not find a way to resolve their conflicts, they would destroy their communities.

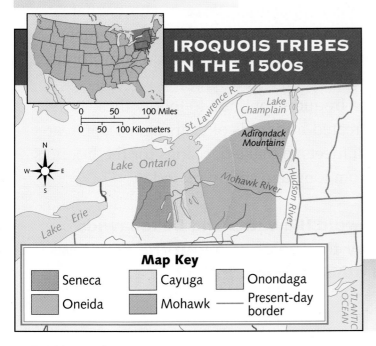

IROQUOIS TRIBES IN THE 1500s

0   50   100 Miles
0   50   100 Kilometers

St. Lawrence R.
Lake Champlain
Adirondack Mountains
Lake Ontario
Mohawk River
Hudson River
Lake Erie
ATLANTIC OCEAN

N W E S

Map Key

Seneca
Oneida
Cayuga
Mohawk
Onondaga
Present-day border

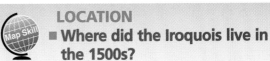

LOCATION
- Where did the Iroquois live in the 1500s?

Lesson 2 • **257**

This wampum belt was made by Iroquois people in the 1800s. It is like the belts made by Hiawatha.

Dekanawida thought of a way to bring peace to the five tribes. He created a set of 13 laws he thought all the Iroquois could follow. The laws would help the tribes resolve their disagreements without fighting wars with one another. He asked all the tribes to accept these laws.

An Iroquois leader named Hiawatha (hy•uh•WAH•thuh) helped Dekanawida tell others about the new laws. To do this, Hiawatha made wampum belts. Wampum (WAHM•puhm) were beads made from polished shells. The beads could be woven into belts in different colors and designs to record a message. Hiawatha's wampum belts told about the laws. By showing these belts to other tribal leaders, Hiawatha and Dekanawida could better explain the new laws.

The tribes agreed to follow the new laws. Each tribe would have its own government. But conflicts among the tribes would be resolved by a Great Council. Members of each tribe would serve on the Great Council. Each council member would have one vote. People use a **vote** to show what they think the group should do. If all the members did not vote the same way, they would compromise until they reached an agreement.

Today the Iroquois continue to follow these laws that were created hundreds of years ago. The Great Council still meets to make decisions for the Iroquois. The laws from long ago still work today.

 How did Hiawatha and Dekanawida carry the message about the new laws to other Iroquois tribes?

Settlers in America Wrote New Laws

In 1620 a group of English settlers known as Pilgrims arrived on a small ship, the *Mayflower*. The Pilgrims had planned to settle in Virginia, where there already was a government. But their ship was blown north by storms. They landed in what is now Massachusetts. Because they were the first settlers, there was no government there yet. So there were no settlers' laws for the Pilgrims to follow.

The Pilgrims wrote a set of laws they called the Mayflower Compact. A compact is a written statement of rules that people sign and agree to follow. The Mayflower Compact said that the Pilgrims would form their own government. They would choose leaders who would make decisions and write new laws that were needed. The people agreed to obey the laws for the good of everyone. The new laws helped the Pilgrims live and work together in their new homeland.

 **What was the Mayflower Compact?**

This painting shows the Pilgrims signing the Mayflower Compact.

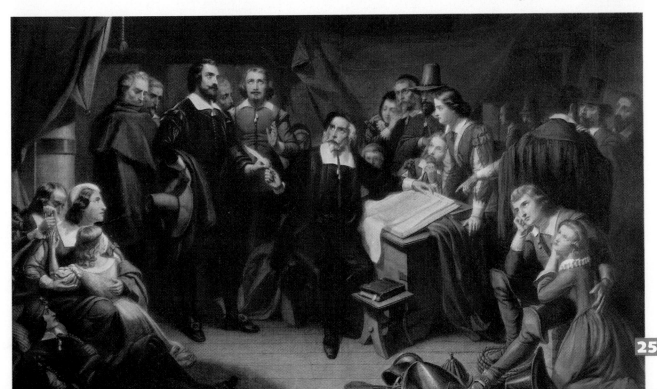

Laws for a New Country

More than 150 years after the Mayflower Compact was signed, many settlers in North America joined together to form one country. They called their new country the United States of America. The country's leaders wrote a set of laws called the United States **Constitution**. The Constitution is more than 200 years old, but it is still the most important set of laws in the United States. It describes how the United States government works. The ideas and laws of the Iroquois and the Pilgrims helped the new country's leaders write the Constitution.

The Constitution also describes the rights, or freedoms, that all citizens have. Americans are free to enjoy their own culture and to practice their religion. American citizens can work at any job they choose and can live and travel where they wish. The Constitution also says that Americans have the right to talk in public about their ideas and the right to vote in elections. In an **election**, people vote to choose leaders. They may also vote for or against new laws.

Students looking at the Constitution

This painting shows leaders meeting to sign the Constitution.

These children are obeying a law that keeps them safe.

Citizens have rights, but they also need to be responsible. A citizen is responsible for obeying the laws. Citizens who do not obey the laws may face the consequences of their actions. The consequences may include paying a fine or going to jail.

 What does the Constitution describe?

LESSON 2 REVIEW

Check Understanding

1. **Recall the Facts** What were the Iroquois laws and the Mayflower Compact? Why were they important?

2. **Focus on the Main Idea** How did communities long ago resolve their conflicts?

Think Critically

3. **Think More About It** How is the Iroquois Great Council like a city council?

Show What You Know

 **Letter-Writing Activity** Imagine that you are one of the Pilgrims. Write a letter that tells why you think people should follow a set of laws. Then make a list of laws for all Pilgrims in the new community to follow. Read your letter to your classmates, and talk over your ideas with them.

How To

Make a Choice by Voting

Why Is This Skill Important?

You make choices every day. You choose what to eat and what to wear. You have different reasons for the choices you make. You can make a choice because you like one thing better than another or because one choice has better consequences than another. Understanding the reasons for your choices will help you make better ones.

Remember What You Have Read

People in communities also make choices. Voting is the way community members make important choices about their government. Perhaps you have voted at your school to choose a school slogan or a mascot.

Before voting, people need to learn as much as they can about the consequences of each choice. The more they know, the better they will be able to make good choices. People should also talk to one another about the good and the bad points of each choice.

Understand the Process

Voting may be our most important right. It allows every citizen to make a choice. Here is how it works.

When people in communities need to make choices about their government, they hold an election. In an election people vote for or against a new law or a candidate. A **candidate** is someone who is running for office.

In some elections people mark paper ballots. A **ballot** lists all the possible choices. A person votes by making a mark next to his or her choice. The ballot is placed in a ballot box. It is kept there with all the other ballots until everyone has voted. Then the votes are counted and the winner is announced.

In an election everyone votes in secret. Each person goes into a voting booth and makes a choice without anyone else watching or listening. Also, the voters do not put their names on the ballots. This way, people can vote without worrying what other people may think about their choices.

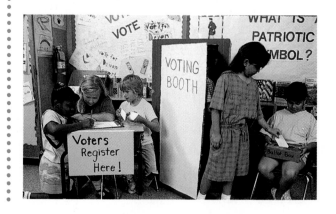

Who wins an election? Often the voter has two or more candidates to choose from. Sometimes voters are asked whether they want to have a new law or to have the government spend money on a certain project. The candidate or the choice that gets the most votes wins. This is called **majority rule** because a majority, or more than half, of the people voting chose one candidate or decision. The people who did not vote for the winner are the minority. With our system of government, even those who do not vote for winners still keep all their rights. We call this idea **minority rights**.

Trying to get the voters to choose one candidate instead of another is called a **campaign**. Candidates look for every chance to tell the public about their ideas. Sometimes candidates make speeches to hundreds of people at dinners or other special events. Often people want to help a candidate get elected. These volunteers pass out posters and buttons with the candidate's name and picture on them.

People who work for a candidate may also call voters on the telephone to tell them why they should vote for that candidate. People may also call voters to tell them why they should or should not vote for a new law. Sometimes candidates discuss and even argue about their ideas in public. Today many candidates spend millions of dollars for television and radio advertisements to tell people about their ideas.

Think and Apply

Hold an election in your school, using what you have learned. You and your classmates should choose two candidates to run for office. Then the class members should form three groups. One group should help each candidate talk to the voters about his or her ideas. A second group should make posters and buttons. The third group should make ballots so each student in the school can vote in secret. This group will also make a ballot box to collect the ballots. Ask for volunteers to count them. Have the winner make a speech accepting the office.

LESSON 3

State Governments

Link to Our World

How is a state government like other kinds of government?

Focus on the Main Idea
Read to find out how state governments affect the lives of citizens.

Preview Vocabulary
governor
public property
private property
jury

National Guard troops help citizens get supplies after a hurricane.

You have read how people and local governments work together to solve problems. Leaders help bring people together, and laws help people know what to do and what not to do. Another government that affects you and your community is your state government. Nearly all people of the United States live in one of the 50 states. And each state has its own government that affects the lives of its citizens.

Not All State Governments Are Alike

The 50 states are different from one another in many ways. Each state has its own climate and landforms, history, and resources. The problems each state faces can be different from the problems in other states, too. Citizens in states like Florida, Texas, and Louisiana must plan ways to deal with hurricanes that may cause damage in their states. Citizens in California and Alaska do not have to worry about hurricanes. But they must plan ways to deal with earthquakes. Since each state has its own problems, each state must have its own government that can work to solve them.

 Why does each state need its own government?

264 • Unit 5

The Governor Leads the State

Each state government has a leader called a **governor**. The governor is elected by the voters in the state. The governor's job is like the job of a city or town mayor in many ways. The governor suggests laws that he or she thinks will be good for the state. A governor also meets with governors from other states to share ideas and talk about common problems.

The governor of a state is also the leader of the state military force, called the National Guard. The National Guard can help citizens in an emergency such as a hurricane or earthquake. When Hurricane Andrew hit Florida in 1992, the Florida National Guard helped protect property. Property is land, buildings, and other things that belong to people. One kind of property is public property. **Public property** belongs to all citizens. Parks and museums are examples of public property. Another kind of property is private property. **Private property** belongs to one person or a small group of people. Homes and businesses are examples of private property.

This girl's bicycle is her private property.

Public property is for all citizens to use and enjoy.

 How is the governor's job like the job of the mayor of a city or a town?

Members of the National Governors' Association meet with President Clinton.

Lawmakers and Judges

Each state government also has lawmakers. The lawmakers are elected by voters in the state. Most states have two groups of lawmakers—representatives and senators—who write laws for the state. Nebraska, however, has only one group of lawmakers. Each state's lawmakers meet in the state capital.

State governments also have state judges. Many judges are not elected. Instead, they are chosen by the governor. Judges decide whether state laws are fair. State judges also help protect private property. If a person breaks the law by stealing or by harming someone else's private property, that person can be brought to court.

In court all the people involved in what happened may have to appear before a judge and a jury. A **jury** is a group of 6 to 12 citizens. The members of the jury listen to what both sides have to say. Then they decide whether the person blamed for the crime is guilty or not guilty. If the person is guilty, the judge will decide the consequences.

A jury listening in a courtroom

 What do state lawmakers and judges do?

Governments Have Different Responsibilities

Your state government and your community government both affect the way you live. Each of these governments can collect taxes from citizens and can make laws. Each one can use tax money to provide services and to buy public property that the people will own.

There are some things only state governments can do. State governments provide citizens with driver's licenses. They also build state highways and care for state parks.

There are certain things only community governments can do. They provide services like fire protection. Garbage collection is another service community governments may provide.

✓ **What are some of the things state governments do?**

LEARNING FROM DIAGRAMS
This diagram gives examples of ways two levels of government affect people who live in Columbia, Missouri. In your own community, what services do citizens receive from each level of government?

TWO LEVELS OF GOVERNMENT

State Government of Missouri

- solves problems in the state
- collects taxes
- provides a court system
- provides money for schools
- builds state highways
- provides state parks
- provides driver's licenses

Community Government of Columbia, Missouri

- solves problems in the community
- collects taxes
- provides community services
- helps protect private property
- provides community parks

LESSON 3 REVIEW

Check Understanding

1. **Recall the Facts** Who is the leader of a state government?
2. **Focus on the Main Idea** In what ways does a state government affect the lives of citizens?

Think Critically

3. **Explore Viewpoints** Why might different governors react to the same problem in different ways?

Show What You Know

Map Activity Draw a map of your state. On your map, show the community where you live. Use symbols to show some different kinds of private property. Also show areas that are public property in and near your community. Make sure your map has a title and a key. Share your map with a classmate.

How To

Measure Distance on a Map

Why Is This Skill Important?

Almost every map is smaller than the part of the Earth it shows. This means that the distance between two places on a map is shorter than the real distance between these places on the Earth. To find out how far apart two places really are, you need a distance scale. A distance scale shows that a certain length on a map stands for some longer, real distance on the Earth.

Understand the Process

Look at the distance scale on the map of the state of Texas. You can see that the top part of the scale has the word *Miles.* The bottom part of the scale has the word *Kilometers.* Kilometers are used in the metric system, which is another way of measuring. You can find distance with either part of the scale.

You can use the distance scale on the map of Texas to find out how far it is from one city to another. Use a ruler to measure the distance scale. It is 1 inch long. Now read the number of miles. On this map, 1 inch stands for 250 miles on the Earth.

If two cities are 1 inch apart on this map, the real distance is 250 miles, or about 400 kilometers. If they are

between 1 and 2 inches apart, you can estimate the real distance, or figure out what it would be. Now use the distance scale to find the distance in miles from El Paso to Austin.

Think and Apply

Use the distance scale and the map of Texas to answer these questions.

1. In miles, how far is it from Corpus Christi to Beaumont?

2. In kilometers, how far is it from the state capital to Dallas?

3. Why is it important to know how to read a distance scale on a map?

How the National Government Works

Link to Our World

How does the national government help you and your community?

Focus on the Main Idea
Read to find out how the national government works.

Preview Vocabulary
Congress
Supreme Court

The governments of a community and of a state help people lead safe and peaceful lives. The government of the United States, our national government, also affects people's lives.

Three Branches of Government

Most of the offices of the United States government are located in Washington, D.C., our nation's capital. The government is made up of three parts, each with a different job to do. The different parts of the government are sometimes called branches. The branches, like those on a tree, are separate but connected. The United States Constitution describes the job of each branch.

 How many parts make up the government of the United States?

THE BRANCHES OF THE UNITED STATES GOVERNMENT

The President

The Congress

The Supreme Court

The President Leads the Government

One branch of the national government includes the President of the United States. The President leads the government and helps keep the country safe and peaceful. These pictures show some duties of the President. They also show how some past Presidents have met those duties.

The President lives and works in the White House.

President Johnson

1. The President can approve a new law by signing it.

President Nixon

2. The President visits other countries and helps build relationships with other nations.

PRESIDENTS OF THE UNITED STATES SINCE 1961

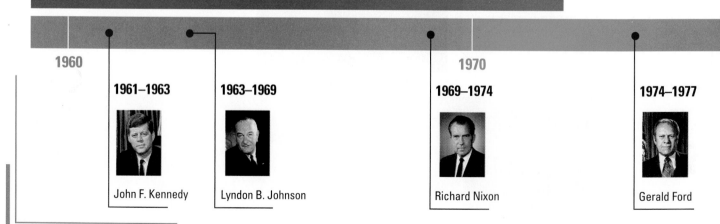

1960

1970

1961–1963
John F. Kennedy

1963–1969
Lyndon B. Johnson

1969–1974
Richard Nixon

1974–1977
Gerald Ford

President Carter

President Reagan

President Bush

3. The President can sign treaties, or agreements with other nations.

4. The President communicates often with U.S. citizens.

5. The President is the leader of the Army, Navy, Air Force, and Marines.

6. The President reports to lawmakers and tells what the government has done and what new laws are needed.

President Clinton

 What are some duties of the President?

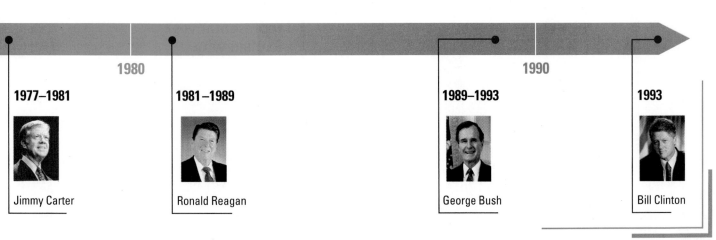

1980

1977–1981

Jimmy Carter

1981–1989

Ronald Reagan

1990

1989–1993

George Bush

1993

Bill Clinton

Congress Makes New Laws

Another branch of the national government includes the Congress. **Congress** makes new laws. Congress has two parts. One is called the House of Representatives, and the other is called the Senate.

The House of Representatives has 435 members. Each state has a certain number of representatives. The more people who live in a state, the more representatives they send to Congress. In 1995 California had the most representatives, 52, because more people lived in California than in any other state. Alaska, Delaware, Montana, North Dakota, South Dakota, Vermont, and Wyoming each had only one representative because they had fewer people than other states.

The Senate has 100 members. Each state, no matter how many people live there, sends two senators to serve in the Senate. Representatives and senators are like the members of a city or town council. They are elected by the people of the United States to meet and to solve national problems.

Congress meets in the Capitol Building.

UNITED STATES REPRESENTATIVES IN FIVE STATES

Bar graph — NUMBER OF REPRESENTATIVES (vertical axis: 0, 10, 20, 30, 40, 50, 60) by state:
- California: 52
- Florida: 23
- Ohio: 19
- Texas: 30
- Vermont: 1

LEARNING FROM BAR GRAPHS
Which two of the states shown here have the most representatives? Explain why.

Members of the House of Representatives

The Capitol Building in Washington, D.C., has two large rooms called chambers. The House of Representatives meets in one chamber, and the Senate meets in the other. Each chamber is large enough so that all the members of the House or the Senate can meet at the same time. The members come together to discuss problems and to vote. They write new laws and decide how much money United States citizens should pay in taxes. Both the House and the Senate must agree on a new law before it can be passed. Then the President can sign the paper telling what the new law is.

Illinois Senator Carol Moseley-Braun is greeting a citizen.

 What are the two parts of Congress called?

The Supreme Court Interprets Laws

A third branch of the national government includes the courts. The **Supreme Court** is the highest, or most important court in the United States. Nine judges, called justices, serve on the Supreme Court. Their leader is called the chief justice.

The Supreme Court is in charge of studying laws and interpreting them, or deciding what they mean. The justices must decide if a law is fair or unfair. If a law is unfair, the justices can ask Congress to change it.

Chief Justice John Marshall once said that the Constitution is "the outline of a government." But this outline does not give answers to many of the questions our lawmakers have about the government. The Supreme Court tells our government what laws it can make when the Constitution is not exactly clear.

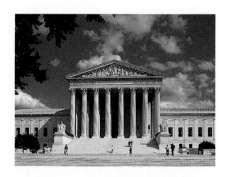

The Supreme Court meets in the Supreme Court Building.

Who?

Sandra Day O'Connor (1930)

Sandra Day O'Connor became the first woman to serve on the Supreme Court. She grew up on the Lazy B Ranch on the border between Arizona and New Mexico. After she received her law degree, she became a senator and an Arizona state judge. President Reagan met her and discovered that as a judge she was tough but fair. He wanted her to serve as a judge on the Supreme Court, and the Senate approved his choice. Sandra Day O'Connor's job has taken her far from the Lazy B Ranch, but she visits whenever she can.

Justices are not elected to the Supreme Court. Instead, they are chosen by the President. The President's choices must be approved by the Senate. A justice serves for life or until he or she resigns. When a justice is chosen to serve on the Supreme Court, he or she promises to "do equal right to the poor and to the rich."

 How are the justices of the Supreme Court chosen?

Nine justices serve on the Supreme Court.

LESSON 4 REVIEW

Check Understanding

1. **Recall the Facts** What are the branches of the United States government?

2. **Focus on the Main Idea** What does each branch of the United States government do?

Think Critically

3. **Think More About It** The United States Constitution gives us "the outline of a government" and leaves the details to be filled in. Why did the writers of the Constitution do this? Explain your answer.

Show What You Know

 **Problem-Solving Activity** Read or listen to news reports to identify a real problem in our nation. The class should form small groups to decide how the problem might be solved. Share your group's ideas with the whole class.

Symbols of Pride

Link to Our World

In what ways can you show that you are proud to be a citizen of your community and country?

Focus on the Main Idea
Read to find out how symbols help people come together and get along in communities in the United States.

Preview Vocabulary
patriotism
anthem
pledge
allegiance

You have probably seen our country's flag in many places—for example, in front of your school, in your classroom, or at the post office. A flag may look like just a piece of cloth with a simple design. However, people in every community honor their country's flag because it is a symbol of patriotism. **Patriotism** is the love that people of many backgrounds have for their country. A flag stands for the ideas that the people of a country believe in.

A Flag for a New Country

There are many kinds of flags. Some rulers, such as the king or the queen of England, have personal flags that stand for them. Other flags stand for cities, states, businesses, or sports teams. Of all the kinds of flags, a national flag is the most important. It stands for people who live in all the communities in a country.

People show pride in their community when they display the flag.

The flag of the United States of America was designed by many people from different communities. Its design has changed over time.

On early United States flags, the number of stars and stripes showed the number of states in the country. But as the country grew, there were too many states to show with stripes. Congress decided that only a new star should be added to the flag when a new state joined the United States. Congress did not say how the stars should be grouped, so there were different designs. In 1912 it was decided that the stars should always be grouped in straight rows. The last change to the flag was in 1960. That year the fiftieth star was added to stand for the state of Hawaii.

1777

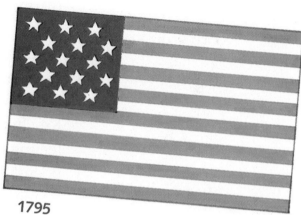

1795

 Why has the design of our country's flag changed many times?

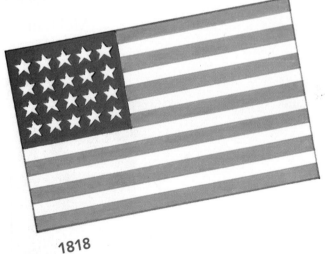

1818

Present day

The National Anthem

Francis Scott Key

Many people, when they look at the flag, think of the freedom it stands for. They also think about the people who fought and died in wars to protect the country's freedom. "The Star-Spangled Banner," the national anthem, was written because of the flag. An **anthem** is a song of patriotism.

Francis Scott Key, a lawyer from Washington, D.C., watched from a distance as Fort McHenry, in Baltimore, Maryland, was attacked by the British during the War of 1812. The battle that had started during the day went on into the night. Even after the fighting had stopped, Key could not see through the darkness to tell who had won. As the sun rose, he could see the American flag flying above the fort. Key knew then that the United States had won. His feeling of patriotism was so strong that he wrote a poem. That poem became the words to "The Star-Spangled Banner."

Most flags are flown only during the day. However, the flag flies day and night over Fort McHenry and over the grave of Francis Scott Key.

 Who wrote "The Star-Spangled Banner"?

THE STAR-SPANGLED BANNER

Oh, say, can you see, by the dawn's early light,
What so proudly we hailed at the twilight's last gleaming?
Whose broad stripes and bright stars, thro' the perilous fight,
O'er the ramparts we watched were so gallantly streaming?
And the rockets' red glare, the bombs bursting in air,
Gave proof thro' the night that our flag was still there.
Oh, say, does that star-spangled banner yet wave
O'er the land of the free and the home of the brave?

The Pledge of Allegiance

Saying the Pledge of Allegiance is a tradition for many citizens in the United States. A **pledge** is a promise. **Allegiance** means being respectful to the flag and to what the flag stands for. When you say that you "pledge allegiance to the flag," you are saying that you promise to honor the flag and our country. People show their respect by standing when they say the pledge. They also place their right hand over their heart in a salute and look at the flag as they say these words.

A third-grade class saluting the flag in 1900

> **"** I pledge allegiance to the Flag of the United States of America, and to the Republic for which it stands, one Nation under God, indivisible, with liberty and justice for all. **"**

The Pledge of Allegiance was said for the very first time in 1892 by children in public schools. Many students all across the United States now join in this salute to the flag every school day.

 What is the Pledge of Allegiance?

A third-grade class saluting the flag today

279

Displaying the Flag

The flag gives people of all ages, in communities across our country, a shared symbol for their homeland. It brings them together and helps them remember the ideas that have made this country great. These photos show some of the places that display our national flag.

The flag is used to honor soldiers and others who have served their country. This flag honored President John F. Kennedy at his funeral.

The flag is flown at voting places on election days.

The nation's flag is used to mark great discoveries. The flag on the moon is held straight by a wire. Because the moon has no air, there is no wind to make the flag wave.

The United States flag is flown at the Olympic Games when someone from the United States wins a medal.

 What are places that display the national flag?

LESSON 5 REVIEW

Check Understanding

1. **Recall the Facts** What are some reasons a flag is displayed?
2. **Focus on the Main Idea** How can a flag help bring people from many communities together to show their pride for their country?

Think Critically

3. **Personally Speaking** In what ways can you show patriotism for your country?

Show What You Know

 **Design Activity** Work with a group to design a flag for your class. Decide what colors and symbols you will use. Each color and symbol should stand for something that you think is important. Then use paper or cloth to make your flag. Explain to your class what the colors and the symbols stand for.

How To

Compare Patriotic Symbols

Why Is This Skill Important?

Symbols are all around you. A flag is a symbol you can see and touch. An anthem is a symbol you can listen to or sing. Symbols are important because they stand for things people believe in. Knowing what symbols mean can help you learn more about the world you live in.

Understand the Process

All countries have their own symbols. Here are a few well-known symbols of the United States.

THE NATIONAL ANTHEM
People sing "The Star-Spangled Banner," our national anthem, at many sports events.

THE BALD EAGLE
The majestic bald eagle is the national bird of the United States. It was chosen as a national symbol because it is found only in North America. This bird has also been seen in every state except Hawaii.

THE GREAT SEAL OF THE UNITED STATES
This became an important symbol in 1782. Both sides of this seal can be seen on a dollar bill. The eagle holds an olive branch, which is a symbol of peace. The arrows the eagle holds are a symbol of strength. The seal is used on important papers and can be seen on the walls of government buildings in the nation's capital.

THE FLAG
Displaying the flag is one way to show patriotism.

Each state also has its symbols. Here are some of the symbols of Texas. How are these symbols different from those of the United States? How are they the same?

Think and Apply

Work with a group. Do research to find out what your state's symbols are.

Then the group should choose one symbol and learn more about it. Make a poster to tell what your group learned about the symbol. Include a picture or drawing of the symbol and a paragraph explaining what it means. Show your poster to the other groups. Discuss with them the differences between state and national symbols.

THE STATE SONG

These are the words to the Texas state song.

TEXAS, OUR TEXAS

Texas, our Texas! All hail the mighty State!
Texas, our Texas! So wonderful, so great!
Boldest and grandest, Withstanding ev'ry test;
O Empire, wide and glorious, You stand supremely blest.
God bless you, Texas! And keep you brave and strong,
That you may grow in pow'r and worth,
Thruout the ages long.

THE STATE BIRD

The mockingbird is the Texas state bird. Mockingbirds are known to be brave when protecting themselves and their young.

THE STATE FLAG

The blue stands for loyalty, and the red shows bravery or courage. The white stands for purity or liberty. The star refers to Texas as the "Lone Star State" because Texas was an independent republic before it was part of the United States.

Pledge to the Flag of Texas
Honor the Texas Flag.
I pledge allegiance to thee,
Texas, one and indivisible.

THE STATE SEAL

The oak branches on the state seal stand for strength, and the olive branches stand for peace. Like the state flag, the seal also has a white star.

Solving Problems in South Africa

Link to Our World

How are governments in other countries like our government?

Focus on the Main Idea

Read to find out how the government of South Africa is solving problems.

Preview Vocabulary

province

Frederick de Klerk was president of South Africa from 1989 to 1994.

There are hundreds of countries in the world. The governments of each community and country work to solve many problems. Now look at one community in the country of South Africa to see how its government is working to solve problems.

An Unfair Government

South Africa is located in the Southern Hemisphere. It lies at the southern tip of the continent of Africa. South Africa touches both the Atlantic Ocean and the Indian Ocean. Near the big city of Johannesburg is the community of Soweto (suh•WAY•toh).

People first settled the land around Soweto and much of southern Africa almost 2,000 years ago. These people were mostly farmers and hunters. They were the ancestors of present-day South Africa's black population.

In the 1600s and 1700s, many white people from Europe came to live in southern Africa. They took over much of the land that the black African people had lived on for hundreds of years. The Europeans set up many communities of their own. In 1910 they formed their own country and called it South Africa.

LOCATION OF SOUTH AFRICA

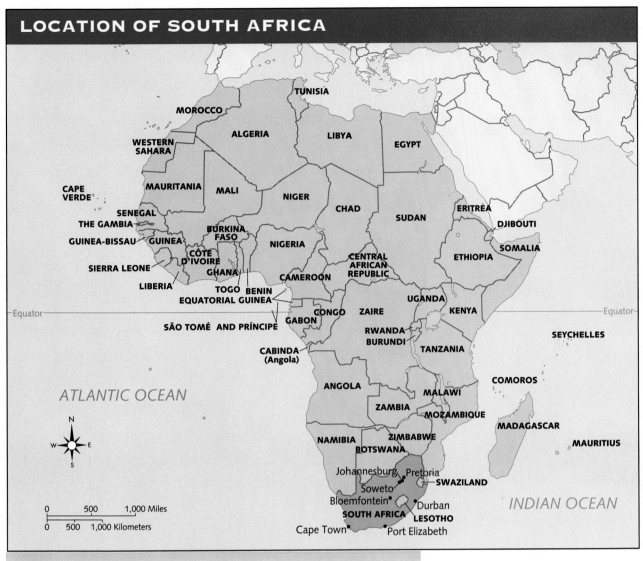

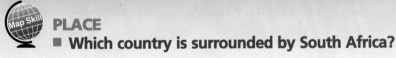

PLACE
- **Which country is surrounded by South Africa?**

Not all the people who lived in South Africa could take part in running the country. Until 1994 only white people were allowed to vote. No black leaders were allowed in the national government. Yet many more black people than white people lived in South Africa. Because of this unfairness, there were many conflicts. Communities such as Soweto were not safe and peaceful places to live. Leaders of South Africa knew these problems had to be solved.

Desmond Tutu is a leader who wanted to change the national government in South Africa.

 **What was the problem in South Africa?**

South African citizens voting in 1994

A New Constitution

In 1993 the leaders of South Africa decided to write a new constitution to stop the unfairness in their country. Like the United States Constitution, the Constitution of South Africa explains how the government will work. It also names the basic rights of all South African citizens in the country's many communities. The South African leaders hoped the new constitution would make the communities in their country peaceful places where all people would be treated the same.

In 1994 South Africa had its first election in which all adult citizens, black and white, were allowed to vote. Voters elected many black representatives to help run the national government. Leaders were also elected in South Africa's provinces. Like states, **provinces** are the large areas that make up some countries. Each province has its own government. Leaders for South Africa's many cities and towns were elected, too.

 What did the new constitution give the citizens of Soweto and other South African communities?

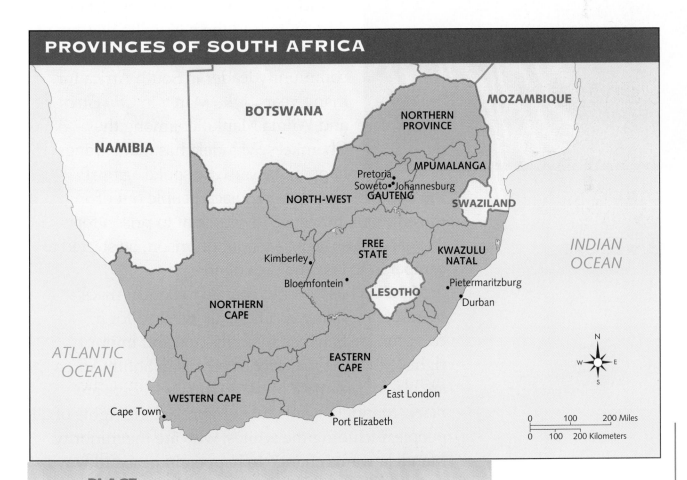

PROVINCES OF SOUTH AFRICA

NAMIBIA

BOTSWANA

MOZAMBIQUE

NORTHERN PROVINCE

MPUMALANGA

Pretoria
Soweto • Johannesburg
GAUTENG

NORTH-WEST

SWAZILAND

FREE STATE

KWAZULU NATAL

INDIAN OCEAN

Kimberley

Bloemfontein

LESOTHO

Pietermaritzburg

Durban

NORTHERN CAPE

ATLANTIC OCEAN

N
W   E
S

EASTERN CAPE

WESTERN CAPE

East London

Cape Town

Port Elizabeth

0   100   200 Miles
0   100   200 Kilometers

PLACE
From 1910 to 1994, South Africa had four provinces. In 1994, the country was divided in a new way.
■ **How many provinces are in South Africa now?**

Map Skill

Nelson Mandela, president of South Africa

The President of South Africa

In 1994 the people of South Africa elected Nelson Mandela as their president. He was the first black South African to lead the national government.

Nelson Mandela has been a community leader in South Africa for many years. Like Marcy in *City Green* and Wilma Mankiller among the Cherokees, Mandela has made things happen. Because he spoke against the unfairness of keeping black people out of government, however, he was sent to prison for 28 years. After he was let out of prison, he started a campaign to become president.

Mandela has brought change to South Africa by resolving many conflicts. He worked for a compromise between majority rule and minority rights. Since the majority of people in South Africa are black, now most of the country's leaders are black. Mandela wants them to protect the rights of all people, including the whites, who are the minority. Mandela wants change to happen in peaceful ways.

 How has Nelson Mandela brought change to South Africa?

Governments Change to Solve Problems

The government of South Africa has made many changes to solve the nation's problems. The biggest change came in 1994. Before then only white people could vote. Now all citizens 18 years and older in every South African community can elect leaders and make other decisions by voting.

Years ago the United States had unfair voting laws, too. At one time only white men who owned land could vote. Africans, Native Americans, and women could not vote. Lawmakers have made changes to the United States Constitution to make voting laws fair for everyone. Today all citizens 18 years and older have the right to vote.

The governments of South Africa and the United States have made many changes. People hope these changes will make the communities in their countries safe and peaceful places for all citizens to live.

 Who has the right to vote in the United States?

Voting Rights

The United States Constitution has been changed several times to give more and more citizens the right to vote. Important years were

1870 Men of all races were allowed to vote.

1920 Women were given the right to vote.

1971 All citizens 18 years and older could vote.

LESSON 6 REVIEW

Check Understanding

1. **Recall the Facts** Who was elected South Africa's first black African president?

2. **Focus on the Main Idea** How is the South African national government working to solve its problems?

Think Critically

3. **Cause and Effect** How do you think changes in the government of South Africa have affected the lives of its citizens?

Show What You Know

 **Creative Writing Activity** Write an essay that shows how you feel about the right to vote. Explain what is meant by the right to vote and whether the law about voting is fair. Read your essay to a classmate, and then discuss it.

THE TURKEY OR THE EAGLE?

For many years lawmakers tried to decide on a design for the Great Seal of the United States. But they could not agree. Finally, on June 20, 1782, Congress chose a design that showed an eagle. On that day, the bald eagle became a national symbol for the United States.

Benjamin Franklin, a member of the committee that chose the design, had wanted the rattlesnake for a national symbol. Later he had agreed that a bird would be a better choice.

The Great Seal of the United States

The Turkey

However, in a letter to his daughter, Sarah, Franklin wrote, "I wish the bald eagle had not been chosen as the representative of our country; he is a bird of bad moral character."

Franklin thought the eagle was a coward because it could be chased away by smaller birds. Also, he had heard that the eagle took food away from other birds. He felt that the turkey would be a better symbol of America because it was a bird with courage. It was also an important food source for settlers.

The turkey–a national symbol?

The Eagle

Over the years many people have disagreed with Franklin. In the 1930s the animal scientist Francis Hobart Herrick wrote that "The bald eagle is an expert fisherman . . . he is never driven from the neighborhood by any other living being excepting a man armed with a gun."

The National Symbol Today

People did not let Franklin's ideas change their minds. The eagle had a long history as a symbol of freedom and power. The choice of the bald eagle as the American symbol was so well liked that pictures of the bird began to be used on quilts, furniture, and dishes. Today the eagle can be seen on coins, paper money, stamps, and government papers.

COMPARE
VIEWPOINTS

1. Why did Benjamin Franklin think the eagle was a bad choice for a national symbol?

2. Why did Francis Hobart Herrick think the eagle was a good choice?

THINK
–AND–
APPLY

Do you agree or disagree with the decision to make the bald eagle a national symbol? Write a letter to Benjamin Franklin to let him know your point of view. Share your letter with your classmates.

BUILDING CITIZENSHIP

These are some of the objects on which an eagle is used.

STORY CLOTH

Follow the pictures shown in this story cloth to help you review the things you read about in Unit 5.

Summarize the Main Ideas

1. People in communities work together to solve their problems.

2. Rules and laws are for the common good of a community.

3. Citizens show pride in their communities in many ways.

4. The parts of a government work together for the common good.

5. People in governments in other countries work together to solve problems.

Write a Motto   Choose one of the main ideas shown in the story cloth. Write a motto, or short saying, about that idea. You can put the motto on a button, an index card, a poster, or a banner. Explain the motto to your classmates.

Draw a Map   Look for the patriotic symbols shown on the story cloth. Now draw a map of your community to show where flags or other patriotic symbols are displayed. Include a title, compass rose, and map key. Then share your map with a family member.

COOPERATIVE LEARNING WORKSHOP

Remember
- Share your ideas.
- Cooperate with others to plan your work.
- Take responsibility for your work.
- Show your group's work to the class.
- Discuss what you learned by working together.

Activity 1

Interview a Leader

Decide which community leader you would like to know more about. Then interview the leader, and ask how young people can become involved with the local government. Put your interview in a class binder for all to read.

Activity 2

Write a Constitution

A constitution is a written set of laws for government. Working in a group, brainstorm a list of rules for your classroom. Then meet with other groups. Vote on which rules to list in a "Classroom Constitution." Write the rules, and display your Classroom Constitution.

Activity 3

Write an Anthem

Francis Scott Key wrote a poem called "The Star-Spangled Banner" to show his feelings of patriotism. Later, his words were set to music, and the song became our national anthem. Work in a group to write an anthem that shows your love for your community. You might write about something that happened in the history of your city or town. Make your words fit the tune of a song you already know. Then sing your song for the class.

CONNECT MAIN IDEAS

Use this graphic organizer to show how the unit's main ideas are connected. First, copy the organizer onto a separate sheet of paper. Then, write a complete sentence to support each group of words.

Lesson 1
Solving community problems
_____
_____

Lesson 6
Solving problems in other countries
_____
_____

Lesson 2
Rules and laws
_____
_____

Living Together in a Community, State, and Nation

Lesson 5
Patriotic symbols
_____
_____

Lesson 3
State governments
_____
_____

Lesson 4
Branches of national government
_____
_____

USE VOCABULARY

Look at the words below. Write a sentence for each word. Then write one more sentence that tells what these words have in common.

allegiance   **patriotism**
anthem   **pledge**

WRITE MORE ABOUT IT

Write a Letter   Think of something that you would like to see changed in your community. Then write a letter to a community leader. In your letter, clearly explain what you think needs to be done differently. Read your letter to a family member.

CHECK UNDERSTANDING

1. What group of people helps a city's mayor make laws?

2. What is the set of laws for our country's government called?

3. What are the jobs of the branches of the national government?

THINK CRITICALLY

1. **Past to Present** How have the lawmakers of the past helped you live your life today?

2. **Think More About It** Why is it important to understand how any government works?

3. **Personally Speaking** If you could hold a government office, which one would you choose? Explain.

APPLY SKILLS

How to Resolve Conflicts

Imagine that two children have a conflict. Each child wants an apple, but there is only one apple. Write a story that tells how the children can resolve the conflict.

How to Compare Patriotic Symbols The design of the United States flag has changed many times. Use the pictures to help you answer these questions.

1. What is the difference between these two flags?

2. Why do you think the flags are so different?

How to Measure Distance on a Map Use the distance scale to answer the following questions. Answer each question using both miles and kilometers.

OHIO

1. What is the distance from Columbus to Portsmouth?
2. What is the distance from Cincinnati to Cleveland?

How to Make Choices by Voting One way citizens help make decisions about their government is by voting in elections. Use the words below to fill in the blanks in the paragraph at the top of the next column. It tells about an election.

**ballot   campaign   candidate
election   vote**

Rebecca Lawson is a _____ for the United States Senate. She will begin her _____ for election in January. She hopes that many people will _____ for her. The voters can choose her name from those on the _____. If most of the people choose her name, she will win the _____.

READ MORE ABOUT IT

Across the Wide Dark Sea: The Mayflower Journey by Jean Van Leeuwen. Putnam. In 1620 a small boy and his father sailed across the ocean to a new life. This story is based on records kept by one of the *Mayflower*'s passengers.

Leaders, Laws, and Citizens by William Wise. Parents' Magazine Press. This book gives a simple history of the United States government.

The President's Cabinet and How It Grew by Nancy Winslow Parker. HarperCollins. Find out about the people who give important advice to the President.

Senator by Richard Sobel. Cobblehill. Read about the work of Connie Mack, a United States Senator from Florida.

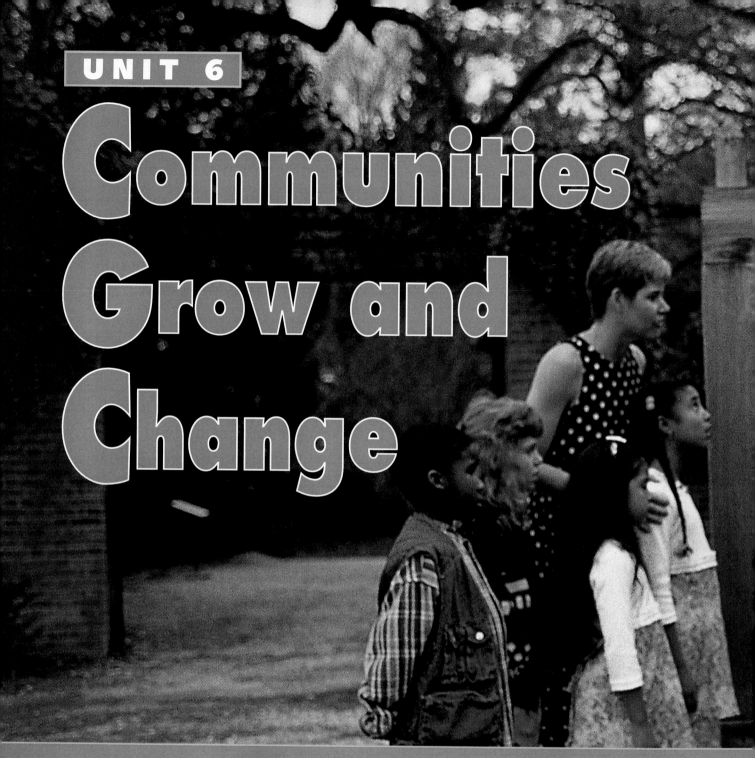

Communities Grow and Change

Communities change in some ways yet stay the same in other ways. ➡

Change in a community can be slow, fast, planned, or unplanned. ➡

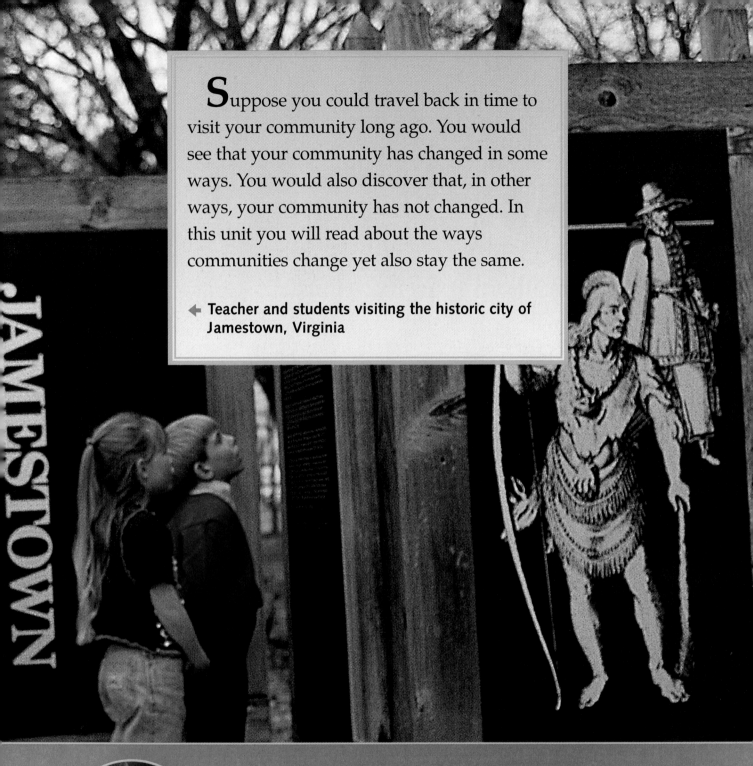

JAMESTOWN

Suppose you could travel back in time to visit your community long ago. You would see that your community has changed in some ways. You would also discover that, in other ways, your community has not changed. In this unit you will read about the ways communities change yet also stay the same.

← Teacher and students visiting the historic city of Jamestown, Virginia

← Growth in a community can sometimes create problems.

Every community has a history. →

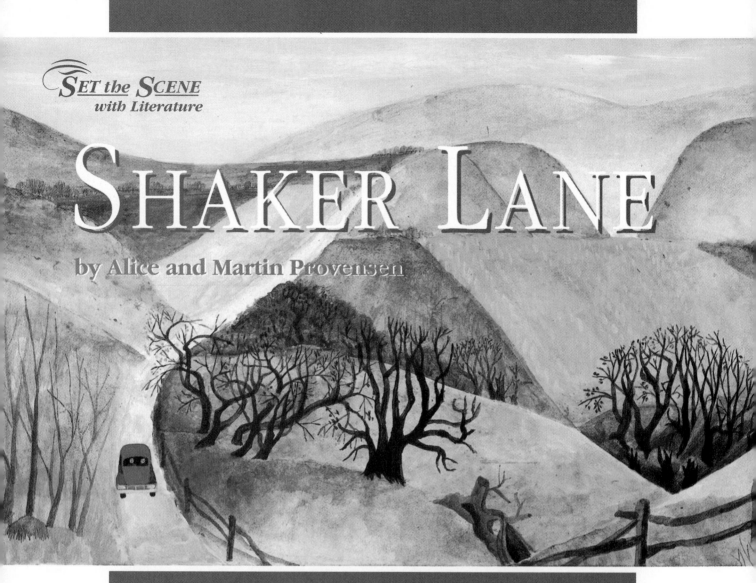

SHAKER LANE

by Alice and Martin Provensen

All communities change over time. Some change takes place slowly. Some change happens quickly. In this story you will have an opportunity to see how change affects the people who live in the tiny community called Shaker Lane.

ot so long ago, if you went down School House Road and crossed Fiddler's Bridge, you would come to Shaker Lane. A Shaker Meeting House once stood at the crossroads. Nothing was left of it but a few stones.

Scrub brush covered the old farmland on both sides of the road. The farm belonged to the Herkimer sisters, Abigail and Priscilla. They were old ladies. They sat all day in their front yard facing the road. No one mowed their fields. No one fixed the fences.

In order to live, the Herkimer sisters sold off pieces of the farm, a half-acre here, an acre there. They sold it cheap. In a year or two there was a row of houses along Shaker Lane.

In the first house along the road lived Virgil Oates
with his wife, Sue Ann, their five kids, and Sue Ann's
brother, Wayne. Next to it was Sam Kulick's place.
Across the road lived Norbert La Rose. His wife's
name was Charlene. They had four kids. They also
had three dogs, five cats, and a duck named Lucy.

The people who lived on Shaker Lane took things easy. Their yards were full of stuff— old dressers waiting to go inside, cars that would never roll again, parts of old trucks, stovepipes, piles of rotten rope, rusty tin, bedsprings, bales of old wire and tin cans. Some people would have liked to see Shaker Lane disappear forever.

When the big yellow school bus came down Shaker Lane, the kids would yell, "Aker, baker, poorhouse shaker!"

Sometimes there were fights.

Here is Old Man Van Sloop's house. Dozens of dogs lived here, as well as chickens and a goat named Shem. The dogs came and went just as they felt like. They fought and slept and chewed on the bones that Old Man Van Sloop found for them somewhere.

Sometimes an angry man showed up, looking for a runaway. Old Man Van Sloop didn't care. "Plenty more where that one came from!" he would shout.

The man would frown and say, "Public nuisance!" and take his dog away.

Next to Old Man Van Sloop lived the Whipple boys, Jesse and Ben. They were twins and did yard work. People never knew if it was Jesse or Ben who weeded their gardens.

Back of the Whipple house was the Peach place. Bobbie Lee Peach and his wife, Violet, lived here with their children—Emma, Zekiel, Sophie, Harvey, and Ralph. Violet's father, Chester Funk, lived with them too.

Here is Big Jake Van der Loon. Big Jake could do anything. He had four helpers: Little Jake, Herman, Matty, and Buddy. Big Jake dug wells, moved barns, put up fences.

He put up a telephone pole for the Herkimer sisters. He moved a chicken coop for Sam Kulick. When an enormous maple tree blew down in a storm, Big Jake cut up firewood for everyone.

The Van der Loon family lived in four houses on Shaker Lane. One for Big Jake, one for his brother-in-law, Harold Prideux; one for LeRoy and Milly Cobb; and one for Big Jake's mother, Big Ethel.

One day Ben Whipple came running up to Big Ethel. "We're going to be flooded out!" he shouted. "They're building a dam on Bosey's Pond!"

It was true. Ed Rikert, the County Land Agent, came to Shaker Lane. "A reservoir is to be built," he said. "Most of you folks will have to move. The county will pay you for your land."

Virgil Oates was the first to leave. "Can't swim," he said. Then the Whipple boys and the Peaches packed up and left. One by one, the other families followed.

The bulldozers came. Huge painted monsters, like
iron dinosaurs, chewed up Shaker Lane. Until, at last,
the excavation was complete.

The water rose slowly but surely. It crept over the
last chimney. Only the Herkimer house was still
there, high on the hill.

What was left of Shaker Lane changed its name to
Reservoir Road. You wouldn't know the place.

Old Man Van Sloop is still here. He has a houseboat. He has his chickens and Shem, the goat.

Lots of dogs still come to visit.

"I like the water," says Old Man Van Sloop.

Communities Change, Yet Stay the Same

Link to Our World

In the time you can remember, how has your community changed and how has it stayed the same?

Focus on the Main Idea
Read to find out about ways communities change and ways they stay the same.

Preview Vocabulary
reservoir
decade
century

Communities change every day. People move into a community, and others leave. Trees are cut down, and flowers are planted. An old building might be torn down to make way for a new building. A new shop might open for business in an old building.

Many Things Change

Many changes took place at Shaker Lane. The Herkimer sisters sold off pieces of their farm, and people built houses on them. Then the people were told they would have to move. A **reservoir**, or lake used for collecting and storing water, was to be built. After the reservoir was built, water covered much of Shaker Lane. A new community soon grew nearby. Many communities in the United States have changed in the same way.

This was Dillon, Colorado, in the 1950s. The state government decided to build a reservoir there. Some buildings were torn down. Others were moved to a new location. ➜

This is Dillon Reservoir. The community of Dillon is now in a new location, several miles away. ➜

Compare the three photographs to see how much Austin, Texas, has changed in nearly a century.

Change can take a day, a decade, or even a century. A **decade** is 10 years. A **century** is 100 years. Some kinds of change take place so slowly that you hardly notice them. To see those changes, you can compare photographs that have been taken of the same place at different times.

 How many years are in a decade? a century?

Then

↑ This photograph of the city hall in Tombstone, Arizona, was taken in 1900. The city hall was built to give the mayor and city workers a place to work.

Now

↑ This photograph was taken in 1995. The mayor and city workers still do their jobs in the city hall.

Now

Many Things Stay the Same

Many changes took place at Shaker Lane, but some things stayed the same. The reservoir was built, but the Herkimer sisters stayed in their house on the hill. Old Man Van Sloop stayed, too. He moved his animals and his belongings onto a houseboat and lived right on the reservoir.

In communities everywhere, many things seem to stay the same. Many old buildings are still used. They may have new technology inside, such as new telephones and computers. But the things people do inside the buildings are much the same as they were a century ago.

↑ This church in St. Marys City, Maryland, was built in 1829. People still go to church there.

Schools have changed a lot over the last century. One hundred years ago, many schools did not have media centers. Now nearly all schools do, and in just the last decade, they have added computers and videotape machines. Schools have changed, but they are still an important part of every community. They provide the same important service they always did—teaching young people what they need to know to be responsible citizens. A century from now every community will still need this service.

 What important service do schools provide?

....

Students in a classroom in 1917. How is your classroom different from this one? How is your classroom the same? ➡

LESSON 1 REVIEW

Check Understanding

1. **Recall the Facts** How is a decade different from a century?
2. **Focus on the Main Idea** How do communities change? How do they stay the same?

Think Critically

3. **Think More About It** What might Shaker Lane be like today if the reservoir had not been built?

Show What You Know

 **Creative Writing Activity** What will your community be like a decade from now? What things will be the same? What things will have changed? Describe how a third grader would live in your community 10 years from today. Share your description with a classmate.

Many Kinds of Change

Link to Our World

What kinds of change have taken place in the community where you live?

Focus on the Main Idea
Read to find out how change takes place in communities in different ways.

Preview Vocabulary
planning
disaster
decline

Communities change in different ways. Some communities change slowly. Change might take decades, even centuries. Other communities change quickly. Sometimes change in a community is planned, while other times change surprises the people who live there.

Slow, Steady Change

Charlotte, North Carolina, is a city that has changed in many ways over the years. Catawba (kuh•TAW•buh) Indians lived where Charlotte is now until European settlers came in the 1740s. The settlers built a town, which soon began to grow. Many people who lived in Charlotte at that time were farmers. Then in 1799 gold was

Charlotte is the largest city in North Carolina. Many businesses are located there.

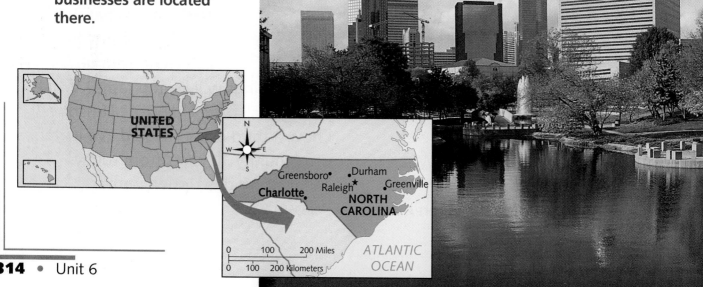

UNITED STATES

NORTH CAROLINA

Greensboro • Durham
Charlotte • Raleigh ★ • Greenville

0   100   200 Miles
0 100 200 Kilometers

ATLANTIC OCEAN

found near Charlotte. Many miners moved to the community to look for gold.

In the late 1800s people began to build factories in Charlotte. Over the next century many more factories and businesses were built there. Many more people moved to Charlotte, and the city continued to grow.

In 250 years Charlotte has grown to become the largest city in North Carolina. More people live there than in any other city in the state. They work in Charlotte's many banks, factories, and other businesses. Charlotte is still growing and changing.

Many people in Charlotte work in factories that make clothing.

 In what ways has Charlotte changed?

LEARNING FROM BAR GRAPHS
How has the population of Charlotte changed since 1900?

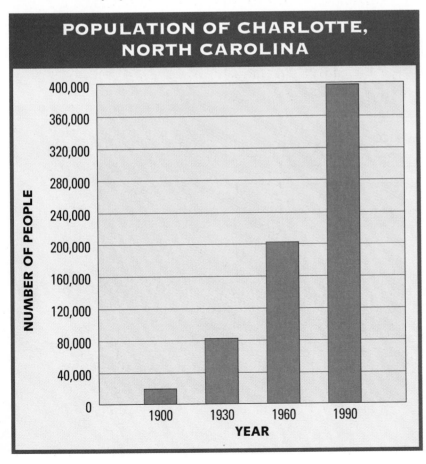

Charlotte is still growing. New buildings are being built there every day.

Fast Change

Some communities change very quickly. As it did in Shaker Lane, sometimes something happens that causes them to disappear.

Terlingua, Texas, grew very quickly near the end of the 1890s. Thousands of people moved there to work in the mercury mines. Mercury is a kind of metal. But by the 1940s the mercury had all been mined. There was no more. The mines closed, and the people left. In just 50 years Terlingua grew from nothing into a busy community and then became a ghost town.

Wagons were once used for transportation in Terlingua.

✓ **Why did Terlingua become a ghost town?**

Though once a busy community, Terlingua, Texas, has become a ghost town.

Citizens work together to make changes in their community.

Planned Change

Sometimes change that takes place in a community is planned. Groups of citizens, including government workers, decide ahead of time what changes should be made. They might decide where to build new neighborhoods, schools, or shopping centers. They might plan how to repair old buildings or highways. **Planning** helps a community grow in an organized way to help its citizens.

 Why is it important to plan changes?

Unplanned Change

Sometimes a change that is not planned happens. A **disaster** is something that happens that causes great harm to a community. An earthquake can be a disaster. So can a flood, a fire, or a hurricane.

In 1992 a powerful hurricane named Andrew slammed into South Florida. The city of Homestead was one of many communities that were changed by the hurricane. Winds as high as 175 miles per hour tossed up boats, trucks, and airplanes. Entire city blocks were flattened. Many businesses were destroyed. The changes caused by the disaster affected all the people who live in the community.

↑ **Many people in Homestead, Florida, lost their homes and their jobs when Hurricane Andrew struck.**

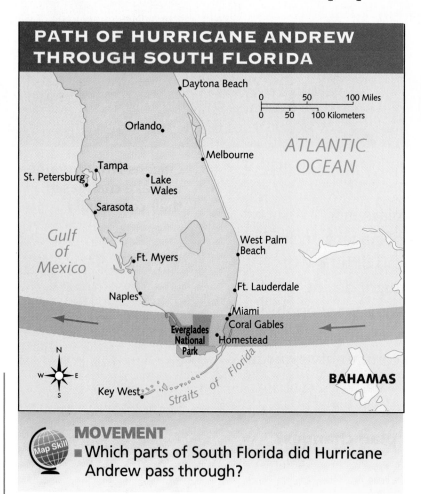

PATH OF HURRICANE ANDREW THROUGH SOUTH FLORIDA

Daytona Beach

0   50   100 Miles
0   50   100 Kilometers

Orlando

Melbourne

ATLANTIC OCEAN

Tampa
St. Petersburg
Lake Wales

Sarasota

Gulf of Mexico

Ft. Myers

West Palm Beach

Naples

Ft. Lauderdale

Miami
Coral Gables
Everglades National Park
Homestead

Key West

Straits of Florida

BAHAMAS

N
W E
S

↑ **After the hurricane, people worked together to rebuild their community.**

MOVEMENT

- Which parts of South Florida did Hurricane Andrew pass through?

Many disasters happen very quickly and without warning. But some unplanned changes happen over a long period of time. For example, in some communities factories close. People must leave the community to find jobs in other places. New families do not come, because there are no jobs for them. So the population of the community stops growing. In such a community, neighborhoods that were once busy now have empty shopping centers and empty homes. When this happens, the community is in **decline** . Some communities are able to recover from a decline. But this can take a long time.

 What are examples of changes that are unplanned?

These empty houses show a neighborhood in decline.

LESSON 2 REVIEW

Check Understanding

1. **Recall the Facts**   What are some kinds of disasters?
2. **Focus on the Main Idea**   In what ways do communities change?

Think Critically

3. **Cause and Effect**   What are some things that can cause communities to change quickly?

Show What You Know

 **News Report Activity** Imagine that you are the first television reporter to arrive in Homestead, Florida, after the hurricane. Write a script for what you will tell your audience. In your script, describe what has happened. Explain how the disaster has affected the community. Read your script to the class.

How To

Compare Maps from Different Times

Why Is This Skill Important?

If you looked through a family photo album, you could see how the people have changed over the years. Comparing maps that show different times in the same place can help you see how that place has changed. You can also see how mapmaking has changed.

How Mapmaking Has Changed

Forty-five years ago, mapmakers made maps by hand, using pen and ink. They made most maps by observing and measuring the area. When they needed to add new information, sometimes the whole map had to be drawn again.

Today, mapmakers use computers to draw maps more quickly and easily. Mapmakers also use photographs taken from space to help them make maps more correct.

Understand the Process

Compare the two maps of the northwestern part of Charlotte, North Carolina. Then answer the following questions to find out how Charlotte has changed.

1. Find the park on each map. How has the area to the west of the park changed?

2. Compare the roads and highways on the maps. What do they tell you about how Charlotte has grown?

3. Find Stewart Creek on each map. What has stayed the same? What has changed?

Think and Apply

Compare an old map of your state or community with a newer map. What do you learn by comparing the two maps?

With a computer, mapmakers can add new information to a map very quickly.

CHARLOTTE, NORTH CAROLINA (NORTHWEST)—1935

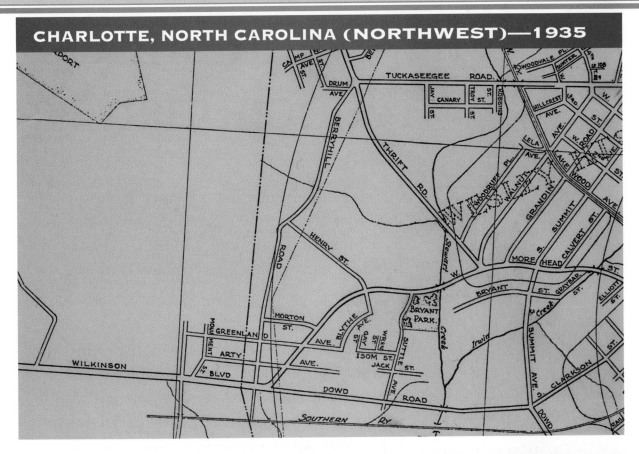

CHARLOTTE, NORTH CAROLINA (NORTHWEST)—1995

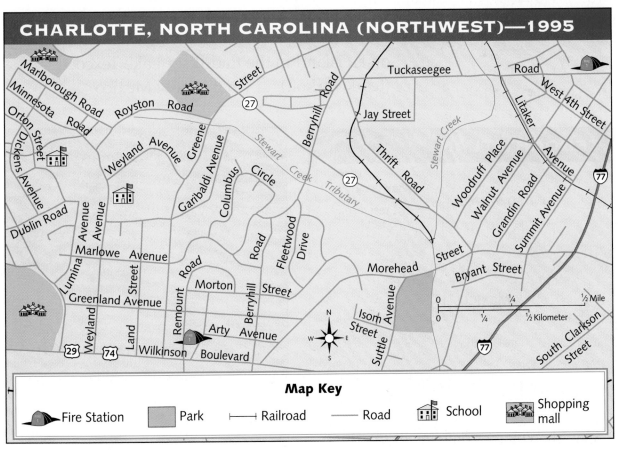

Map Key

Fire Station | Park | Railroad | Road | School | Shopping mall

The Community of Tenochtitlán

LESSON 3

Link to Our World

In what ways did communities change many centuries ago?

Focus on the Main Idea
Find out how a community in Mexico changed many centuries ago.

Preview Vocabulary
canal
causeway
empire

Every community has a history. Its history tells how that community has changed in many ways over time. One community in Mexico has been through many changes over many centuries.

A City on a Lake

The city of Tenochtitlán (tay•nohch•teet•LAHN) was started almost 700 years ago by the Aztec Indians. The Aztecs believed that their gods wanted them to build a city in a special place. When they saw an eagle sitting on a cactus eating a snake, it would be a sign that they had found the right place. The Aztecs saw this sign on an island in the middle of Lake Texcoco (tes•KOH•koh), in what is now Mexico.

A Spanish explorer's drawing of the city ➜

A painting of the great city of Tenochtitlán, one of the largest cities in the world

The Aztecs built Tenochtitlán on that island. Many years passed, and it became a great city. The Aztecs built huge temples and many homes. People traveled through the city on roads and canals. **Canals** are waterways that are built by people. Canoes were used on the canals to carry products to market. There were also wide roads over the water called **causeways** . The causeways joined Tenochtitlán with other cities that were located on the land around the lake.

The Aztecs used soil and reeds, or grasses that grow in water, to build floating gardens. These gardens floated like large rafts in the shallow waters around the city. The Aztecs planted them with crops, such as corn, beans, and tomatoes. These human-made "islands" produced a lot of food.

This painting shows Aztecs building a floating garden.

 How did canals and causeways help people in Tenochtitlán travel?

Changes in Government

Tenochtitlán was the capital city of the huge Aztec Empire. An **empire** is all the land and people under the control of a powerful nation. In the early 1500s, there were millions of people in the Aztec Empire.

By 1521, however, the Aztec Empire was in ruins. Hernando Cortés (er•NAN•doh kawr•TEZ), a Spanish explorer, led soldiers into Tenochtitlán. They fought a war with the Aztecs and destroyed the city. The Spanish built a new city in place of Tenochtitlán and called it Mexico City. It became the capital of the Spanish Empire in Mexico. The Spanish began draining Lake Texcoco in the 1600s to make room for their growing city.

The Spanish ruled until the Mexican people formed their own government. Mexico became an independent country in 1821.

Hernando Cortés

A drawing of Mexico City in the 1600s. This city was built on top of the ruins of Tenochtitlán.

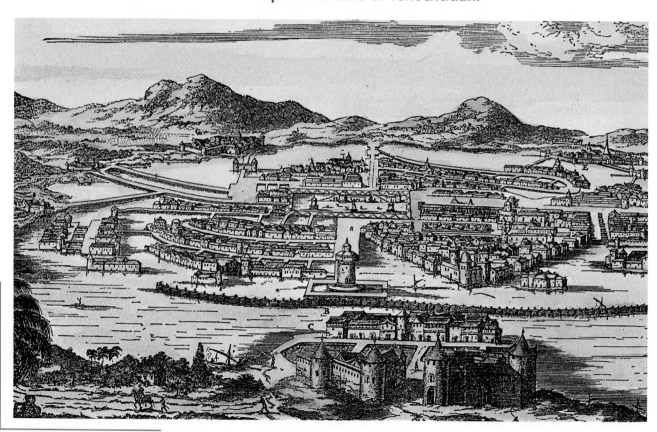

The time line below shows some of the ways that Tenochtitlán has changed over time. However, some things have not changed. This city, which was built in the middle of a lake, has stayed a capital city for nearly 700 years. Mexico City is the capital of Mexico.

 What new name did the Spanish explorers give to Tenochtitlán?

↑ **A church built by the Spanish in the 1600s**

LEARNING FROM TIME LINES
For how long did each group—the Aztecs, the Spanish, and the Mexicans—use Tenochtitlán as their capital city?

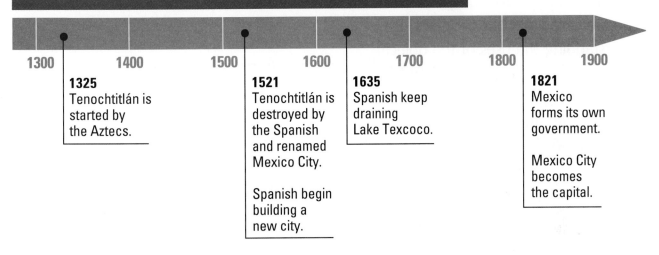

TIME LINE OF TENOCHTITLÁN'S HISTORY

1300	1400	1500	1600	1700	1800	1900

1325
Tenochtitlán is started by the Aztecs.

1521
Tenochtitlán is destroyed by the Spanish and renamed Mexico City.

Spanish begin building a new city.

1635
Spanish keep draining Lake Texcoco.

1821
Mexico forms its own government.

Mexico City becomes the capital.

LESSON 3 REVIEW

Check Understanding

1. **Recall the Facts** How did the Aztecs find the location for Tenochtitlán?
2. **Focus on the Main Idea** How has Tenochtitlán changed over time?

Think Critically

3. **Cause and Effect** How did people change Lake Texcoco over the years?

Show What You Know

Art Activity Paint or draw a scene from Tenochtitlán when it was a great city. Your drawing might be of a temple or a floating garden. Use the pictures in this lesson and pictures from encyclopedias and other books for ideas. Add your artwork to a bulletin board display.

How To

Learn from Artifacts

Why Is This Skill Important?

Objects that we find that were used by people in the past are called **artifacts**. A tool, a piece of jewelry, or a bowl are examples of artifacts.

Scientists who look for artifacts and try to explain how they were used are called **archaeologists**. By understanding the uses of the objects they find, they help us learn about the past. Knowing how to explain artifacts can give clues about how people lived long ago.

Understand the Process

Look at the picture below and read the description of the artifacts. Then answer the questions in the next column.

↑ Archaeologists found these tools in the Aztec ruins of Tenochtitlán. They are made of stone. Long ago, people put kernels of corn on the flat surface and used the round stone to grind the corn into powder.

1. Where were these tools found? What are they made of?

2. What present-day tools do they look like?

3. How did people use these tools?

4. What do these tools tell you about how people lived long ago?

Think and Apply

The corn-grinding tools have changed over time. Some of the features, however, have stayed the same. Compare the two pictures. Make one list of the features that have changed and another of the features that have stayed the same.

↑ Some Mexicans use tools like these to prepare food.

LESSON 4

Mexico City Today

Link to Our World

What problems do cities face today?

Focus on the Main Idea
Find out what problem Mexico City faces today.

Preview Vocabulary
pollution

Today, Mexico City is in the place where Tenochtitlán once stood. Over many years the beautiful capital of the Aztec Empire has changed into another great city. Mexico City has many interesting buildings, parks, and museums.

The Largest City in the World

Mexico City is the largest city in the world. The population of the city and its surrounding area is more than 21 million.

A scene in one of the many beautiful parks in Mexico City. The Latin American Tower is in the background.

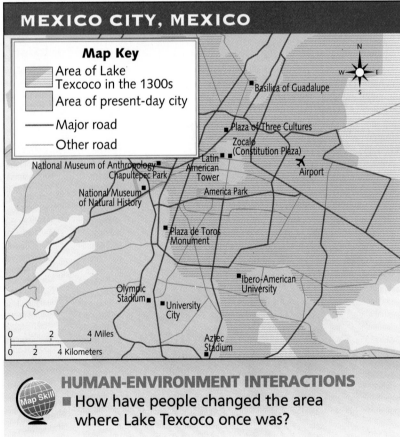

MEXICO CITY, MEXICO

Map Key
- Area of Lake Texcoco in the 1300s
- Area of present-day city
- Major road
- Other road

Basilica of Guadalupe

Plaza of Three Cultures

Zócalo (Constitution Plaza)

National Museum of Anthropology
Chapultepec Park

Latin American Tower

Airport

National Museum of Natural History

America Park

Plaza de Toros Monument

Ibero-American University

Olympic Stadium

University City

Aztec Stadium

0   2   4 Miles
0   2   4 Kilometers

HUMAN-ENVIRONMENT INTERACTIONS
- How have people changed the area where Lake Texcoco once was?

Like that of most large cities in the world, Mexico City's large population has created problems. The people living in the city use many vehicles— buses, trucks, and cars. All of these vehicles produce exhaust, a kind of smoke. This exhaust, along with smoke from factories, causes pollution. **Pollution** is anything that makes the air, land, or water unclean.

The air in Mexico City is so thick with pollution at times that the citizens cannot see the mountains around their city. The air is not healthful for people to breathe.

 How many people live in Mexico City?

Exhaust from vehicles is the main cause of air pollution.

Air pollution over Mexico City

Solving the Pollution Problem

The people in Mexico City are working to solve their pollution problem. Some factories that produced harmful smoke have been closed. Many vehicles now use special fuels and engines that produce less pollution. There is also a law called "No driving today." This means that car owners may not drive their cars at least one day each week.

Using public transportation has also helped. In the 1960s, the people of Mexico City voted to build a subway. A subway is a set of tunnels with trains that run under the city. Many people now use the subway, and this has helped cut down on the number of vehicles on city streets.

Building the subway also gave Mexico City's people a new way to enjoy the history of their city. While working underground, subway builders found part of an Aztec temple. The pieces of the temple were carefully uncovered and left where they were found. An underground museum was built around them. Now people can visit the museum on their way to work or school.

Pieces of an Aztec temple can be seen in this museum, which is located in a subway station.

What?

The Mexican Flag

The Mexican flag reminds people of Mexico's history. The center of the flag shows an eagle sitting on a cactus with a snake in its mouth. This symbol reminds people of the Aztec city of Tenochtitlán, which is now Mexico City.

The people of Mexico City have many reasons to be proud of their city. It has had a long and interesting history.

 Why are the subways in Mexico City important?

The Plaza of Three Cultures has the ruins of an Aztec temple as well as a Spanish church and several modern buildings. It is a place where people can see some of the many ways Mexico City has changed.

LESSON 4 REVIEW

Check Understanding

1. **Recall the Facts** What did workers find when they were building the subway?
2. **Focus on the Main Idea** How are people working to solve Mexico City's air pollution problem?

Think Critically

3. **Cause and Effect** Why does Mexico City have a problem with air pollution?

Show What You Know

Write a Postcard
Take an imaginary trip to Mexico City. Visit the many beautiful parks and museums. Design a postcard you can send to your family or friends. On the back, describe the things you have seen and done in Mexico City. After sharing your postcard with family members, put your postcard in a class scrapbook.

How To

Solve a Problem

Why Is This Skill Important?

You probably have to solve problems every day. You can use a set of steps to help you solve problems. Knowing the steps can help you be ready to solve most problems when they happen.

Remember What You Have Read

The citizens of Mexico City had a big problem. The polluted air in their city was not healthful for people to breathe.

Understand the Process

Here are some steps to use to solve a problem.

Step 1 Identify the problem.

The Mexicans saw that the air in their city was not healthful.

Step 2 Think of solutions to the problem.

A big problem like air pollution needs many **solutions**, or ways to solve it. The Mexicans thought of many things they could do. They could shut down the factories that caused pollution. They could have vehicles use fuels that cause less pollution. They could have people leave their cars at home one day each week. They could build a subway.

Step 3 Compare the solutions.

What are the good points and bad points of each solution? A good point of closing down some of the factories is that there is less air pollution. A bad point is that many people lose their jobs. Name the good and bad points of each solution that was named in Step 2.

Step 4 Carry out one solution.

The Mexican people are working together to make each solution work. One group of citizens designed the subway. Another group worked to make special fuels.

Step 5 Solve the problem. Then think about how well the solution worked.

The problem of air pollution in Mexico City is not yet solved, but the solutions are helping. The air is much cleaner today than it was 10 years ago.

Think and Apply

The problems you face every day may not be as big as Mexico City's, but they are important to you. Imagine that you need to pay for your lunch but do not have enough money. Use the five steps to find a solution.

Every Community Has a History

Link to Our World

What are some ways to find out about a community's history?

Focus on the Main Idea
Find out how you can learn about the history of your community.

Preview Vocabulary
historical society

History is the story of what happens to people and their communities over time. In this book you have found out what communities are and why communities are built where they are. You have seen how people celebrate their heritage and culture and how they work together. You have learned how people organize their governments. In this unit you have looked at how change affects communities. You have also seen that some things do not change. Now use what you have learned to discover more about the community where you live.

Learning About the History of Your Community

There are many ways you can learn about the history of your community. Every community has places where you can find information.

Older family members can tell you what life was like before you were born.

A neighbor talks about the history of a community.

A good place to start is with your family. Maybe you have older family members you can interview to discover things about yourself and your community. Ask them questions. Find out what life was like when they were your age. Look at old family photos or movies. Some family members might be able to show you artifacts that were used long ago.

Maybe your family has just moved to a new community or your family members do not live in your community. Then you might interview other members of your community—perhaps some of the workers at your school. Your neighbors may also share what they know about your community.

Family members may have artifacts that can provide information about life long ago.

People who work in libraries and museums often have a special interest in history. They may have a lot of information about your community.

Many communities have special places where you can gather information. The library may have books, maps, and other displays that you can learn from. Your community may also have a museum or a historical society. A **historical society** is a group of people, usually volunteers, who have a special interest in the history of their community. They may have collections of photographs and artifacts.

 Who can provide you with information about the history of your community?

Using Social Studies Skills

You can use your social studies skills as you learn about the history of your community. You could make a time line that shows when important events happened in your community. You could also compare maps or photographs from different times to see how things have changed. You might make a graph to show how the population of your community has grown or declined.

Soccer Team Wins Championship

By Toby Taylor
Daily News Sports Correspondent

It was a very close game, but the Doraville Eagles defeated the Fairburn Bluejays 5-4 to win the district soccer championship. The Eagles were behind 4-1 at the half, with the only goal scored by Brittany Williams. In the beginning of the second half, an outstanding pass by Marquis Wilson to Sal Mendoza helped pull the Eagles within one point. Then, in a scoring frenzy, the Eagles netted 3 more to win in the last two minutes of the game. Goalie Scott Tow had an outstanding day with 4 saves. William Mendoza, Wilson, Andrea Garza, and Andrew Weekes each scored one goal.

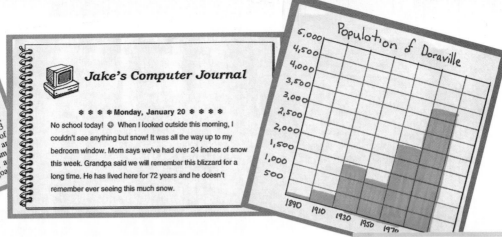

Jake's Computer Journal

✳ ✳ ✳ ✳ **Monday, January 20** ✳ ✳ ✳ ✳

No school today! ☺ When I looked outside this morning, I couldn't see anything but snow! It was all the way up to my bedroom window. Mom says we've had over 24 inches of snow this week. Grandpa said we will remember this blizzard for a long time. He has lived here for 72 years and he doesn't remember ever seeing this much snow.

As you study your community's history, remember that history is happening every day. And *you* are a part of that history. You may wish to keep a journal or scrapbook of events that are important to you. Someday, when you become an older member of your community, a group of third graders may ask you what life was like years ago. Just think how much fun it would be to tell them about it!

 What social studies skills can you use to tell others about the history of your community?

Students Help Plan New City Park

By Peggy Hamilton
Daily News Staff Writer

Third grade students at Dora Heights Elementary School met with city planners yesterday to provide input for the new park. The park will be located in the vacant lot on the west side of City Hall and will include a playground. The students were asked to describe the kinds of features they'd like to see in the playground, and the kids had plenty to say.

"We hope there will be lots of slides," said Zachary Herbst. "And many places for climbing."

Tamika Watson described how her sister, a wheel-chair user, has enjoyed the playground at the park in nearby Westville. That playground has specially designed ramps and areas that are built for wheel chair access.

"We want our new playground to have places where *all* children can play and have fun," said Tamika.

City officials will be looking for volunteers to help build the park, beginning sometime in May.

LESSON 5 REVIEW

Check Understanding

1. **Recall the Facts** What are the members of a historical society interested in?
2. **Focus on the Main Idea** Name three ways you can learn about the history of your community.

Think Critically

3. **Explore Viewpoints** Would two older members of your community tell the same story about your community's past? Explain.

Show What You Know

Make a List A time capsule is a container that holds papers and other objects that tell about life in a certain time. The time capsule is put in a safe place for people to open years later. What would you put in a time capsule to be opened a century from now? Make a list of 10 things, and explain why you chose each one.

MELISSA POE FIGHTS POLLUTION

When Melissa Poe was 9 years old, she wrote a letter to the President and asked him to stop pollution. Many weeks went by, but she did not hear from the President. So she came up with another idea.

She called an advertising company and asked to have a copy of her letter put on a billboard. The company put her letter on several billboards. Adults and children wrote to Melissa and asked how they could help.

Melissa started a club and called it Kids For A Clean Environment (Kids FACE®). Today it has more than 30,000 members around the world. All of them are working to stop pollution in their communities.

The President finally did write back. But, his letter was not very helpful. It was a letter that told Melissa to stay in school. The letter did not say anything about fighting pollution. By the time Melissa got the letter, she had already started Kids FACE.

Since Melissa has started Kids FACE, she has been invited to speak at many places, including the White House. Melissa hopes to become President someday!

Dear Mr. President,
   Please will you do something about pollution.
I want to live till I am a 100 years old.
   Mr. President, if you ignore this letter
We will all die of pollution.
                              Please Help!
                              Melissa Poe, Age 9
                              Nashville, Tennessee

THINK AND APPLY

Is there something you would like to do for your community? Write down your idea, and think of a plan. Then write a paragraph that will persuade people to follow your plan. Read your paragraph to your classmates. When all of you have read your paragraphs, vote for two plans you would like to follow.

◄ Melissa Poe shakes hands with Vice-President Al Gore. He helped in the Kid's Earth Flag celebration. The boy below signs a piece of the Kid's Earth Flag which was started by Kids FACE. The flag, made by children around the world, shows how they feel about the environment. ▼

UNIT 6

STORY CLOTH

Follow the pictures shown in this Story Cloth to help you review what you have learned in Unit 6.

Summarize the Main Ideas

1. Some things in a community change, and some things stay the same.

2. Changes in a community can be slow, fast, planned, or unplanned.

3. Growth in a community can sometimes create problems.

4. Every community has a history.

Write a Poem   Choose any of the events in this story cloth, and write a poem about how the community changed and what affect those changes had on the people in the community. Read your poem to the class.

Make a Class Scrapbook   Find out how your community got started. Perhaps some of the community streets, buildings, or schools are named after founders or early settlers. Ask local or state libraries and historical societies to help you get information. Then write a one-page report that describes your findings. Include any pictures or maps you could find. Put your report in a class scrapbook. Share the scrapbook with community leaders.

COOPERATIVE LEARNING WORKSHOP

Remember
- Share your ideas.
- Cooperate with others to plan your work.
- Take responsibility for your work.
- Show your group's work to the class.
- Discuss what you learned by working together.

Activity 1

Make a Diary of a Disaster

Choose a disaster that has happened to a community. Collect newspaper and magazine articles about the disaster. Then use the information you have gathered to make a diary about it. In your diary, explain what caused the disaster and how it affected the community. Tell how people in the community worked together to help each other.

Activity 2

Make a History Minibook

Make a minibook that shows how Mexico City has changed over time. Your minibook should have 12 or more pages with pictures on them.

The pictures should be in order from the earliest time to the latest time. Staple the pages together. Then ask other groups to look through the pages to find out how the city has changed.

Activity 3

Use a Computer

Visit your library to gather information about the population of your community. Find out the populations of as many years as possible. Then use a computer to put the numbers into tables and graphs. You can study the graphs to see how the population of your community has changed over time.

CONNECT MAIN IDEAS

Use this graphic organizer to show how the unit's main ideas are connected. First, copy the organizer onto a separate sheet of paper. Then, write one detail for each main idea.

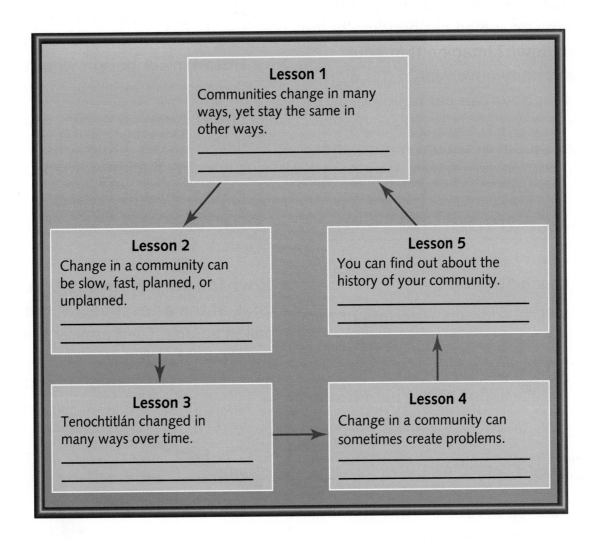

Lesson 1
Communities change in many ways, yet stay the same in other ways.
_____
_____

Lesson 2
Change in a community can be slow, fast, planned, or unplanned.
_____
_____

Lesson 5
You can find out about the history of your community.
_____
_____

Lesson 3
Tenochtitlán changed in many ways over time.
_____
_____

Lesson 4
Change in a community can sometimes create problems.
_____
_____

USE VOCABULARY

Words that describe time and culture are important when you write about history. Write a paragraph about your community using each of the following words in a sentence.

ancestor   century   custom   decade   tradition

WRITE MORE ABOUT IT

Write a Letter   How do you feel when you see an old building being torn down? Imagine that your community government has plans to tear down an old building. Write a letter to persuade others that they should or should not go ahead with the government's plans.

CHECK UNDERSTANDING

1. What can cause a community to change quickly?

2. Which is longer, a decade or a century?

3. Who were the people who built Tenochtitlán? Who built Mexico City?

THINK CRITICALLY

1. **Past to Present**   How can studying artifacts help you learn about people who lived long ago?

2. **Think More About It**   History is the story of people and how communities have changed over time. How can you help make sure that the changes in your community will make it better?

3. **Personally Speaking**   Which of the following jobs would you choose to do? Tell how your job would help your community.

   Historian—A person who studies the past and writes about it.

   City Planner—A person who helps citizens decide where their city's new buildings, roads, and parks should be built.

APPLY SKILLS

How to Learn from Artifacts
Look at the artifact below. It is called an *adz.* Then answer the questions that follow.

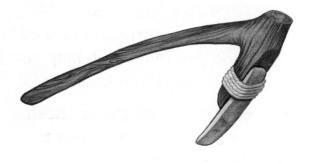

1. What do you think this tool is made of?

2. What present-day tool does it look like?

3. How do you think people long ago used this tool?

How to Compare Maps from Different Times

Compare this map to the map on pages A2–A3, and answer the following questions.

NORTH AND SOUTH AMERICA, 1546

1. Which map makes it easier to tell where countries are located?
2. How do you think each map was made? Why do you think that?

How to Solve a Problem Read these paragraphs, and answer the questions that follow.

An oil spill in Valdez, Alaska, caused many problems for the otters that lived there. When an otter is covered with oil, its body cannot stay warm. Unless the oil is removed, the otter will die.

To solve this problem, volunteers decided to remove the oil from the otters. They captured otters and brought them to special cleaning areas. The otters were washed gently with soap and water. Then their fur was allowed to dry. The washings were repeated until all the oil was removed. During the first summer after the spill, 348 otters were captured and cleaned. Of those otters, 226 lived.

1. What steps did volunteers take to help solve the problem?
2. Do you think the rescue workers were successful in solving the problem? Why or why not?

READ MORE ABOUT IT

Letting Swift River Go by Jane Yolen. Illustrated by Barbara Cooney. Little, Brown. A young girl tells how the Swift River in Massachusetts formed the Quabbin Reservoir.

McCrephy's Field by Christopher A. Myers and Lynne Born Myers. Houghton Mifflin. After 50 years, Joe McCrephy returns to his family's land.

Under the Moon by Dyan Sheldon. Dial. After she finds an artifact in her backyard, a girl dreams about what the area was once like.

FOR YOUR REFERENCE

CONTENTS

GAZETTEER

This gazetteer is a geographical dictionary that will help you locate places discussed in this book. The page number tells where each place appears on a map.

A

Adirondack Mountains (ad•uh•RAHN•dak) A mountain range in northeastern New York. *p. 257*

Afghanistan A country in western Asia. *p. 166*

Africa The second-largest continent. *p. 35*

Alabama A state in the southeastern United States. *p. 33*

Alaska A state of the United States, in the northwestern corner of North America. *p. 33*

Albany The capital of New York. *p. 117*

Algeria A country in northwest Africa. *p. 285*

Amarillo A city in northwestern Texas. *p. 268*

Amazon River A river in South America; second-longest in the world. *p. 119*

Annapolis The capital of Maryland. *p. 117*

Antarctica A continent surrounding the South Pole; covered by an ice cap. *p. 35*

Appalachian Mountains (a•puh•LAY•chuhn) A mountain range in the eastern United States. *p. 87*

Arctic Ocean The body of water north of the Arctic Circle. *p. 34*

Arizona A state in the southwestern United States. *p. 33*

Arkansas A state in the south central United States. *p. 33*

Asia The largest continent. *p. 35*

Atlanta The capital of Georgia. *p. 117*

Atlantic Ocean The ocean that separates North and South America from Europe and Africa. *p. 33*

Augusta The capital of Maine. *p. 117*

Aurora A city in Ohio. *p. 78*

Austin The capital of Texas. *p. 117*

Australia The smallest continent. *p. 35*

B

Baltimore A city on the Chesapeake Bay in Maryland. *p. 148*

Bangladesh (bahn•gluh•DESH) A country in southern Asia. *p. 166*

Baton Rouge (bat•uhn ROOZH) The capital of Louisiana. *p. 117*

Beaumont (BOH•mahnt) An industrial city in southeastern Texas. *p. 268*

Bell A city in Oklahoma. *p. 253*

Bhutan (boo•TAN) A kingdom on the northeastern border of India. *p. 166*

Billings A city on the Yellowstone River in south central Montana. *p. 98*

Bismarck The capital of North Dakota. *p. 98*

Boise The capital of Idaho. *p. 129*

Bombay The capital of Maharashtra, India. *p. 166*

Boston The capital of Massachusetts. *p. 87*

Botswana (baht•SWAHN•uh) A country in southern Africa. *p. 285*

Brasília (bruh•ZIL•yuh) The capital of Brazil; designed by Lúcio Costa. *p. 119*

Brazil A country in South America; covers about half of the continent. *p. 119*

British Columbia A province on the Pacific coast of Canada. *p. 57*

Burundi (bu•ROON•dee) A country in east central Africa. *p. 285*

C

Cahokia (kuh•HOH•kee•uh) A village in Illinois located where the Missouri River joins the Mississippi River. *p. 98*

Calcutta (kal•KUH•tuh) The capital of West Bengal, in eastern India. *p. 166*

California A state in the southwestern United States. *p. 33*

Canada A country in North America. *p. 33*

Cape Town A seaport city in the Cape Province of South Africa. *p. 285*

Cape Verde Islands A string of volcanic islands in the Atlantic Ocean. *p. 285*

Caribbean Sea (kar•uh•BEE•uhn) A part of the Atlantic Ocean; the West Indies and Central and South Americas form its boundaries on three sides. *p. 142*

Carson City The capital of Nevada. *p. 117*

Casper A city in central Wyoming. *p. 98*

Central America Countries between North and South America, from Mexico to Colombia. *p. 142*

Chad A country in north central Africa. *p. 285*

Charleston A seaport city in South Carolina. *p. 148*

Charlotte The largest city in North Carolina. *p. 321*

Cheyenne (shy•AN) The capital of Wyoming. *p. 117*

Chicago A city in northeastern Illinois. *p. 87*

China A country in eastern Asia. *p. 142*

Cincinnati A city in southwestern Ohio. *p. 98*

Cleveland The second-largest city in Ohio; located in the northern part of the state. *p. 78*

coastal plain One of the two major plains along the coast in the United States. *p. 87*

Colorado A state in the western United States. *p. 33*

Colorado River A river in the southwestern United States. *p. 49*

Columbia The capital of South Carolina. *p. 117*

Columbus The capital of Ohio. *p. 117*

Concord The capital of New Hampshire. *p. 117*

Congo A country in central Africa. *p. 285*

Connecticut A state in the northeastern United States. *p. 33*

Coral Gables A city in southeastern Florida, on the Biscayne Bay. *p. 318*

Corpus Christi (KAWR•puhs KRIS•tee) A city in southern Texas. *p. 268*

Cuba An island in the West Indies. *p. A2*

D

Dallas A city in northeastern Texas. *p. 87*

Delaware A state in the eastern United States. *p. 33*

Delhi (DEL•ee) A city in northern India, on the banks of the Yamuna River. *p. 166*

Denver The capital of Colorado. *p. 117*

Des Moines (dih•MOYN) The capital of Iowa; the largest city in the state. *p. 117*

Detroit The largest city in Michigan. *p. 148*

Dover The capital of Delaware. *p. 117*

Durham A city in northeastern North Carolina. *p. 314*

E

Eastern Cape A province in South Africa. *p. 287*

Eastern Hemisphere (HEHM•uh•sfeer) The eastern half of the Earth. *p. 36*

East Los Angeles A neighborhood in Los Angeles, California. *p. 143*

Egypt A country in northeastern Africa; the Nile River, the longest river in the world, is here. *p. 285*

El Paso A city in western Texas. *p. 105*

equator An imaginary line on the Earth that is halfway between the poles. *p. 35*

Ethiopia (ee•thee•OH•pee•uh) A country in eastern Africa. *p. 285*

Europe The second-smallest continent. *p. 35*

Everglades National Park A large marshland in southern Florida. *p. 318*

F

Florida A state in the southeastern United States. *p. 33*

Frankfort The capital of Kentucky. *p. 117*

Free State A province in South Africa. *p. 287*

G

Galveston A port city in southeastern Texas; on Galveston Island. *p. 268*

Ganges River (GAN•jeez) A river in northern and northeastern India. *p. 166*

Georgia A state in the southeastern United States. *p. 33*

Ghana A country in western Africa. *p. 285*

Great Basin An area of low, dry land in the western United States. *p. 87*

Great Lakes Chain of five lakes between the United States and Canada. *p. 33*

Great Plains A large area of plains in the west central United States. *p. 87*

Greenland An island off northeast North America. *p. 141*

Greensboro A city in north central North Carolina. *p. 314*

Greenville A city in eastern North Carolina. *p. 314*

Guinea (GIN•ee) A country in western Africa, on the Atlantic Ocean. *p. 285*

Gulf of Mexico A body of water on the southeastern coast of North America. *p. 33*

H

Harlem A neighborhood in New York City. *p. 148*

Harrisburg The capital of Pennsylvania. *p. 117*

Hartford The capital of Connecticut. *p. 117*

Hawaii A state made up of a string of volcanic islands in the north central Pacific Ocean. *p. 33*

Helena The capital of Montana. *p. 117*

Homestead A city in southeast Florida. *p. 318*

Honolulu The capital of Hawaii. *p. 117*

Hudson River A river in New York; begins in the Adirondack Mountains. *p. 257*

I

Idaho A state in the northwestern United States. *p. 33*

Illinois A state in the central United States. *p. 33*

India A country in Asia. *p. 142*

Indiana A state in the north central United States. *p. 33*

Indianapolis The capital of Indiana. *p. 117*

Indus River A river in Asia. *p. 166*

Iowa A state in the north central United States. *p. 33*

Iran An Islamic country in southwestern Asia; formerly known as Persia. *p. 166*

J

Japan A country in the western Pacific Ocean, off the east coast of Asia. *p. 142*

Jefferson City The capital of Missouri. *p. 117*

Johannesburg A city in northeastern South Africa. *p. 285*

Juneau (JOO•noh) The capital of Alaska. *p. 117*

K

Kansas A state in the central United States. *p. 33*

Kansas City A city in Kansas. *p. 148*

Kentucky A state in the east central United States. *p. 33*

Kenya A country in eastern Africa; borders the Indian Ocean. *p. 285*

Knoxville A city in Tennessee, on the Tennessee River. *p. 87*

Krishna River A river in southern India; empties into the Bay of Bengal. *p. 166*

L

Lake Texcoco A dry lake near Mexico City; used to be the site of Tenochtitlán. *p. 327*

Lansing The capital of Michigan. *p. 117*

Laredo A city in southern Texas. *p. 268*

Lesotho (luh•SOH•toh) A kingdom in southern Africa. *p. 285*

Libya A country in northern Africa. *p. 285*

Lincoln The capital of Nebraska. *p. 107*

Little Rock The capital of Arkansas. *p. 117*

London A city in England. The Thames River flows through this city. *p. 95*

Los Angeles A city in California. *p. 105*

Louisiana A state in the southern United States. *p. 33*

Louisville A city in north central Kentucky, on the Ohio River. *p. 148*

Lubbock A city in Texas. *p. 268*

M

Madagascar (mad•uh•GAS•ker) A country off the southeastern coast of Africa. *p. 285*

Madison The capital of Wisconsin. *p. 117*

Madras A city in India on the Coromandel Coast; main port for southeastern India. *p. 166*

Maine A state in the northeastern United States. *p. 33*

Mali A country in western Africa. *p. 285*

Maryland A state in the eastern United States. *p. 33*

Massachusetts A state in the northeastern United States. *p. 33*

Memphis A city in southwestern Tennessee, on the Mississippi River. *p. 98*

Mexico A country in southern North America; borders on the Pacific Ocean and the Gulf of Mexico. *p. 33*

Mexico City The capital of Mexico. *p. 327*

Miami A city in southeastern Florida, on the Biscayne Bay. *p. 142*

Michigan A state in the north central United States. *p. 33*

Minneapolis A city in southeastern Minnesota. *p. 87*

Minnesota A state in the northern United States. *p. 33*

Mississippi A state in the southern United States. *p. 33*

Mississippi River The longest river in the United States. *p. 87*

Missouri A state in the central United States. *p. 33*

Missouri River A river in the western United States; joins the Mississippi. *p. 87*

Montana A state in the northwestern United States. *p. 33*

Montgomery The capital of Alabama. *p. 117*

Montpelier (mahnt•PEEL•yer) The capital of Vermont. *p. 117*

N

Nashville The capital of Tennessee. *p. 117*

Nebraska A state in the central United States. *p. 33*

Nepal A kingdom on the northeastern border of India. *p. 166*

Nevada A state in the western United States. *p. 33*

New Hampshire A state in the northeastern United States. *p. 33*

New Jersey A state in the eastern United States. *p. 33*

New Mexico A state in the southwestern United States. *p. 33*

New Orleans A city in southeastern Louisiana. *p. 87*

New York A state in the northeastern United States. *p. 33*

New York City A city in New York. *p. 105*

Nigeria (ny•JIR•ee•uh) A country in western Africa. *p. 285*

North America A continent; includes the United States, Canada, and Mexico. *p. 34*

North Carolina A state in the southeastern United States. *p. 33*

North Dakota A state in the northwestern United States. *p. 33*

Northern Hemisphere The northern half of the Earth. *p. 37*

North Korea A country on the eastern coast of Asia. *p. 142*

North Pole The northernmost place on Earth; surrounded by the Arctic Ocean. *p. 36*

O

Ohio A north central state in the United States; borders on Lake Erie. *p. 33*

Ohio River A river in the north central United States. *p. 87*

Oklahoma A state in the southwestern United States. *p. 33*

Oklahoma City The capital of Oklahoma; largest city in the state. *p. 117*

Olympia The capital of Washington. *p. 117*

Omaha A city on the plains of Nebraska. *p. 107*

Oregon A state in the northwestern United States. *p. 33*

Orlando A city in central Florida. *p. 87*

P

Pacific Ocean A body of water that extends from between the western coasts of the North and South Americas to Australia and the eastern coast of Asia. *p. 33*

Pakistan (PAK•ih•stan) A country in southern Asia. *p. 166*

Pennsylvania A state in the northeastern United States. *p. 33*

Philadelphia A city in southeastern Pennsylvania. *p. 148*

Philippines A country made up of islands off the southeastern coast of China. *p. 142*

Phoenix The capital of Arizona. *p. 49*

Pierre (PIH•er) The capital of South Dakota, on the Missouri River. *p. 117*

Pittsburgh A city in southwestern Pennsylvania. *p. 98*

Platte River A river in the central United States; joins the Missouri River. *p. 98*

Pretoria (prih•TOHR•ee•uh) The capital of South Africa. *p. 285*

Providence The capital of Rhode Island. *p. 117*

R

Raleigh (RAHL•ee) The capital of North Carolina. *p. 117*

Rhode Island A state in the northeastern United States. *p. 33*

Richmond The capital of Virginia. *p. 117*

Rio de Janeiro (REE•oh DAY zhun•NAIR•oh) A city in Brazil; famous for its beaches and mountains. *p. 119*

Rio Grande River A river in the southwestern United States. *p. 78*

Rocky Mountains A mountain range in western North America. *p. 87*

Rwanda (roo•AHN•duh) A country in east central Africa. *p. 285*

S

Sacramento The capital of California. *p. 87*

Salem The capital of Oregon. *p. 117*

Salt Lake City The capital of Utah. *p. 117*

San Francisco A large port city in California. *p. 89*

Santa Fe The capital of New Mexico. *p. 117*

Seattle A large port city in western Washington. *p. 105*

Senegal (sen•ih•GAWL) A country in western Africa. *p. 285*

Somalia (soh•MAHL•ee•uh) A country in eastern Africa. *p. 285*

South Africa A country in southern Africa. *p. 285*

South America A continent in the Western Hemisphere; includes most of Latin America. *p. 35*

South Carolina A state in the southeastern United States. *p. 33*

South Dakota A state in the northwestern United States. *p. 33*

Southern Hemisphere The southern half of the Earth. *p. 37*

South Korea A country on the eastern coast of Asia. *p. 142*

South Pole The southernmost place on Earth; located in west central Antarctica. *p. 36*

Springfield The capital of Illinois. *p. 117*

Sri Lanka An island in the Indian Ocean, south of India. *p. 166*

St. Lawrence River A river in Canada that forms a border between Canada and New York. *p. 257*

St. Louis A large city in Missouri. *p. 87*

St. Paul The capital of Minnesota. *p. 117*

Sudan (SOO•DAN) A country in northeastern Africa. *p. 285*

T

Tahlequah (TAL•uh•qwaw) A city in northeastern Oklahoma. *p. 253*

Tallahassee The capital of Florida. *p. 117*

Tampa A city in west Florida; on Tampa Bay. *p. 318*

Tanzania (tan•zuh•NEE•uh) A country in eastern Africa. *p. 285*

Tennessee A state in the southeast central United States. *p. 33*

Tennessee River A river in the southeastern United States. *p. 98*

Tenochtitlán (tay•nawch•tee•TLAHN) The capital of the Aztec Empire; Mexico City is now in the same location. *p. 322*

Terlingua A ghost town in Texas. *p. 316*

Texas A state in the southern United States. *p. 33*

Thames River A river in London, England. *p. 95*

Togo A country in western Africa. *p. 285*

Topeka The capital of Kansas. *p. 117*

Trenton The capital of New Jersey. *p. 117*

Tucson (TOO•sahn) A city in Arizona. *p. 49*

Tunisia (t(y)oo•NEE•zhee•uh) A country in northern Africa. *p. 285*

U

Uganda (y)oo•GAN•duh) A country in eastern Africa. *p. 285*

Utah A state in the western United States. *p. 33*

V

Vancouver A city in Canada. *p. 57*

Vermont A state in the northeastern United States. *p. 33*

Vietnam A country in southeastern Asia. *p. 142*

Virginia A state in the eastern United States. *p. 33*

W–Z

Washington A state in the northwestern United States. *p. 33*

Washington, DC The capital of the United States. *p. 117*

Western Hemisphere The western half of the Earth. *p. 36*

West Virginia A state in the eastern United States. *p. 33*

Wichita A city in south central Kansas. *p. 98*

Wisconsin A state in the north central United States. *p. 33*

Wyoming A state in the northwestern United States. *p. 33*

Yellowstone River A river in the northwestern United States. *p. 98*

Yuma A city in Arizona, along the Colorado River. *p. 33*

Zaire (ZY•er) A country in Africa. *p. 285*

Zimbabwe (zim•BAHB•way) A country in south central Africa. *p. 285*

GLOSSARY

This glossary contains important social studies words and their definitions. Each word is respelled as it would be in a dictionary. When you see this mark ´ after a syllable, pronounce that syllable with more force than the other syllables. The page number at the end of the definition tells where to find the word in your book.

add, āce, câre, pälm; end, ēqual; it, īce; odd, ōpen, ôrder; tŏŏk, pōōl; up, bûrn; yōō as *u* in *fuse*; oil; pout; ə as *a* in *above*, *e* in *sicken*, *i* in *possible*, *o* in *melon*, *u* in *circus*; **ch**eck; ri**ng**; **th**in; **th**is; **zh** as in *vision*

A

advertisement (ad•vər•tīz´mənt) Information that a producer provides about products and services *p. 210*

agriculture (ag´rə•kul•chər) The raising of crops and farm animals *p. 174*

allegiance (ə•lē´jəns) Respect for the flag and for what the flag represents *p. 279*

ancestor (an´ses•tər) A member of a person's family who lived a long time ago, such as a great-great-grandparent *p. 48*

anthem (an´thəm) A song of patriotism *p. 278*

archaeologist (är•kē•ol´ə•jist) A scientist who looks for artifacts and tries to explain how they were used *p. 326*

artifact (är´tə•fakt) Object that we find that was used by people in the past *p. 326*

B

ballot (bal´ət) A list that shows all the possible choices in an election *p. 262*

bar graph (bär graf) A graph with bars of different heights that show amounts of things *p. 200*

barter (bär´tər) To trade one product or service for another *p. 214*

basic needs (bā´sik nēdz) Food, clothing, and shelter *p. 194*

border (bôr´dər) The lines that are drawn on the map to show where one state or country ends and another begins *p. 116*

boundary (boun´də•rē) Another word for border *p. 116*

branch (branch) A smaller river that flows into a larger one *p. 98*

C

campaign (kam•pān´) A way to get voters to choose one candidate instead of another *p. 263*

canal (kə•nal´) A waterway that is built by people *p. 323*

candidate (kan´də•dāt) Someone who is running for office *p. 262*

capital city (kap´ə•təl sit´ē) Where the leaders of the country or state meet and work *p. 111*

capitol (kap´ə•təl) The building where lawmakers meet *p. 113*

cardinal directions (kär´də•nəl di•rek´shənz) The main directions: **N** means north, **S** means south, **E** means east, and **W** means west *p. 39*

causeway (kôz´wā) A wide road built over the water *p. 323*

century (sen´chə•rē) A length of time that is 100 years *p. 311*

citizen (sit´ə•zən) A person who lives in a community *p. 40*

climate (klī´mət) The kind of weather a place has in each season year after year *p. 83*

coast (kōst) The land next to oceans, or on the shores of lakes, or along rivers *p. 82*

communication links (kə•myōō•nə•kā´shen lingks) Machines that let people who are far apart communicate with one another *p. 226*

compass rose (kum´pəs rōz) The symbol on a map that tells you directions, or which way to go *p. 39*

competition (kom•pə•tish´ən) What happens when companies produce and sell the same product *p. 208*

compromise (kom´prə•mīz) Giving up some of the things you want in order to resolve a disagreement *p. 256*

conflict (kän´flikt) A disagreement *p. 256*

conflict resolution (kän´flikt re•zə•lü´shən) A way to try to solve the problems between people or groups *p. 256*

Congress (kong´grəs) The part of the government that makes new laws for the nation *p. 272*

consequence (kän´sə•kwens) Something that happens as a result of an action *p. 41*

Constitution (kon•stə•tōō´shən) The set of laws the government of the United States follows *p. 260*

consumer (kən•sōō´mər) The person who buys a product or a service *p. 207*

continent (kon´tə•nənt) One of the seven main land areas on the Earth *p. 34*

cooperate (kō•ä´pə•rāt) How people work together to keep their community a safe and peaceful place *p. 40*

council (koun´səl) A group of people who have been chosen by citizens to meet and solve problems *p. 251*

county (koun´tē) A part of a state *p. 114*

county seat (koun´tē sēt) A city or town where the leaders meet *p. 114*

crop (krop) A plant used by people for food or other needs *p. 106*

cross section (krôs sek´shən) A drawing or photo that shows what an object would look like if it were cut open *p. 206*

crossroads (krôs´rōdz) A place where two routes cross *p. 93*

culture (kul´chər) A people's way of life *p. 55*

custom (kus´təm) A way of doing something *p. 54*

D

decade (dek´ād) A length of time that is 10 years *p. 311*

decline (di•klīn´) Neighborhoods that were once busy but that now have empty shopping centers and empty homes *p. 319*

demand (di•mand´) The wish that people have for a product or a service *p. 209*

desert (dez´ərt) A place with a hot, dry climate *p. 84*

disaster (di•zas´tər) Something that happens that causes great harm to a community *p. 318*

distance scale (dis´təns skāl) The scale on a map that measures the distance, or how far it is, between two places *p. 38*

E

election (i•lek´shən) An event in which people vote to choose leaders or vote for or against new laws *p. 260*

empire (em´pīr) The land and people under the control of a powerful nation *p. 324*

equator (i•kwā´tər) An imaginary line that is halfway between the North Pole and the South Pole *p. 36*

export (eks´pôrt) To send a product or resource out of a country to another country *p. 227*

F

fact (fakt) Statement that is true *p. 213*

ferry (fer´ē) A boat that carries people and goods across a waterway *p. 94*

folktale (fōk´tāl) A traditional story that often teaches a lesson *p. 168*

ford (fôrd) A shallow place in a waterway that can be crossed by walking, riding, or driving *p. 94*

founders (faûn´dərz) The people who start a community *p. 56*

fuel (fyo͝ol) A resource, such as oil, that is found inside the Earth *p. 108*

G

gateway (gāt´wā) An entrance *p. 101*

ghost town (gōst toun) A town with buildings but no people *p. 110*

globe (glōb) A round model of the Earth *p. 36*

government (guv´ərn•mənt) A group of elected citizens who make the rules for a community *p. 40*

government services (guv´ərn•mənt sər´va•səz) Services that are provided for all the citizens of a community *p. 252*

governor (guv´ər•nər) The elected leader of a state's government *p. 265*

grid (grid) A set of lines the same distance apart that cross one another to form boxes *p. 222*

growing season (grō´ing sē´zən) The months in which crops can grow *p. 107*

H

harbor (här´bər) A protected place where ships can stay safe from high waves and strong winds *p. 89*

hemisphere (hem´ə•sfi(ə)r) Another way of saying "half of the Earth" *p. 36*

heritage (her´ə•tij) The culture left to someone by his or her ancestors *p. 149*

historical society (his•tôr´ə•kəl sə•sī´ə•tē) A group of people, usually volunteers, who have a special interest in the history of their community *p. 334*

history (his´tə•rē) The story of what has happened in a place *p. 48*

holiday (hä´lə•dā) A special day for remembering a person or an event that has importance for the people in a community *p. 158*

human-made features (hyo͞o´mən•mād fē´chərz) The buildings, bridges, or roads that people have added to a place *p. 85*

human resources (hyo͞o´mən rē´sôr•səz) The people who work for a company *p. 204*

I

immigrant (im´ə•grənt) A person who moves from one country to live in another *p. 141*

import (im´pôrt) To bring a product or resource into a country from another country *p. 227*

industry (in´dus•trē) All the companies that make the same product or provide the same service *p. 205*

intermediate directions (in•tər•mē´dē•it di•rek´shənz) The directions that are midway between two cardinal directions: northeast, southeast, southwest, and northwest *p. 105*

international trade (in•tər•nash´ən•el trād) Trade between people in different countries *p. 225*

invention (in•ven´shən) Something that has been made for the first time *p. 211*

J

judge (juj) A citizen who is chosen to work as a leader in the courts *p. 43*

jury (jûr´ē) A group of 6 to 12 citizens who sit in the courtroom and listen to what both sides have to say *p. 266*

L

landform (land´fôrm) The natural feature, or shape, of land. *p. 80*

law (lô) A rule that helps make a community a safe place to live *p. 41*

literature (lit´ə•rə•chər) The books, poetry, stories, and plays written by people to share ideas *p. 149*

location (lō•kā´shən) Where something is found *p. 31*

M

majority rule (mə•jôr´ə•tē rōol) When more than half of the people voting choose one candidate or decision *p. 263*

manufacture (man•yə•fak´chər) To make all kinds of goods *p. 102*

map (map) A picture that shows the location of something *p. 31*

map key (map kē) A box that tells what the symbols on the map stand for *p. 38*

marketing (mär´kit•ing) Planning how to sell a product to the community *p. 203*

mayor (mā´ər) The leader of a city or town government *p. 42*

mediator (mē´dē•ā•tər) A person who works to help both sides settle their disagreement *p. 256*

mineral (min´ər•əl) A resource, such as gold, that is found inside the Earth *p. 108*

minority rights (mə•nor´ə•tē rīts) When those who did not vote for the winner still keep all their rights *p. 263*

missionary (mish´ən•er•ē) A person who is sent to tell others about his or her beliefs *p. 50*

mountain range (moun´tən rānj) A large group of mountains *p. 80*

N

natural resource (nach´ər•əl rē´sôrs) Something found in nature that is useful to people *p. 106*

O

opinions (ə•pin´yənz) What someone believes or thinks *p. 213*

opportunity (ä•pər•tōō´nə•tē) The chance to find a job, get an education, or have a better way of life *p. 140*

P

patriotism (pā´trē•ə•ti•zəm) The love that people have for their country *p. 276*

peninsula (pə•nin´sə•lə) A piece of land that has water almost all the way around it *p. 82*

petition (pə•tish´ən) A written request for government action that people sign *p. 250*

physical feature (fiz´i•kəl fē´chər) Something found in nature such as weather, plant life, land, and water *p. 79*

pictograph (pik´tə•graf) A graph that has small pictures that stand for groups of things *p. 200*

plain (plān) A landform that is flat or gently rolling *p. 81*

planning (plan´ing) A way to help communities grow in an organized way *p. 317*

plateau (pla•tō´) A landform that has steep sides and a flat top *p. 81*

pledge (plej) A promise *p. 279*

point of view (point əv vyōō) The way a person feels about something *p. 156*

pollution (pə•lü´shən) Anything that makes the air, land, or water unclean *p. 328*

population (pop•yə•lā´shən) The number of people who live in a place *p. 146*

port (pôrt) A place that has deep water where ships can dock *p. 88*

price (prīs) The amount of money needed to buy a product or service *p. 208*

private property (prī´vit prop´ər•tē) Something that belongs to one person or a smaller group of people *p. 265*

producer (prə•dōō´sər) The person who makes a product *p. 201*

product (prod´əkt) Something that people make or grow, often to sell *p. 198*

province (prov´ins) The large area that forms part of some countries *p. 287*

public property (pub´lik prop´ər•tē) Something that belongs to all citizens *p. 265*

R

rain forest (rān fôr´əst) A thick forest that has a hot, wet climate *p. 119*

rapids (ra´pəds) The parts of rivers where the water runs very fast, often over rocks *p. 90*

raw materials (rô mə•tir´ē•əlz) Resources needed to make a product *p. 202*

religion (ri•li´jən) What a person believes about God or a set of gods *p. 140*

reservoir (rez´ər•vwär) A lake used for collecting and storing water *p. 310*

resource (rē´sôrs) Something that people use to make what they need *p. 45*

responsibility (ri•spon•sə•bil´ə•tē) A duty that citizens have *p. 44*

riverbank (riv´ər•bangk) The land beside the river *p. 97*

route (rōot) path from one place to another *p. 92*

rural (rŏor´əl) An area that is out in the countryside, away from cities and towns *p. 194*

S

sequence (sē´kwəns) The order in which things happen *p. 164*

service (sûr´vəs) Something one person does for another *p. 197*

solution (sə•lōo´shən) Way to solve a problem *p. 331*

state capital (stāt kap´ə•təl) A place where the lawmakers meet to make laws for a state *p. 114*

supply (sə•plī´) The amount of a product or service there is to be sold *p. 209*

Supreme Court (sə•prēm´ kôrt) The most important court in the United States *p. 274*

symbol (sim´bəl) An item that is used to stand for something that is real on the Earth *p. 38*

T

table (tā´bəl) A way to organize information *p. 146*

tax (taks) The money paid to the government to run a city, state, or country *p. 252*

technology (tek•nol´ə•jē) The use of machines, tools, and materials to make products faster and more easily *p. 201*

time line (tīm līn) A way to show when important events took place *p. 53*

trade center (trād sen´tər) A community where buying and selling goods is the main work *p. 90*

tradition (trə•dish´ən) The custom, or way of doing something, that is passed on from parents to children *p. 159*

V

valley (val´ē) The landform between a hill and a mountain range *p. 80*

volunteer (vol•ən•tir´) The people who work in a community without being paid *p. 47*

vote (vōt) The way people show what they think a group should do *p. 258*

W

wage (wāj) The money a worker is paid *p. 204*

INDEX

Page references for illustrations are set in italic type. An italic m indicates a map. Page references set in boldface type indicate the pages on which vocabulary words are defined.

A

Advertisement, 210, *210,* 213, *213*
Africa. *See* South Africa
African Americans
 art of, 149, *149*
 in dance, 151, *151*
 holiday customs and traditions of, 161, *161*
 literature of, 149, *149,* 152-155, *152-155*
 migration from South to North, 147-148, *147, m148*
 music of, 150-151, *150*
Agriculture (farming), **174**
 communities built near, 106-108, *106, m107, 108*
 product map of India, *m175*
Air pollution, 328-329, *328,* 331
Alaska, *88,* 115, *115,* 264, 272
Allegiance, 279
Amazon River, 119
American Indians. *See* Indians, American
Amish community, 186-199, *m195*
 barn raising in, 191-193, *192,* 196-197, *196*
 firefighting service in, 186-193, 197
 products and services traded with outside world, 197-199, *197-199*
 way of life in, 194-195, *194, 195*
Ancestor, 48
Andrew, Hurricane, 318, *318*
Anglos, 50, 52
Anthem, national, 278, 282
Anza, Juan Bautista de, 49
Appalachian Mountains, *80*
Archaeologists, 326
Arizona
 city hall in, *312*
 diverse cultures in, 50-51, 52, *52,* 54-55, *54-55*
 Indians in, 48, *48,* 49-51
 rivers of, *m49*
 See also Yuma, Arizona
Art, African American, 149
Artifacts, 326, *326*

B

Bald eagle, *282,* 290-291
Ballot, 262. *See also* Votes and voting; Voting rights
Baltimore, Maryland, 230-231
Banneker, Benjamin, 113, *113*
Bar graph, 200, *200*
Barn raising, 191-193, *192,* 196-197, *196*
Barrio, 144
Barter, 214, 215-221
Basic needs, 194
Bell, Oklahoma, 253-254, *m253*
Bell Sports, 202-204, *202-204*
Bicycle helmet, 202-204, *202-206*
Bicycles, trade in, 236
Big Sur, California, *82*
Bombay, India, *165*
Border, 116, *m117*
Boston, Massachusetts, 89, *m89*
Boundary, 116, *m117*
Branch (of river), 98, *m98*
Branches
 of national government, 269
Brasília, Brazil, 118-121, *m119, 120-121*
Brazil
 capital city of, 118-121, *m119, 120-121*
 exports and imports of, 228
Bridges, 94-95, *94, m95,* 102, *102*
British Columbia, 56-59, *56, m57, 58-59*
Bush, George, *271*
Business. *See* Industry; Trade
Butter churn, *100*
Buying, 207-209, *207-209*

C

Cahokia, 97-99, *97, m98*
California, *82*
 diversity in, 143-145, *143-145*
 natural disasters in, 122
 port cities in, 89, *m89,* 109
 representatives in Congress, 272, *272*
 state government in, 264
Campaign, 263
Canada, 56-59, *56, m57, 58-59,* 61
Canada Day, 61
Canal, 323
Candidate, 262
Capital city, 111
 of Brazil, 118-121, *m119, 120*
 of state, 114-115, *m114, 115-116, m117*
 of United States, 111-113, *112*
Capitol, 113, *115,* 272, 273, *311*
Cardinal directions, 39
Carter, Jimmy, *271*
Catawba Indians, 314
Causeway, 323
Century, 311
Changes
 in communities, *92,* 122-123, *122-123,* 298, 299-311, *299, 310-311,* 314-319, *314-318*
 fast, 316, *316*
 in land, 122-123, *122, 123*
 planned, 317, *317*
 in schools, 313, *313*
 slow and steady, 314-315, *314*
 unplanned, *298,* 318-319, *318*
Charlotte, North Carolina, 314-315, *314-315,* 320, *m321*
Cherokee Indians, 253-254, *253-254,* 255
Chinatown (Los Angeles), *143*
Chinese Americans
 in Arizona, 51, 52
 in California, *143*
 in Vancouver, 60, *60*
Chouteau, René Auguste, 99-100, *99*
Churches, *121, 312, 325*

For permission to reprint copyrighted material, grateful acknowledgment is made to the following sources:

Margaret Walker Alexander: From "Lineage" in *For My People* by Margaret Walker. Published by Yale University Press, 1942.

The Archives of Claude McKay, Carl Cowl, Administrator: "The Tropics in New York" by Claude McKay from *Selected Poems of Claude McKay.* Text copyright 1953 by Bookman Associates; text copyright © 1981 by Twayne Publishers.

Farrar, Straus & Giroux, Inc.: From *Saturday Sancocho* by Leyla Torres. Copyright © 1995 by Leyla Torres.

Good Books: From *Reuben and the Fire* by Merle Good, illustrated by P. Buckley Moss. Text copyright © 1993 by Merle Good; illustrations copyright © 1993 by P. Buckley Moss.

Mary C. Hearne and Owen Edward Thomas: Texas State Song, "Texas, Our Texas," by William J. Marsh. Lyrics copyright © 1925 by W. J. Marsh; lyrics copyright renewed 1953 by William J. Marsh. Published by Southern Music Company.

Houghton Mifflin Company: Grandfather's Journey by Allen Say. Copyright © 1993 by Allen Say.

Alfred A. Knopf, Inc.: "Color" from *The Panther and the Lash* by Langston Hughes. Text copyright © 1967 by Arna Bontemps and George Houston Bass.

Lothrop, Lee & Shepard Books, a division of William Morrow & Company, Inc.: Roxaboxen by Alice McLerran, illustrated by Barbara Cooney. Text copyright © 1991 by Alice McLerran; illustrations copyright © 1991 by Barbara Cooney.

Morrow Junior Books, a division of William Morrow & Company, Inc.: "Knoxville, Tennessee" from *Black Feelings, Black Talk, Black Judgment* by Nikki Giovanni. Text copyright © 1968, 1970 by Nikki Giovanni. From *City Green* by DyAnne DiSalvo-Ryan. Copyright © 1994 by DyAnne DiSalvo-Ryan.

Simon & Schuster Books for Young Readers, Simon & Schuster Children's Publishing Division: Aurora Means Dawn by Scott Russell Sanders, illustrated by Jill Kastner. Text copyright © 1989 by Scott Russell Sanders; illustrations copyright © 1989 by Jill Kastner.

Third World Press, Chicago: Haiku from *I've Been a Woman* by Sonia Sanchez. Text © 1978, 1985 by Sonia Sanchez.

Viking Penguin, a division of Penguin Books USA Inc.: Shaker Lane by Alice and Martin Provensen. Copyright © 1987 by Alice Provensen.

ILLUSTRATION CREDITS:

Jason Dowd, pp. 64–65; Katy Farmer, pp. 91, 92–93; Barbara Ericksen, pp. 124–125; Katy Farmer, pp. 152–155, 169; Uldis Klavins, pp. 178–179; Katy Farmer, pp. 206, 210, 213, 223, 227; Barbara Ericksen, pp. 232–233; Katy Farmer, pp. 237, 267 (right), 277; Uldis Klavins, pp. 292–293; David Schleinkoff, 338–339; Katy Farmer, p. 342

COVER CREDIT:

Keith Gold & Associates
All maps by GeoSystems

PHOTO CREDITS:

Key: Page positions are shown in abbreviated form as follows: (t)-top, (b)-bottom, (l)-left, (r)-right, (c)-center, (bg)-background, (fg)-foreground

Unit 1

Page iii Timothy Fuller; iv Beverly Brosius/Harcourt Brace & Company; v Michael Newman/PhotoEdit; vi Lawrence Migdale/Photo Researchers; vii Harcourt Brace & Company/Terry D. Sinclair; viii Ron Kunzman/Harcourt Brace & Company; 16 (bl) Buddy Mays/International Stock Photography; 16 (br) David Young-Wolff/PhotoEdit; 16-17 Terry D. Sinclair/Harcourt Brace & Company; 17 (bl) Timothy Fuller; 30 Harcourt Brace & Company; 40 Terry D. Sinclair/Harcourt Brace & Company; 41 Timothy Fuller; 42 Timothy Fuller; 43 Timothy Fuller; 44 Richard Hutchings/Photo Researchers, Inc.; 45 Timothy Fuller; 46 Timothy Fuller; 47 (t) Stephen McBrady/PhotoEdit; 47 (b) Timothy Fuller; 48 E.T. Corson-Clarissa Winsor Collection/Arizona Historical Society; 50 Yuma County Historical Society/Arizona Historical Society; 51 (t) Timothy Fuller; 51 (b) Yuma County Historical Society/Arizona Historical Society.; 52 (l) Timothy Fuller; 52 (r) Timothy Fuller; 54 Timothy Fuller; 55 (t) Margaret Finefrock/Unicorn Stock Photos; 55 (b) David Husten/Woodfin Camp & Associates; 56 City Of Vancouver Archives; 58 (l) Vancouver Public Library; 58 (r) Vancouver Public Library; 59 Greg Kinch/Black Star/Harcourt Brace & Company; 60 (t) Ed Gifford/Masterfile; 60 (b) Yvonne McDougall/Diarama Stock Photos; 61 Stock Montage; 62-63 James Magdanz; 62 (b) Harcourt Brace & Company/Ron Kunzman; 63 (t) James Magdanz; 63 (b) James Magdanz; 66 Ron Kunzman/Harcourt Brace & Company.

Unit 2

Page 70 (bl) Tibor Bognar/The Stock Market; 70 (br) Rathe 1990/FPG; 70-71 Mark Segal/Panoramic Images; 71 (bl) Bill Varie/The Image Bank; 71 (br) J.G. Edmanson/International Stock Photography; 79 Ranes Lynn/Photo Researchers, Inc.; 80-81 (t) Jeff Foott/DRK Photo; 80 (bl) David Muench Photography, Inc.; 80 (br) Jerry Whaley/Natural Selection Stock Photography; 80 (cr) Pat O'Hara/DRK; 81 (b) David Lissy/Natural Selection Stock Photography; 81 (tr) Stephen J. Krasemann/DRK; 82 (t) Stephen J. Krasemann/DRK; 82 (bl) David Muench Photography, Inc.; 82 (br) David Muench Photography, Inc.; 83 (l) Beverly Brosius/Harcourt Brace & Company; 83 (r) Myrleen Ferguson Cate/Index Stock Photography; 84 Telegraph Colour Library/FPG; 85 R. Mastroianni/Black Star/Harcourt Brace & Company; 88 Grant Heilman Photography; 90 (t) Runk/Schoenberger/Grant Heilman Photography; 90 (b) K. Vreeland/H. Armstrong Roberts, Inc.; 94 (t) Matthew McVay/Tony Stone Images; 94 (bl) Archive Photo/Popperfoto;

94 (br) Calvin Larsen/Photo Researchers, Inc.; 97 William Iseminger; 99 (b) Missouri Historical Society; 99 (tc) Jim Richardson/Westlight; 99 (tr) Ray Bial; 100 (l) Ray Bial; 100 (r) Chuck Schmeiser/Unicorn Stock Photos; 100 (c) Ray Bial; 101 Denver Public Library, Western History Department.; 102 Culver Pictures, Inc.; 103 J. Blank/H. Armstrong Roberts, Inc.; 104 International News Photos/UPI/Bettmann; 106 Tom Bean/DRK; 107 (t) Tony Stone Images; 107 (b) Robert Frerck/Tony Stone Images; 108 (b) Peter Christopher/Masterfile; 108 (tl) Grant Heilman Photography; 108 (tr) Dave Schaefer/The Picture Cube; 109 David L. Brown/The Picture Cube; 110 Tom Bean/DRK; 111 The Granger Collection; 112 (t) The Granger Collection; 112 (b) Andre Jenny/International Stock Photography; 113 (t) The Granger Collection; 113 (b) Schomburg Center for Research in Black Culture/Harcourt Brace & Company; 114 G. Ahrens/H. Armstrong Roberts; 115 Jeff Schultz/Alaska Stock Images; 118 Tony Stone Images; 120 Columbus Memorial Library at the Organization of American States; 121 Jose Fuste Raga/The Stock Market; 122-123 (inset) Wide World Photos; 122-123 Leverett Bradley/Tony Stone Images; 123 (inset) AP Photo; 126 Harcourt Brace & Company.

Unit 3

Page 130 (bl) Tom & Deeann McCarthy/The Stock Market; 130 (br) © 1995 Dale Higgins; 130-131 Tony Freeman/PhotoEdit; 131 (bl) Chris Boylan/Unicorn Stock Photos; 131 (br) Chromosohm/Sohm MCMXCII/Unicorn Stock Photos; 140 New York Daily News/Harcourt Brace & Company; 141 Harcourt Brace & Company; 142 Bruce Coleman, Inc.; 143 John Elk III/Bruce Coleman, Inc.; 144 (t) Michael Newman/PhotoEdit; 144 (c) Michael Newman/PhotoEdit; 144 (b) Mary Kate Denny/PhotoEdit; 145 (l) Gary Conner/PhotoEdit; 145 (r) Michael Newman/PhotoEdit; 147 Schomburg Center for Research in Black Culture; 149 (t) Schomburg Center for Research in Black Culture/WPA Photograph Collection; 149 (c) Culver Pictures, Inc.; 149 (b) Wide World Photos; 150 Archive Photos/Frank Driggs Collection; 151 Wide World Photos; 152 Wide World Photos; 153 The Granger Collection; 154 Wide World Photos; 155 (t) Schomburg Center for Research in Black Culture; 155 (b) Leandre Jackson; 157 National Portrait Gallery/Smithsonian Institution/Art Resource, NY; 159 (t) Ron Kunzman/Harcourt Brace & Company; 159 (b) Lawrence Migdale/Harcourt Brace & Company; 160 (t) Lawrence Migdale; 160 (bl) Lawrence Migdale/Harcourt Brace & Company; 160 (br) Harcourt Brace & Company; 161 (t) Lawrence Migdale; 161 (c) Lawrence Migdale; 161 (b) Lawrence Migdale/Harcourt Brace & Company; 162 (b) Lawrence Migdale/Harcourt Brace & Company; 163 Roy Morsch/The Stock Market; 165 Dallas & John Heaton/Westlight; 167 Frank Grant/International Stock Photography; 168 (t) Nick Wheeler/Westlight; 168 (b) Viviane Moos/The Stock

Market; 170 (t) Dinodia Picture Agency; 170 (b) Amy Reichman/Envision; 171 (tl) Terry D. Sinclair/Harcourt Brace & Company; 171 (tr) Brian Yarvin/Photo Researchers; 171 (bl) Pramod Mistry/Dinodia Picture Agency; 171 (br) Dinodia Picture Agency; 172 (t) Tom & Michele Grimm/International Stock Photography; 172 (b) Michael Howell/Envision; 173 Dinodia Picture Agency; 176 Lewis W. Hine/New York Public Library; 177 AP/Wide World Photos; 180 Terry Sinclair/Harcourt Brace & Company; 183 Auguste Renoir, *Woman with a Cat*, c. 1875, National Gallery of Art, Washington, D.C. Gift of Mr. and Mrs. Benjamin E. Levy. © 1995 National Gallery of Art Board of Trustees.

Unit 4

Page 184 (bl) Ron Kunzman/Harcourt Brace & Company; 184 (br) Ron Kunzman/Harcourt Brace & Company; 184-185 Ron Kunzman/Harcourt Brace & Company; 185 (bl) Ron Kunzman/Harcourt Brace & Company; 185 (br) Dilip/Mehta/The Stock Market; 194 Kevin O'Mooney/Odyssey; 195 Owen Franken/Stock, Boston; 196 Lisa Loucks Christenson/Absolute Stock & Assignment; 197 (t) Comstock; 197 (bl) Lee F. Snyder/Photo Researchers, Inc.; 197 (br) Michael J. Chimpf; 198 (t) Vanessa Vick/Photo Researchers, Inc.; 198 (b) Kevin O'Mooney/Odyssey/Chicago; 199 (t) W. Lynn Seldon, Jr.; 199 (b) Jon Feingersh/Stock, Boston; 201 (l) Paul Chauncey/The Stock Market; 201 (r) Ron Kunzman/Harcourt Brace & Company; 202-204 (all) © 1995 Matt Gilson; 205 Lawrence Migdale/Photo Researchers, Inc.; 207-211 (all) Ron Kunzman/Harcourt Brace & Company; 212 Mike Hall; 224 (l) Churchill & Klehr; 224 (r) Martha Cooper/Peter Arnold, Inc.; 225 (l) Harcourt Brace & Company/Terry D. Sinclair; 225 (r) Giraudon/Art Resource, NY; 226 (t) Charles Thatcher/Tony Stone Images; 226 (b) Terry D. Sinclair/Harcourt Brace & Company; 228 (c) Ron Kunzman/Harcourt Brace & Company; 228 (tl) Ron Kunzman/Harcourt Brace & Company; 228 (tr) Tony Freeman/PhotoEdit; 228 (bl) Tony Freeman/PhotoEdit; 228 (br) David Young-Wolff/PhotoEdit; 229 (c) Ron Kunzman/Harcourt Brace & Company; 229 (tl) Ron Kunzman/Harcourt Brace & Company; 229 (tr) Bradley Simmons/Bruce Coleman, Inc.; 229 (br) Ron Kunzman/Harcourt Brace & Company; 229 (cr) Ron Kunzman/Harcourt Brace & Company; 230 Harcourt Brace & Company/Black Star/John Troha; 231(all) courtesy, Umoja Children, Inc., Baltimore, Maryland; 233 Terry Sinclair/Harcourt Brace & Company.

Unit 5

Page 238 (bl) Will & Deni McIntyre/Photo Researchers, Inc.; 238 (br) Richard Hutchings/Photo Researchers, Inc.; 238-239 Ron Kunzman/Harcourt Brace & Company; 239 (bl) Jim Pickerell/Tony Stone Images; 239 (br) Aneal Vohra/Unicorn Stock Photos; 250 Harcourt Brace & Company/Terry D. Sinclair; 251 (l) Craig Blouin/Tony Stone Images; 251 (r) Daniel J. Schaefer/PhotoEdit; 252 (t) Harcourt Brace & Company/Ron Kunzman; 252 (b) Gary Irving/Tony Stone Images; 253 James Schnepf/Gamma Liaison; 254 T. Campion/Sygma Photo News; 255 Paula Lerner/Woodfin Camp & Associates; 258 The Granger Collection; 259 The Granger Collection; 260 (t) Michael Evans/Sygma Photo News; 260 (b) The Granger Collection; 261 David Young-Wolff/PhotoEdit; 262 Bachmann/Photo Researchers, Inc.; 263 Bob Daemmrich Photography, Inc.; 264 Bill Wisser/Gamma Liaison; 265 (t) Ron Kunzman/Harcourt Brace & Company; 265 (b) Susan Van Etten/PhotoEdit; 265 (b) AP/Wide World Photos; 266 Jim Pickerell/Tony Stone Images; 269 (bl) Everett Johnson/Folio; 269 (br) Patricia Fisher/Folio; 270 (l) Wide World Photos; 270 (br) AP/Wide World Photos; 270-271Timeline (l to r) Alfred Eisenstaedt/Life; Malak/Photo Researchers; The White House; Gerald R. Ford Library; Michael Evans/Liaison International; David Valdez/The White House; The White House; Bill Fitz-Patrick/The White House; 271 (b) Wally McNamee/Sygma Photo News; 271 (tl) Henri Bureau/Sygma Photo News; 271 (tc) J.L. Atlan/Sygma Photo News; 271 (tr) J.L. Atlan/Sygma Photo News; 273 (t) UPI/Bettmann; 273 (b) Steve Leonard/Black Star; 274 (b) Theo Westenberger/Gamma Liaison; 275 Supreme Court Historical Society; 276 J.M. Mejuto; 278 Archive Photos; 279 (t) Bettmann; 279 (b) Russell D. Curtis/Photo Researchers, Inc.; 280 (l) Dan Budnik/Woodfin Camp & Associates; 280 (r) Norman A. Petersen/Unicorn Stock Photos; 280-281 Nasa/Harcourt Brace & Company; 281 William R. Sallaz/Duomo Photography; 282 (tl) H. Mark Weidman; 282 (tr) Florent Flipper/Unicorn Stock Photos; 282 (bl) The Bettmann Archive; 282 (br) David Cummings/Unicorn Stock Photos; 283 (l) John Shaw/Tom Stack & Associates; 283 (tr) Wayne Floyd/Unicorn Stock Photos; 283 (br) Bob Daemmrich Photography, Inc.; 284 The Bettmann Archive; 285 AP/Wide World Photos; 286 Wide World Photos; 288 The Bettmann Archive; 290 (t) The Bettmann Archive; 290 (b) Larry Lefever/Grant Heilman Photography; 291 (l) H. Schmeiser/Unicorn Stock Photos; 291 (tr) Harcourt Brace & Company/Carroll Morgan; 291 (br) A. Gurmankin/Unicorn Stock Photos; 291 (cr) Paraskevas Photography; 294 Terry D. Sinclair/Harcourt Brace & Company; 296 (t) Smithsonian Institution; 298-299 Harcourt Brace & Company/Don Rutledge/Black Star.

Unit 6

Page 298 (bl) Judy Gurovciz/International Stock Photography; 298 (br) Judy Griesedieck/Black Star; 299 (bl) Murray Alcosser/The Image Bank; 299 (br) Miwako Ikeda/International Stock Photography; 310 (t) Summit Historical Society; 310 (b) Summit Historical Society; 311 (t) PICA02460, Austin History Center, Austin Public Library; 311 (bl) Bollaty Lomeo/The Image Bank; 311 (br) C03181, Austin History Center, Austin Public LIbrary; 312 (b) Marilyn David/Folio; 312 (tl) Allen A. Dutton; 312 (tr) Al Gordon/Profiles West; 313 Culver Pictures, Inc.; 314 Andre Jenny/International Stock Photography; 315 (t) Will & Deni McIntyre/Photo Researchers, Inc.; 315 (b) Terry Parke/Transparencies, Inc.; 316 (t) John Boykin; 316 (b) John Boykin; 317 Ken Karp/Omni-Photo; 318 (b) Ben Van Hook/Black Star; 319 R. Krubner/H. Armstrong Roberts, Inc.; 320 Sal Dimarco/Black Star/Harcourt Brace & Company; 321 (t) Charlotte Mecklenburg Public Library, Robinson-Spangler Carolina Room; 322 The Granger Collection; 323 (t) Schalkwijk/Art Resource, NY; 323 (b) Museo de la Ciudad de Mexico/Nicolas Sapieha/Art Resource, NY; 324 (b) The Granger Collection; 324 (b) The Granger Collection; 325 Cliff Hollenbeck/International Photography; 326 (l) Aneal F. Vohra/Unicorn; 326 (r) George Ancona; 327 M. Thonig/H. Armstrong Roberts; 328 (inset) A. Reininger/Woodfin Camp & Associates; 328 Piero Guerrini/Woodfin Camp & Associates; 329 (t) Robert Frerck/Woodfin Camp & Associates; 329 (b) Victoria Bowen/Harcourt Brace & Company; 330 Kal Muller/Woodfin Camp & Associates; 332 Harcourt Brace & Company/Terry D. Sinclair; 333 (t) Harcourt Brace & Company/Ron Kunzman; 333 (b) Ron Kunzman/Harcourt Brace & Company; 334 Harcourt Brace & Company/Ron Kunzman; 336 Kids For A Clean Environment; 337 (t) Kids For A Clean Environment; 337 (b) Ap Photo/Dennis Paquin; 340 Harcourt Brace & Company/Terry D. Sinclair; A1 NASA; 344 G. Ahrens/H. Armstrong Roberts; R1 (t) Victoria Bowen/Harcourt Brace & Company; R1 (b) Dinodia Picture Agency.

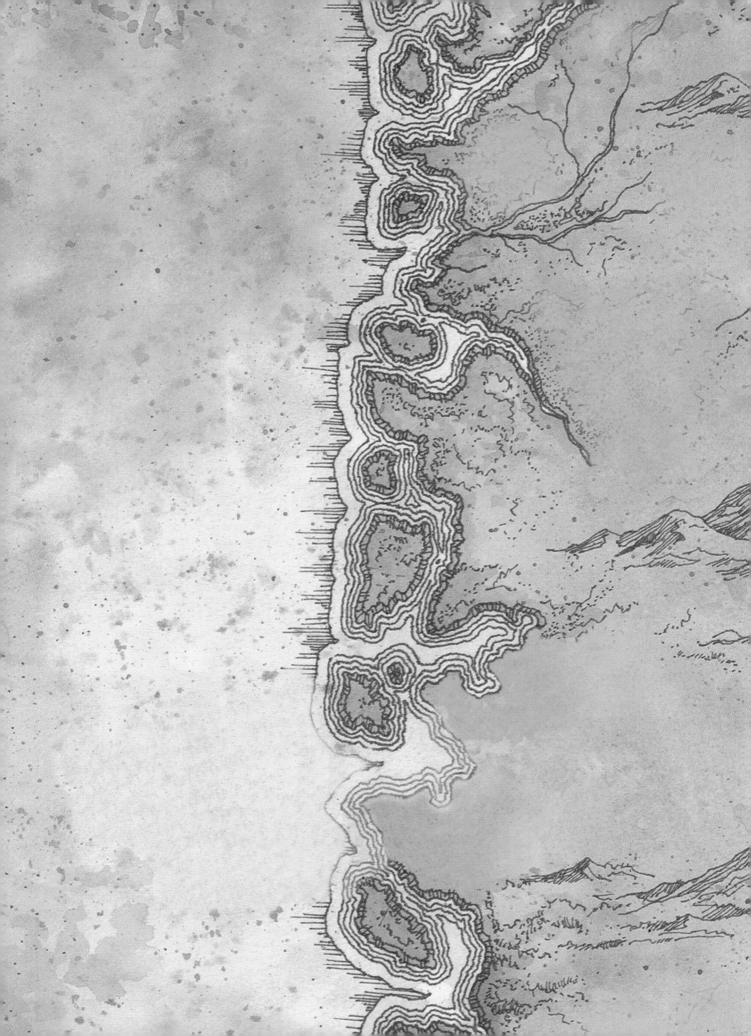